Jane's Addiction:

SHOCKINGLY HABITUAL

The Extraordinary Rock 'n' Roll Tale

First published by Media - 11 PUBLISHING February 7, 2025

First edition
ISBN (paperback): 9798348348496
ISBN (hardcover): 9781088010006
This book was professionally typeset on Reedsy.
Find out more at reedsy.com

5

For Perry, Dave, Stephen, Eric, Chris, Flea, Martyn, Peter, Etty, Josh, and all the brilliant musicians who came before you, influencing you to pick up an instrument and create, so that you may bring joy to us all. On behalf of all the fans around the world and" ASP AS AFE",

WE THANK YOU!

"There is nothing conceptually better than Rock 'n' Roll."

-John Lennon

MICAH R. GUIDRY

Jane's Addiction: SHOCKINGLY HABITUAL

The Extraordinary Rock 'n 'Roll Tale

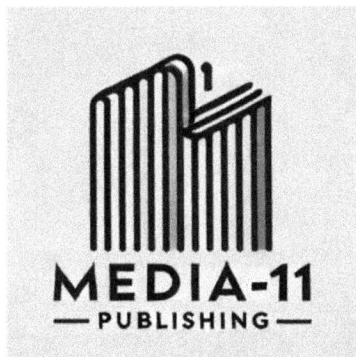

MEDIA-11
— PUBLISHING —

Preface

Within my innermost heart, there's a moment where a song, an album, or a band became so much more than just sound but a lifeline, a beacon, a part of my soul. For me, that happened in 1987 when I was 14 and handed a cassette tape. On that dubbed, slightly grainy recording was Jane's Addiction. Raw, hypnotic, untamed, it wasn't just music; it was a revelation.

From the incessant groove of "Trip Away" to the haunted vulnerability of "I Would for You, "through the incendiary cover of the Rolling Stones' "Sympathy for the Devil" to the eternally ethereal "Jane Says, "that tape became my constant companion, blaring from my Walkman and home stereo alike. It wasn't just a collection of songs; it was an awakening.

A cassette lit that flame, and *Nothing's Shocking* sealed it as a lifetime relationship in 1988. That album wasn't just played; it was passed around like a relic among friends, defining our youth and connecting us to a secret rhythm that only we seemed to understand. In 1990, *Ritual de lo Habitual* stitched its way into the very fabric of our lives.

Jane's Addiction wasn't just the soundtrack to our days; they were a revolution, a heartbeat, a banner under which we found ourselves and each other.

Then, of course, was the live experience: from ditching school to catch a flight and see them in Dallas in 1990, to the inaugural Lollapalooza festival, Perry Farrell's audacious brainchild, it wasn't just music; it was a movement that broke boundaries, recast culture, and encouraged us all to live larger, louder, and freer.

This book is my appreciation letter to the band that has been the constant in my life's chaos, a steady reminder of the beauty in rawness, the art in vulnerability, and the power in defiance. It's for the fans like me who've danced, screamed, and cried through their music, who've found a piece of themselves in Perry's eccentric brilliance, Dave's soaring riffs, Eric's resonant bass lines, and Stephen's thunderous rhythms.

Every page of this book is a labor of love, thoroughly researched and deeply imagined. I strove to ensure each moment, each timeline, event, and every story is deeply rooted in history, researched, and sewn into this story with the fervor of a fan and an artist's heart. When facts fell silent, I leaned into the essence of these personalities, drawing from the countless biographies and interviews and my decades of connection.

From the live, independent debut record on Triple-X, to *Ritual de lo Habitual*, from *Strays* to *The Great Escape Artist* and up to their latest singles "True Love" and "Imminent Redemption, "Jane's Addiction has never stopped growing. It's an art that's as fearless and vulnerable as it gets, a real manifestation of not being like anything but themselves. This book is for you, the fans. For all of us who felt that first electric jolt of "Jane Says, "who lost themselves in the anthem "Stop!" and who to this day chase that magic into live shows and shared memory. It's for the dreamers, the rebels, the believers, or anyone who found home in the wild, beautiful chaos that is Jane's Addiction.

Jane's Addiction has always been more than a band. It was an idea, a dare, to embrace life in its messiest, most magical form. This is an idea for us, the ones who dared answer that call. Welcome to the incredible story of Jane's Addiction.

PART ONE

A Boy's Tragedy

The jewelry store was a refuge of silence and glinting metal in the heart of Queens, New York, a small, polished space tucked between the chaotic pulse of the city streets. Outside, car horns blared and voices shouted over the dull rumble of traffic. But inside, the world was calm, a shrine to precision and beauty.

The fluorescent lights hummed softly overhead, glowing across the glass display cases. Beneath the surface of the counters lay treasures: rows of delicate gold bands, necklaces that shimmered like liquid light, and brooches encrusted with stones that glittered like fragments of a kaleidoscope. To an outsider, it was a place of quiet reverence, where beauty was crafted by hand and displayed like artifacts in a museum.

For young Perry Bernstein, perched on a stool by the counter, it was magical and maddening. His small hands were pressed flat against the cool glass, leaving faint smudges that would be wiped away within moments by his father's watchful hand. His legs swung idly, not quite reaching the floor, as he stared at the contents of the display with a mixture of awe and frustration.

The jewels seemed to call to him, their brilliance drawing his gaze like a moth to a flame. But they were always out of reach, locked away behind the glass. Even at three, Perry felt the quiet sting of being on the outside looking in, of wanting something he wasn't allowed to touch.

Across the counter, his father worked in focused silence, bent over a small velvet cloth spread across the workbench. Jacob Bernstein was a large man, with thick, calloused fingers that moved with surprising precision as he adjusted the prongs on a diamond ring. A jeweler's lope perched on his eye, its thick lens magnifying the glint of the stone he held. Around him lay an array of tools, tiny hammers, needle-thin tweezers, a magnifying glass, and an assortment of calipers, each laid out in careful order, as though they were sacred instruments of his trade.

"Come here, Perry, "Jacob said, his voice low but firm, breaking the stillness.

Perry slid off the stool, his feet making a soft thud against the linoleum floor. He moved closer, craning his neck to see what his father was working on. The diamond in Jacob's hand caught the light, sending tiny rainbows scattering across the counter.

"These tools", Jacob said, gesturing to the array spread before him", each one has a purpose. Everything has its place. You understand?"

Perry nodded; his dark eyes wide as he stared at the tools. To him, they looked like objects of magic, capable of transforming something ordinary into something extraordinary. He didn't fully grasp the weight of his father's words, but he felt the gravity of the moment, the quiet pride in Jacob's voice, the sense of mastery that radiated from his steady hands.

"Um, but if it um, does not fit?" Perry asked, his voice small but curious, his gaze fixed on the ring.

Jacob paused, his fingers stilling momentarily as a faint smile tugged at the corners of his mouth. "Then we make it fit, "he said, the conviction in his tone unshakable.

Perry stared at his father, sensing something in those words that went beyond the craft of jewelry. There was a certainty in Jacob, a quiet determination that Perry admired even if he couldn't articulate it. But beneath his fascination with the tools and the glittering jewels, a restless energy simmered.

With its quiet order and polished surfaces, the jewelry store felt stifling. Perry could sense the world's pulse beyond its walls, the chaotic energy of Queens calling to him with a voice he couldn't yet ignore. This was his father's domain, a world of precision and boundaries. But even at three years old, Perry felt the stirrings of a need for something wilder, untamed.

The Bernstein family's apartment in Queens was a far cry from the polished elegance of the jewelry store. It was small and cluttered, filled with the remnants of their daily lives, a worn couch with sunken cushions, mismatched chairs pulled up to a scarred wooden table, and stacks of papers and books that never seemed to find a home.

The walls were paper-thin, peeling in places to reveal faded layers of paint beneath. Framed photographs hung crookedly in the hallway, their edges curling slightly, snapshots of family gatherings and moments now frozen in time. There was a warmth to the space, but it was overshadowed by a sense of weariness, as though the walls themselves carried the weight of unspoken struggles.

Perry's corner of the apartment was little more than a bed pushed up against the wall beneath a small window. At night, he would lie awake, staring at the ceiling as the sounds of the city filtered through the thin glass. The distant hum of traffic, the occasional shout from the street, and the muffled laughter of neighbors created a strange symphony that lulled him to sleep.

But some nights, the noise inside the apartment drowned out the sounds of the city.

His parents' arguments had a rhythm of their own, a familiar rise and fall that Perry had learned to endure in silence. His mother's voice, sharp and brittle, cut through the walls like the edge of a knife.

"I can't keep doing this, "she would say, her tone trembling with exhaustion. "This isn't a life, Jacob. We're stuck." She paused, turned her back, "And those 'characters' you do business with? They scare the hell out of me, dammit!"

His father's voice was softer, steadier, but no less strained. "You don't need to worry about those people. It's just business. We're building something. For the boys. Don't you see that?"

The arguments would rise like a storm, voices clashing and overlapping until, suddenly, they stopped. The silence that followed was heavier than the shouting, a quiet that seemed to seep into every corner of the apartment.

On those nights, Perry would lie in bed, clutching a small Star of David pendant his mother had given him. Its edges were smooth, worn down from years of being handled, and it felt cool against his palm. To him, it was more than just a symbol of faith, it was a talisman, something to hold onto when the world felt too big, too chaotic.

He spent his days painting on a small easel, right next to his mother, who was always painting or repairing 'treasures' that Perry and her would find during their outings in the city. They'd spend time looking through alleys, dumpsters and second-hand stores for items that could be repaired and put to use or transformed into art, an activity Perry loved, and he would continue to engage in throughout his adulthood.

He had a habit during any uncomfortable moment, in which he would hum softly to himself, a melody without words, something that came from deep inside him. It wasn't much, but it was enough to fill the silence, to drown out the tension that hung in the air like a storm waiting to break.

One morning, Perry woke to an eerie sound. The usual sounds of the apartment, his father moving about in the kitchen, the faint clatter of dishes, were absent. On this particular morning he heard commotion from downstairs, and the light filtering through the blinds cast pale stripes of red and blur across his bed. The atmosphere felt heavy, and very wrong.

Slipping out of bed, he padded softly down the hallway, his feet cold against the wooden floor. He stopped outside his mother's bedroom door, his small hand hovering just above the handle. Slowly, he pushed the door open.

The bed was unmade, the sheets tangled and empty. On the nightstand, a row of orange pill bottles caught the morning light, their labels peeling slightly. A glass of water sat beside them, untouched. The faint scent of his mother's perfume lingered in the air, a ghostly reminder of her presence.

"Perry… come here, son". His father's voice drifted from the kitchen, soft and broken.

Perry followed the sound, his heart pounding. He found his father at the kitchen table, his head in his hands, a bottle of whiskey sitting half-empty beside him. Jacob looked up slowly as Perry entered, his eyes red-rimmed and glassy with grief. Perry watched as a two paramedics wheeled a body, covered in a white sheet, slowly out the front door.

In his high-pitched, toddler-speak", What wong, Papa? Where mamma? He walked quickly towards the open front door, lifting his little finger as he pointed at the body on a stretcher, which was being lifted into an ambulance. Is dat my momma?" Perry's voice was cracking and uncertain, his words trembling in the quiet as his watery eyes stared in confusion.

Jacob didn't answer. Instead, he stood from his chair, reached out and pulled Perry into a rough embrace, holding him tightly. For a moment, Perry allowed himself to be held, to feel the warmth of his father's arms. But even then, a part of him began to pull away, to retreat behind an invisible wall. In that moment, at a mere three years old-his mother, his best friend, and a part of his tiny beating heart, was gone forever.

That morning stayed with Perry, etched into his memory. It was the beginning of an understanding, of loss, of fragility, of the cracks that ran beneath the surface of their lives.

It Ignites

The night air was thick with the pungent smell of cigarette smoke, spilled beer, and the sweat of a hundred bodies crammed into a crumbling punk club on the Sunset Strip. The walls seemed to vibrate, pulsating with the distorted roar of amplifiers and the thunderous beat of drums as the Sex Pistols cover band tore through another track. Neon signs flickered outside, throwing harsh washes of electric pink, blue, and yellow through the narrow doorway, colors spilling onto the dirty pavement like the fractured remnants of a neon war.

Perry Farrell staggered out into the night, his body damp with sweat and his face alight with a feral energy that refused to die down even as the music faded behind him. He wasn't drunk, at least, not entirely but the night felt thick and hazy, the Strip was bending and breathing around him, alive with chaos. The sounds of laughter, shouting, and engines revving melded into one discordant hum. Cigarette butts littered the sidewalk like tiny corpses, crushed beneath the heels of those who stumbled out of the club before him.

He pulled a joint from his pocket, his hands trembling slightly as he fumbled with the matchbook. The thin flame sparked and danced in the breeze, casting flickering light across his angular face. For a moment, the light caught on the faint track marks along his arm, barely visible but undeniable. Perry inhaled deeply, the sharp burn filling his lungs as he exhaled into the cool night air. The plume of smoke twisted and dissipated above him, joining the haze that hung low over the Strip.

"That was some performance in there, "a voice called out from behind him, raspy and tinged with the telltale gravel of someone who had screamed through more than her fair share of concerts.

He turned, squinting through the dim light. A girl stood in the doorway of the club; her shoulder pressed casually against the frame. She wore a shredded "The Damned" T-shirt that clung to her slight frame, her eyeliner smeared into messy streaks that gave her an unhinged edge. There was something feral in her wide, bloodshot eyes, a spark that matched the unfiltered energy still burning in Perry's veins.

Perry smirked, his half-smoked joint dangling from the corner of his mouth. "What performance?" he asked, his voice dry and dismissive, as if he hadn't just thrown himself into a wild, frenzied dance that had left the entire club mesmerized.

She laughed, a low, throaty sound that turned into a cough halfway through. "The way you danced?" she said, stepping closer. "It was like you were fucking possessed or something."

Perry's smirk widened, his lips curling upward as he exhaled another plume of smoke. "Well, maybe I was, "he replied, his voice soft but tinged with defiance, as if daring her to say otherwise.

She stopped a few feet away, her gaze sweeping over him with a curiosity that bordered on intensity. "You should seriously start a band", she said, her tone blunt but earnest. "And not one of those bullshit Van Halen wannabes with their lipstick and leather pants. Do something real. Something that actually matters, for once. I swear, these bands have gotten fucking lazy".

Her words hung in the air like a challenge, sparking something deep within him. Perry didn't respond right away, his gaze flickering back toward the glow of the Strip. He could feel the weight of her challenge settling into his chest like an ember, feeding the hunger that had been gnawing at him for as long as he could remember.

"Ha! No…Fuck that, "he said finally, his voice low but charged with conviction. He turned back to face her, his eyes glinting in the pale light of the neon signs. "No, no…I'm gonna do something fucking better. Something none of these cats have experienced. Something that, you know, can't be fucking typecast… or put in box." He takes a hit, and as he's inhaling, "start a damn revolution, ya dig?"

She tilted her head, her expression skeptical but amused. She giggles, "Sure kid, that's what they all say, "she muttered, her voice laced with a cynicism that came from years of broken promises and empty words. As she turns and walks back toward the club entrance, she shouts, "Every asshole with a guitar thinks they're gonna change the fuckin' world."

Perry's gaze hardened, his jaw tightening as he took a final drag from his joint. He turns around, her back to him strolling through the club door, and yells, "Then they're all lying, "he said, his voice steady and unyielding. "But I'm not. I swear to God, except me! Besides, I can't play guitar for-shit!"

A siren wailed in the distance, its piercing cry slicing through the noise of the Strip. The girl flinched, her head snapping toward the sound, but Perry didn't move. He stood rooted to the spot, his mind already racing with ideas and visions that seemed too big to contain.

The next morning, sunlight streamed through the tall industrial windows of a photography studio, filling the room with a cold, unforgiving light. Dust motes hung suspended in the air, caught in the beams that slanted across the concrete floor. The space smelled faintly of chemicals and stale coffee; the remnants of late nights spent developing prints.

Perry stood on a raised platform in the center of the room, his shirtless torso gleaming with a fine sheen of sweat. His body twisted into an impossible shape, his arms outstretched and his muscles taut, as though he were straining against some invisible force. Around him, photography students moved in a slow, deliberate orbit, their cameras clicking in rapid succession.

"Notice the interplay of light and shadow, "the instructor said, her voice calm and clinical as she circled the group. Her silver hair was pulled back into a severe bun, her glasses perched low on her nose. "The tension in his posture, the way his muscles strain against the limits of his body. This is what you're trying to capture. Not just the form, but the struggle".

Perry didn't hear her. His mind was elsewhere, caught in a loop of the girl's words from the night before: "You should seriously start a band." The phrase repeated itself over and over, growing louder each time, until it drowned out the soft click of the cameras and the murmurs of the students around him.

The idea was like a splinter lodged in his brain, small but impossible to ignore. He could feel it digging deeper, wrapping itself around the restless energy that buzzed inside him, demanding to be turned into something tangible.

Back in the real world, at a restaurant Perry couldn't stand, yet worked -

"Farrell!" The sharp bark of the kitchen manager's voice snapped him out of his thoughts.

Perry blinked, the memory of the Strip dissolving as he turned to face the older man standing in the doorway of the greasy diner. His apron was streaked with stains, and his face was flushed with irritation.

"These dishes aren't gonna wash themselves!"

Perry sighed, dragging his feet as he stepped away from the delivery truck he'd been leaning against. The sun beat down on the cracked pavement, the heat radiating in shimmering waves as he trudged toward the back of the diner.

Later, as he climbed back into the truck, he let out a long breath and rested his hands on the steering wheel. The radio crackled with static before settling on a punk rock station, the familiar screech of distorted guitars filling the cab.

Perry tapped his fingers against the wheel in time with the music, his mind already drifting back to the night before. He could see the girl's face, her wild eyes and sharp words. Her challenge.

He didn't know how or when, but he could feel it in his bones: the revolution he'd promised her was coming.

The Leap

The air in the warehouse was electric, thick with a raw energy that made it hard to breathe. It wasn't just the heat of the packed bodies, though the press of the crowd against the unpainted cinder block walls made the room feel like a furnace. It was the anticipation, the unspoken understanding that something was about to break loose, something uncontainable.

Dim bulbs hung from wires strung across the ceiling, their pale light barely cutting through the faint haze of cigarette smoke that hung in the air. Shadows danced across the crowd, flickering across faces glistening with sweat. The room felt alive, pulsing with the restless energy of a hundred people feeding off each other's tension.

Perry Farrell was the center of it all. Shirtless, slick with sweat, and moving like a man possessed, he was a blur of frenetic energy. His pale skin gleamed under the faint light, his hair hanging in wild black tufts that clung to his damp forehead. Every movement he made was erratic and unpredictable, arms flailing, body twisting, legs kicking as though he were trying to exorcise some inner demon.

His voice cut through the chaos like a blade, a raw, piercing scream that climbed in pitch until it hit something primal, something almost otherworldly. It wasn't just singing; it was a call to something darker and deeper than any music that had come before it.

The band behind him, Psi-Com, churned out an unrelenting wall of sound, drums pounding with tribal intensity, guitars shrieking and snarling, every note a challenge to the crowd. It was music stripped of polish, raw and visceral, refusing to follow any recognizable rhythm. The sound crashed into the crowd like waves, pushing them into a jagged, chaotic sway that mirrored Perry's own erratic movements.

In the middle of the crowd, Eric Avery stood rooted to the spot, his gaze locked on Perry. His jaw was tight, his brow furrowed in concentration, but there was something in his eyes, a flicker of curiosity, of fascination, that betrayed his outward stoicism. His fingers moved unconsciously against his thigh, tracing phantom bass-lines to the music in his head. He wasn't just watching; he was studying, dissecting, trying to make sense of the wild, unfiltered chaos in front of him.

Beside him, Casey Niccoli stood with a sketchbook propped against her arm, her pencil moving furiously across the page. She didn't look down as she drew, her gaze fixed on Perry, her hand working as though it were moving on instinct alone. Her sketches were wild, unrestrained, each line capturing a fleeting moment of Perry's performance, the tension in his limbs, the manic intensity in his eyes, the raw, unhinged energy that radiated from him.

Casey was beautiful, but not in the conventional sense. There was an edge to her beauty, something sharp and dangerous. Her dark eyes glinted with an intensity that matched Perry's own, and her movements carried the same unspoken defiance. She was chaos given form, a force of nature that seemed to thrive on the same reckless energy that drove Perry to throw himself into the music.

The music built to a frenzied crescendo, the sound swelling until it filled every inch of the warehouse, pressing down on the crowd like a physical force. Perry climbed onto a stack of speakers, his movements jerky and unsteady, his body silhouetted against the dim light. Every muscle in his frame was taut, his chest heaving as he teetered on the edge.

The crowd below watched in rapt silence; their breath collectively caught in their throats. Perry's gaze swept over them, his wild eyes daring them to look away. A reckless grin spread across his face, a flash of white teeth against the sheen of sweat on his skin.

"Get down from there!" a voice called out sharply from below. The sound guy's tone was urgent, cutting through the din.

Perry ignored him. He took a step forward, his arms outstretched, his grin widening as if he were reveling in the chaos. Then, without warning, he leaped.

For a heartbeat, time seemed to slow. Perry's body arched through the air, a blur of pale skin and dark hair. The crowd seemed to recoil instinctively, parting just enough to let him hit the concrete floor.

The impact was brutal, the sound of his body hitting the ground cutting through the music like a gunshot. A ripple of unease spread through the crowd, a low murmur that grew as Perry lay still for a moment, dazed and crumpled on the floor. Blood trickled from his nose, pooling beneath him.

Slowly, he pushed himself to his knees, his movements shaky but deliberate. His voice broke the silence, raw and unsteady but still fierce, refusing to falter. He kept singing, his words cutting through the lingering tension in the air, dragging the song to its chaotic, discordant end.

The instruments fell silent, leaving only Perry's voice hanging in the air, a haunting, unsteady echo that seemed to linger long after it faded. For a moment, the warehouse was silent, the crowd frozen, unsure of what to do.

Then the applause started. It began as a low murmur, a few scattered claps, before swelling into a thunderous roar. Cheers erupted from the crowd, the noise crashing over Perry as he stumbled to his feet, wiping the blood from his face with the back of his hand.

Perry pushed through the crowd, brushing off the hands that reached out to steady him. His vision swam, his body aching from the fall, but the adrenaline still coursing through him numbed the pain. He ignored the concerned murmurs, the wide-eyed stares of admiration and disbelief, his focus locked on a single figure at the edge of the room.

Casey Niccoli stood waiting; her sketchbook clutched tightly in her hands. Her dark eyes followed him as he approached, her expression unreadable.

"That was fucking terrible, "she said as he stopped in front of her, her voice cutting through the noise with sharp precision.

Perry grinned, with blood still smeared across his lips. "Thanks, "he replied, his voice rough but tinged with amusement. "Kind of… fucking hurts, though." He winced, gingerly touching his ribs. "What do you have, babe?"

Casey snapped her sketchbook shut, with her gaze steady as she looked him over. "Depends, "she said, her tone calm but challenging. "What are you running from, baby?"

The grin slipped from Perry's face, replaced by a flicker of confusion. He frowned, his eyes narrowing as he glanced at her. "What?" he muttered, wiping his nose with the back of his hand. "What does that mean, Case? Who says I'm running?"

Casey tilted her head, her gaze unwavering. "Your eyes do, "she said quietly, her voice steady and matter-of-fact.

Perry blinked, caught off guard. He glanced at his reflection in a cracked mirror on the wall. His own eyes stared back at him, wild and bloodshot, framed by the smudges of blood on his face.

He turned back to Casey, searching her expression for an answer he didn't have. But her gaze remained calm, steady, and unnervingly certain, leaving him feeling exposed in a way he couldn't explain.

In her rendering, Perry was a deity, half-beautiful, half-decaying. His face was split down the middle, one side flawless and ethereal, his features sharp and godlike, his eyes piercing and filled with light. The other side was a mask of decay, the skin cracked and rotting, the eye hollow and dark, a symbol of something beyond life, beyond humanity.

The lines of the drawing were sharp, deliberate, as though each stroke of the pencil had been carved with intent. The beautiful side of his face radiated something untouchable, a perfection that felt almost cruel in its distance. The decayed side seemed to seep into the air around it, pulling the viewer closer, forcing them to confront the inevitability of ruin.

Perry studied the image in silence, his lips curling into a faint smile that didn't quite reach his eyes. "Is that how you see me?" he asked, his voice soft, almost reverent.

Casey finally looked up from where she sat, her dark eyes meeting his with an intensity that felt like a challenge. Her expression was calm, steady, as though she had been waiting for the question. "It's how you see yourself, "she replied, her voice unwavering, the words sharp enough to cut through the dim haze of the room.

The smile on Perry's lips faltered slightly, his gaze lingering on the drawing. There was something unsettling about it, something that gnawed at the edges of his composure. It was too close to a truth he wasn't ready to name, a reflection of something he buried deep inside himself, even as it clawed to break free.

He ran a hand through his damp hair, the flickering candlelight throwing shadows across his sharp features. The air in the apartment was heavy, thick with the scent of incense and smoke, but it was Casey's presence that felt suffocating. She saw him too clearly, peeled back the layers he worked so hard to keep in place.

She set her pencil down with deliberate care, leaning back on her hands, her posture relaxed but her gaze unwavering. "You're wasting your fucking time with that band, "she said, her words blunt and surgical, cutting through the dim, dreamlike quality of the room.

Perry let out a sharp exhale, leaning forward and rubbing the back of his neck. The words stung, not because they surprised him, but because he knew she was right. "Yeah, well, tell me something I don't know, "he muttered, his voice tinged with frustration and just a hint of resignation.

Casey straightened, her movements fluid but charged with purpose. Her dark eyes locked onto his, her voice steady but electric. "You need to go bigger, "she said, her words carrying a weight that made them impossible to ignore. "Weirder. You need to scare people into excitement. You're not 'sad, ' Perry. You're not fucking miserable. So stop pretending to be."

Wilton House

Wilton House loomed like a ghost from another time, a crumbling relic of Victorian opulence that seemed to mock the modern city sprawling around it. Its steep gables and ornate woodwork were cloaked in years of neglect, the dark paint peeling away in long, curling strips. Ivy crept along its facade, twisting and curling as though it sought to reclaim the house for nature. The windows were cloudy with dust and grime, obscuring whatever lay behind them, and the once-grand front porch sagged slightly, the wood creaking beneath the weight of its own decay.

It was a place that refused to be ignored. The kind of house that made passersby pause and stare, drawn to its eerie beauty despite themselves. It stood as a monument to faded glory, a ruin that seemed alive with secrets, as though the walls had absorbed decades of memories and refused to let them go.

Inside, Wilton House buzzed with life. Dust motes hung like tiny stars, caught in the weak sunlight filtering through the dirty panes. The smell of turpentine, candle wax, and faint cigarette smoke clung to the walls, mingling with something more primal, the metallic tang of creativity, the electric charge of minds working furiously, unbound by convention.

The foyer was a riot of color. A massive canvas leaned against the far wall, an explosion of paint that seemed almost alive, its chaotic swirls and jagged lines drawing the eye and refusing to let go. The painter stood in front of it, shirtless and covered in streaks of blue and red, his hands moving in furious strokes. His face was twisted with emotion, his movements alternately confident and desperate as though he were locked in battle with the painting itself.

In the dimly lit hallway, two poets were locked in a heated argument, their voices echoing off the peeling wallpaper.

"Bukowski was a fucking fraud!" one shouted, gesturing wildly with a cigarette clutched between his fingers. "All he ever did was glorify misery!"

The other jabbed a finger in the air, his voice trembling with passion. "No, man, he owned it! That's the point! He stared it in the face and made it poetry!"

Their words rose and fell like the tide, charged with the kind of conviction only artists could muster. For them, it wasn't just an argument; it was a matter of salvation, a fight to prove that their understanding of the world through art was correct.

In a corner of the parlor, a topless girl sat cross-legged on the floor, her long hair falling in dark waves over her bare shoulders. A deck of tarot cards was spread out in front of her, their intricate designs catching the weak light. Her hands moved slowly, shuffling and rearranging the cards with a deliberate rhythm. Her eyes were closed, her lips moving in a silent incantation, her entire presence radiating an otherworldly calm. She had become a fixture in the house, a kind of modern oracle whose fortunes were sought after by anyone who dared to ask. Her voice, when she spoke, was soft and measured, laced with a mystery that made people lean closer, desperate to catch every word.

The entire house seemed to hum with energy. Each room held its own world, a self-contained universe of art and chaos, where the lines between genius and madness blurred.

Music drifted from somewhere upstairs, a haunting, half-finished melody played on repeat, the raw edges of its creation still exposed. Sculptures, some elegant, others grotesque, were scattered across the floor like forgotten toys, their forms both captivating and unsettling.

Perry Farrell moved through it all with the ease of someone who belonged, someone who had not just claimed this space but had shaped it, molded it into an extension of himself. His steps were confident, measured, his sharp eyes darting from one scene to the next, taking in the chaos with a satisfied gleam. To him, Wilton House wasn't just a home, it was a sanctuary, a kingdom for the misfits and the dreamers, for those who couldn't, or wouldn't, fit into the ordinary.

Eric Avery followed behind him, his gaze darting around as though he couldn't decide where to look. The house overwhelmed the senses, its strange energy pressing in from all sides. The peeling wallpaper, stained with time and faded patterns, seemed to close in on him. Every corner held something strange, abstract canvases smeared with violent colors, sculptures that looked as though they had been torn from nightmares, and the steady murmur of voices that ebbed and flowed like an undertow.

Eric's face was a mixture of intrigue and unease, his jaw tightening as he passed the tarot girl. Her eyes flicked open briefly as he walked by, dark and sharp, as though she were pulling threads from his soul. He looked away quickly, muttering something under his breath. Somewhere behind them, someone laughed, a sharp, discordant sound that cut through the murmur of conversation and left a chill in the air.

"Welcome to the madhouse, "Perry said, his voice low but tinged with amusement. His words carried a strange reverence, as though he were introducing Eric to a cathedral rather than a decaying mansion filled with misfits. A smirk tugged at the corners of his mouth as he turned back to Eric, his eyes gleaming with mischief.

Eric gave a short, uneasy laugh, his lips curling into a half-smile. "Jesus, you live here?" he asked, his voice tinged with disbelief.

Perry nodded without hesitation, his grin widening. He swept his arm around, gesturing to the expanse of rooms, each filled with its own strange scene. "We all live here, "he said, his voice brimming with pride and defiance. "That's the point. No boundaries, man. No rules. Just pure, fucking creation." His voice rose slightly on the last words, the intensity of his conviction bleeding through.

Eric's eyes lingered on the massive painting in the foyer, its chaotic lines seeming to ripple as he stared at it. "No rules, huh?" he said, his tone half-skeptical, half-resigned. "Looks like no one's cleaned the place in years, either."

Perry laughed, a sharp, sudden sound that carried through the room. "Cleanliness isn't exactly the fucking priority here, man. You want clean, go find yourself a suburban garage band."

Eric cracked a small smile, his discomfort easing slightly. "Fair enough, "he said, his voice dry. "So this is where the magic happens, huh?"

"Magic?" Perry's grin widened, his eyes glinting. "This place *is* magic, man. It's alive. You feel it, don't you?" He gestured toward the painter in the foyer, who was now muttering under his breath as he smeared a streak of crimson across the canvas. "You don't get that in some sterile studio. That's raw. That's real."

Eric glanced around again, his gaze landing briefly on the topless girl in the corner before flicking back to Perry. "I don't know, man, "he said, shaking his head slightly. "It's a lot."

Perry smirked, clapping a hand on Eric's shoulder. "That's the point. If it doesn't feel like too much, you're not fucking doing it right."

Somewhere in the distance, the haunting melody looped again, a fragmented song that felt like it was reaching for something just out of reach.

As they moved deeper into the house, the air seemed to grow heavier, thick with a cocktail of incense, sweat, and cigarette smoke. They passed a dimly lit room where a group of junkies lay sprawled across a mismatched assortment of vintage furniture. The upholstery, once ornate and vibrant, was now stained and threadbare, the patterns worn to faded ghosts of their former selves.

The junkies' bodies were limp, their heads lolling against the backs of couches and armrests. Shadows stretched across their hollowed cheeks and sunken eyes, exaggerating the gauntness of their faces. Their breathing was shallow, slow, as if they teetered on the edge of consciousness. One of them cradled an empty syringe in his hand, his fingers barely gripping it, as though it were the last thread tethering him to the world around him.

Eric grimaced; his discomfort palpable. His gaze darted across the scene, landing briefly on a girl slumped in the corner, her arms dotted with fresh bruises, her eyes half-closed as she swayed in and out of some distant reality. He shook his head and muttered under his breath, "And pure destruction?"

Perry, who was already a step ahead, glanced over his shoulder at Eric. The faint amber glow of a nearby lamp caught his face, lighting up the mischievous grin that spread across his lips. His eyes glinted with that wild, reckless energy that Eric had come to know so well, a chaotic magnetism that both attracted and repelled him. "Same thing, isn't it?" Perry said, his tone almost playful, but with an undercurrent of something darker.

Eric's jaw tightened, a flicker of skepticism crossing his face, but he said nothing. He simply stared at Perry, his expression unreadable. Perry's grin widened, his confidence unwavering, as though daring Eric to challenge his worldview.

And yet, as unsettling as Perry's logic was, Eric felt the pull of it, the intoxicating gravity of Perry's conviction, that unwavering belief that he was onto something bigger than all of this chaos, something that transcended the ruin and madness around him. It was dangerous, maybe even insane, but it was impossible to ignore. He was in. And they swiftly got to work writing. But launching this new project would not be pleasant.

Eric had some good riffs, and Perry's outlandish yet humble lyrics seemed to be a good fit. It was during this first, raw period of the band that would-be classics like "Mountain Song, ""Pigs in Zen," and "Kettle Whistle" were born.

They rehearsed, held auditions for guitarists and drummers, and booked shows. However, by the spring of 1986, the first incarnation of Jane's Addiction was already teetering on the edge of collapse. For six months, they'd been playing scattered gigs around L.A., trying to carve out a sound that felt like it could shake the city's foundations. But their lineup was a revolving door of frustration. They'd gone through three guitarists already, and the latest one, a wiry guy with hollow eyes, spent more time shooting speedballs in the bathroom than rehearsing. His sloppy, stumbling playing turned their live shows into endurance tests. The drummer, Matt Chaikin, was hardly better. He'd skip rehearsals altogether, leaving Perry and Eric sitting in a damp, smoke-filled room, waiting, their irritation palpable.

Magnificence Brewing

Casey's walls were alive with her art. Every inch of space was covered in her drawings, each one a strange amalgamation of beauty and darkness. Some pieces were intricate and hauntingly detailed, others wild and erratic, their jagged lines and heavy shading giving them a raw, visceral energy. Together, they painted a picture of Casey's inner world, a mind filled with contradictions, where chaos and precision lived side by side.

Eric sat cross-legged on the floor of Perry's tiny apartment, his bass propped on his lap as his fingers worked through a jagged, hypnotic riff. Perry lounged against the wall, scribbling lyrics in a battered notebook, his expression detached but focused. The room smelled of stale cigarettes and turpentine, remnants of Casey's latest art project scattered across the space like abandoned thoughts.

Eric's riff faltered, the notes cutting off abruptly as he let out a frustrated sigh. "Dude, we need a drummer, "he said, his voice clipped, the words carrying the weight of too many wasted hours. He leaned back, rubbing his temples, trying to calm the frustration building inside him. "Like, someone who can actually fucking keep up. And show up. What a concept, right?"

Perry looked up from his notebook, a sly grin tugging at the corners of his mouth. "What about your sister's boyfriend?" he asked casually, as if the thought had just drifted into his head.

Eric shot him a look, his dark eyes narrowing. "Stephen? Seriously?" He shook his head, scoffing. "The guy's all about that Iron Maiden, double-kick, metal shit. He's not what we're after."

Perry shrugged, unfazed. "Metal or not, the dude can play. And let's be honest, he's not gonna flake like Chaikin." He raised an eyebrow, his grin sharpening into something more challenging. "Unless you've got some magical drummer hidden up your sleeve?"

Before Eric could respond, soft footsteps echoed from the hallway. Rebecca, Eric's younger sister, leaned against the door frame, arms crossed over her chest. She had the same sharp features as her brother, the same intense eyes, though hers carried a confidence that felt unshakable. Rebecca was striking, her presence filling the room even before she spoke.

"Stephen can handle it, "she said, her tone steady, her words leaving no room for argument. Her gaze flicked to Eric, daring him to disagree. "And you know it."

Eric groaned, running a hand through his hair. "Jesus, Rebecca. You weren't even at the last show, "

"I didn't have to be, "Rebecca cut him off, her voice calm but firm. "I heard all about it. Your guitarist is a fucking mess, and Chaikin's a no-show half the time. Stephen's solid, Eric. He's not gonna pull that shit." She glanced at Perry, a knowing smile tugging at the corner of her mouth. "And he can probably get Dave to audition, too."

Perry perked up at that, confused. "Wait, 'Dave?' As in that kid?" To himself, thinking, "Oh whats his fucking name… Oh, 'Navarro' ?" he asked, his interest clear.

Rebecca nodded, her confidence unwavering. "Yeah. They played together in that band, what was it… Dizastre? He's a killer guitarist. You want to fix this mess you've got? Stephen and Dave are your guys."

Perry, a bit concerned, laughs, "Sure but isn't he like 16?" He can't get in to the major spots. He's a minor. Those kids play fucking backyard parties and 'warehouse gigs.'

Rebecca responded, "Oh for fucks-sake, he's 18. And he can play your 'hot-spots'….as long as he comes through the backdoor and doesn't touch the floor of the place, other than the stage. He'll have to wear one of those green, ya know, 'no fucking alcohol wristbands. Christ Perry, The Runaways were playing the Whiskey and CBGB'S when they were like 14! Don't worry about it. Its non fucking- issue. She rolls her eyes.

Eric let out a long, frustrated exhale, his fingers tapping an absent rhythm against his bass. He hated to admit it, but she wasn't wrong. The guitarist was a disaster, and Chaikin was a lost cause. He got to his feet abruptly, slinging his bass over his shoulder. "You know what, Perry? Fuck it. Do whatever you want, "he snapped, heading for the door. "I'm done wasting my time on this shit."

"Eric, "Perry called after him, his tone sharp enough to stop Eric in his tracks. "You walk out that door, it's over. You really want to throw this away because we can't sort out a lineup?"

Eric hesitated, one hand on the doorknob. He glanced back at Perry, then at Rebecca, who was watching him with a raised eyebrow, her expression daring him to give up. The tension in the room was thick, every second dragging out longer than the last.

Finally, Eric let out a frustrated laugh, turning back to face them. "Alright, fine, "he muttered, his tone begrudging. "Call Stephen. But if he can't keep up, we're not wasting more time."

Rebecca smirked, pushing off the door-frame. "He'll keep up, "she said confidently. "And Dave will blow your mind. Just wait."

Perry leaned back against the wall, his grin triumphant. "Looks like we've got ourselves a plan." He flipped his notebook closed, his mind already racing ahead to what could come next.

Eric rolled his eyes, muttering something under his breath as he sat back down, his bass resting against his knee. "This better not be another fucking disaster, "he grumbled.

Perry just laughed, a low, mischievous sound that filled the room. "Relax, man. The universe always provides. You'll see."

Later, Stephen and Dave arrived, both carrying the unmistakable energy of metal kids who had been waiting for their shot. Stephen was tall and lanky, with long, extremely curly hair that hung in his face and an Iron Maiden patch stitched to the back of his jacket. Dave, by contrast, was smaller and wiry, his hands twitching with nervous energy as he unpacked his guitar.

"So, "Eric began, leaning against his amp with a skeptical look. "What kind of fuckin' music you guys into?"

Dave's eyes lit up, and he grinned like an eager teenager. "Fuckin' Maiden, man!" he said, his voice bright with enthusiasm.

"Some Dio, Ratt… you know, the hard stuff, "Stephen added, his voice casual but confident.

Eric groaned, running a hand down his face. "Great, "he muttered under his breath. "Just great."

He turned to Perry, giving him the 'finger, ' his expression somewhere between irritation and disbelief. "You planned this, "he said flatly.

Perry's grin widened, his eyes gleaming with that familiar spark of mischief. "Okay, okay. Its gonna work. Trust me man. These cats bring a different element, sure…but everything's planned, "he replied smoothly. "Even a nonsensical band like this ."

Eric shook his head but didn't argue. Instead, he grabbed his bass, testing the strings. Of course, it was perfectly tuned. Perry hadn't left anything to chance.

They started to play, and for a moment, it felt like a collision of worlds that shouldn't have worked. Metal riffs clashed against post-punk rhythms, Perry's haunting vocals rising above it all, strange and hypnotic. But then something happened, an electric charge that seemed to ripple through the room. The sound began to take shape, raw and unfamiliar, a thing that refused to conform to any genre or expectation.

It wasn't metal, It wasn't punk, and it wasn't anything the world had heard before. But it was alive. In that room, beneath the peeling wallpaper of Wilton House, Jane's Addiction was born. It was messy, chaotic, and entirely new.

The old rehearsal space was perfect for this unique "thing" they were attempting. A converted Victorian house in the heart of Los Angeles, it had seen decades of life, and now it housed the storm of creativity that was Jane's Addiction. Instruments were scattered across the wooden floors, amps buzzing faintly, and the air smelled of sweat, coffee, and cigarette smoke. It was chaotic, alive, just like the band itself.

Perry stood in the center of the room, barefoot, shirtless, and radiating manic energy. His hair was wild, and his movements were sharper than usual, his body vibrating like a live wire.

The band was running through an early version of "Pigs in Zen, "the arrangement still raw, the pieces not quite fitting together. Perry abruptly stopped singing, throwing up his hands.

"No, no, no! Like this!" he shouted, cutting through the sound of Dave's guitar.

The band froze, instruments dangling from their shoulders as Perry crossed the room. He grabbed the mic stand and began demonstrating a vocal run, his voice stretching, cracking slightly but still carrying the raw, urgent energy that made him magnetic.

"Do you hear that? That rise, right there? That's what we need! It has to pull you in, like a fucking undertow, "he said, his eyes darting from Dave to Stephen. "And you, "he pointed at Stephen, "the drums need to feel heavier there. Like a goddamn heart attack. Boom, BOOM! Not just tapping your way through it, man."

Stephen sighed but nodded, picking up his sticks again. "Yeah, alright, Perry. I get it. Let's run it again."

Dave leaned against his amp, watching Perry with a mixture of amusement and annoyance. "You realize you sound like a fucking lunatic, right?"

Perry grinned, unfazed. "Yeah, but I'm a lunatic who knows what he wants. Now hit it!"

Stephen rolled his eyes but counted them in, the crash of the drums signaling the start of the song. This time, the energy felt tighter, more focused, and Perry let himself lose control again, his voice cutting through the air like a blade.

Across the room, Casey Niccoli sat cross-legged on the floor, surrounded by a sea of sketches and paints. Her long hair fell over her face as she worked, her hands smudged with charcoal and ink. Perry wandered over during a break, towel draped around his neck, his curiosity piqued by her intensity.

"What are you making, Case?" he asked, crouching down beside her.

She didn't look up, her focus unwavering as she added details to an intricate design. "Just some ideas for the fliers. Something weird, something that'll make people stop and stare."

Perry tilted his head, studying the artwork. The sketches were wild, twisting faces, abstract shapes, and sharp, jagged lines that seemed to leap off the page.

"I love it, "he said finally, his voice softer than usual. "But what if we added… this?" He grabbed a nearby pencil and began sketching over her design, adding swirling patterns and strange, distorted figures.

Casey shot him a look, half-annoyed but mostly amused. "You're impossible, you know that?"

He grinned, leaning closer. "Yeah, but you fucking love me for it."

She shook her head but didn't stop him, their creative energies blending seamlessly on the page.

Dave and Stephen were huddled near the drum kit, hashing out a particularly tricky section of "I Would for You." Stephen tapped out a rhythm on the snare, his brow furrowed in concentration, while Dave picked at his guitar, the notes sharp and melancholic.

"Okay, but what if you held back here?" Dave suggested, pointing at the sheet music in Stephen's lap. "Let the vocals breathe a little before we bring it back up."

Stephen nodded slowly, trying the adjustment. The sound shifted, suddenly feeling more spacious, more vulnerable.

"Yeah, "Dave said, his voice tinged with excitement. "That's it. That's the vibe."

In the corner of the room, Eric Avery sat on an old, battered couch, his bass in his lap and a journal balanced on his knee. He was scribbling notes furiously, occasionally pausing to pluck out a bass line. He glanced up at the others, his expression unreadable.

"Eric, "Perry called out from across the room, "you got something for us, or are you just writing your memoirs over there?"

Eric smirked, his pen still moving. "Just wait. You'll hear it when it's ready."

By midnight, the house was alive again, the sound of Perry's voice echoing through the halls as the band returned to the music. He stood in the center of the room, the mic clutched tightly in his hand, his eyes closed as he sang. His voice was raw, filled with an aching intensity that seemed to pull the others along with him

The band followed his lead, their instruments weaving together in a way that felt almost instinctual. The music was messy, imperfect, but it was theirs. It was a reflection of everything they were, chaotic, passionate, and undeniably alive.

Perry stepped out onto the patio, the cool night air brushing against his skin. The faint glow of the moon lit up the space, and the smell of tobacco hit him. He paused in the doorway, his eyes adjusting to the dim light. Dave Navarro was slouched in a chair, a cigarette dangling from his lips. Perry's gaze dropped to Dave's arm, catching the faint glint of a syringe lying on the table beside him.

Perry froze for a moment, the sight taking the wind out of him. He sighed, then turned back toward the kitchen. He grabbed a bottle of wine and a beer from the fridge, uncorking the wine as he walked back outside. The pop of the cork made Dave glance up, his eyes slightly glassy but still sharp.

"I see we've got another smack-head in the group, "Perry said, his voice light but edged with something sharper. He handed the beer to Dave, who took it without a word, his cigarette still hanging loosely from his lips.

Dave leaned back in the chair, taking a long drag before exhaling through his nose. "Guess I fit the profile, huh?" he said, cracking a faint, humorless smile.

Perry slid into the chair across from him, wine glass in hand. He leaned forward, studying the younger man. "How long you been chasing the dragon?" he asked, his tone casual, but his eyes betrayed his concern.

Dave took a swig of beer, his fingers absently tapping the side of the can. "Couple years. Started when I was about 17. You know, just messing around at first." He shrugged. "Then it kinda… stuck."

Perry shook his head, swirling the wine in his glass. "Seventeen? Jesus, kid. You're what, 19 now?"

"Yeah, "Dave said, looking out into the night. "A real fuckin' overachiever, huh?"

Perry let out a dry laugh, leaning back in his chair. "I'm not going to preach kid. As I'm sure you've figured out, I'm no stranger to the dope. I suppose I'll be done with it one day. I honestly don't even know why I do that shit in the first place. But you, well you're too goddamn talented for this shit, Navarro. Seriously. I hear you play, and I think, 'This kid's gonna change the fucking world.' I wish I had a third of your talent. But pace yourself brother. We can't change the world if you're nodding off in some alley."

Dave looked down, his cigarette smoldering between his fingers. "Talent doesn't mean much when your head's all fucked up, "he muttered.

Perry raised an eyebrow, tilting his head. "And what's got your head so fucked up, huh? You're 19. You should be chasing girls, not smack."

Dave hesitated, his jaw tightening. After a long pause, he finally spoke. "My mom's boyfriend killed her when I was 15. Shot her. Right in front of me."

Perry's expression softened, his usual quick wit replaced by something quieter, more somber. "Jesus, kid, "he said softly. "I'm sorry."

"They never caught him, "Dave continued, his voice flat. "And after that… I don't know. Music was the only thing that made any sense. It was the only thing that didn't hurt."

Perry nodded slowly, taking a sip of wine. "I get it, "he said after a moment. "Maybe more than you'd think."

Dave glanced at him, curiosity flickering in his eyes. "Yeah? How?"

Perry stared out into the darkness, his voice quieter now. "My mom killed herself when I was three." He paused, swallowing hard. "I don't remember much about her, other than making art with her. Going on dumpster-diving outings, looking for 'treasures." But I remember the feeling very much. That fucking hole it left in my world when she was gone. Like something's missing, and you know you're never gonna get it back."

Dave blinked, his cigarette frozen halfway to his mouth. "Shit, "he muttered. "I didn't know."

"Not something I go around sharing, "Perry admitted, offering a faint smile. "But it's why I eventually got out of New York. Needed to leave all that darkness behind. My dad ran this shady jewelry shop, real sketchy shit. My brother worked with him. He made a lot of jewelry for a lot of famous people. If wasn't for me, man. I just had to fucking get out here. I wanted to surf, to paint…write. Shit, singing didn't even come into the picture until I was 21."

Dave, a bit surprised, mumbles, "No shit?"

Perry, "Yup. I used to get work doing god-awe full fucking impressions of famous people, sometimes singers. One night this lovely girl; don't recall her name…well, she tells me I should start my eon band and be a singer! Craziest shit I'd ever heard at the time."

Dave snorted, shaking his head. "And now you're running the craziest band I've ever been in."

Perry chuckled, raising his glass. "To crazy bands and crazy people, huh?"

Dave clinked his beer against Perry's glass, a faint smile tugging at the corners of his mouth. For a moment, the weight between them lifted, replaced by something lighter, a quiet understanding between two men who had seen more than their fair share of darkness.

"You're gonna be okay, Navarro, "Perry said after a moment, his tone serious. "But you gotta want it. You can't let this shit take you under."

Dave nodded, though his gaze stayed distant. "Yeah. Maybe."

The two of them sat in silence for a while, the night wrapping around them like a blanket. In the quiet, with the city lights twinkling in the distance, it felt like an unspoken truce had been made, a fragile bond between two lost souls finding their way through the chaos.

Realizing the Dream

The small, cluttered office of Triple X Records was alive with a sense of tension that was almost palpable. Afternoon sunlight streamed through dusty Venetian blinds, cutting across the room and casting streaks of light over the cluttered desk. A vinyl copy of Jane's Addiction's live album sat in the center, pristine and important, as if it were a sacred relic.

Peter Heur and Dean Naleway, sat across from Perry and Eric. Peter leaned forward in his chair, resting his elbows on the desk as he carefully measured his words. Dean, leaning back, fiddled with a pen. The atmosphere was heavy, with the stakes higher than they had ever been.

"Look, "Peter began, taking a deep breath, "what you guys are doing… it's special. Different. But, "

Perry cut him off, his voice sharp and biting. "Look, Pete, you're our label, for now. And our management. But Warner is ready to ink a deal. Can you even begin to do this fucking band the justice that they can?"

Dean interjected, his voice a little too defensive. "You can't expect, "

"Then fuck off, Dean!" Perry snapped, standing abruptly and jabbing a finger in his direction. His frustration was spilling over. "You've already said the industry won't be able to place us in a certain 'genre' for marketing. Which tells us you've already made up your minds that we'll always be a 'small-time' act. And maybe so. But we'll spread, organically if we have to, our goddamn way. The people are ready for something new that doesn't fit into a neatly packed little box. They will find us. Whether it's with you, Warner, or who the fuck ever."

Eric shifted uncomfortably in his chair, glancing between Perry and the two label heads. Outside, a secretary slowed her steps as she passed the office, clearly eavesdropping on the escalating argument.

Peter leaned back, his face a mixture of frustration and weariness. "Perry, be reasonable. The majors? Warner, Atlantic… they won't give you what we will. They'll drop you like a bag of shit and tear up your contract without a care if you guys don't go gold."

Perry leaned forward, hands planted on the desk. "And you, Pete? What can you provide for us at this point? A tiny advance and smaller royalties?"

Peter sighed deeply, clearly exasperated. "Independence, "he said firmly. "Room to grow, for crying out loud. Two very important things you simply will not get with a major… not for a hell of a long time, at least."

"Oh yeah?" Perry said, standing up straight and crossing his arms. "Well my brothers, you'll just have to fucking watch us. Come on, E." He motioned to Eric, who hesitated before slowly standing, clearly conflicted.

Dean stood as well, his voice rising as he tried to get through to Perry. "Perry, wait. Just… listen to me."

Perry stopped at the door, his back to them, and sighed. "What is it, Dean?" His voice was calmer now, almost resigned.

Dean glanced at Peter, then back at Perry. "If we can't keep you from going to Warner…" He paused, choosing his words carefully. "At least keep us on as your managers. Long enough to make this deal. I don't want to see you guys get fucking eaten alive."

Perry crossed his arms and began pacing, his frustration evident.

Eric cleared his throat, attempting to speak. "Maybe we should, "

"Fine, "Perry said abruptly, cutting Eric off. He gestured toward the door. "Let's go, buddy."

Eric stood, clearly still unsure, and followed Perry out. Just as they reached the door, Perry stopped and turned back to face Dean and Peter.

"Thanks for the demo money, guys, "he said, his tone softer now, almost sincere. "Really. And for pressing the record. We do appreciate it. But we're not punk rock. We're something else. If you're going to make this deal with those assholes, you need to understand that."

With that, Perry turned and strode out of the room, leaving Peter and Dean sitting in stunned silence.

In the dimly lit hallway of Triple X Records, Perry marched ahead, his movements purposeful and brisk. Eric hurried to keep up, his journal clutched tightly in one hand.

"That was our best fucking offer so far, Perry, "Eric said, his voice low and tense. "You sure you want to chance Warner?"

Perry stopped abruptly, turning to face Eric with fire in his eyes. "No, that was our safest offer, "he said, jabbing a finger at Eric's chest. "Do you want to be safe, or do you want to be great, Eric? Huh?"

Before Eric could answer, Perry turned and shoved open the exit door, the sunlight blinding as they stepped outside.

The band's new van, courtesy of Triple X, crawled down Sunset Strip, as it passed the iconic Whiskey a Go Go. The street was alive with energy, a line of suits stretching around the block. Perry was behind the wheel, Casey beside him in the passenger seat, scribbling in her notebook. In the back, Dave and Stephen lounged, their conversations drowned out by the noise of the city.

"The fuck is this?" Dave asked, peering out the window as they rolled past the line of industry types.

Stephen pulled out a flier he had snagged earlier and scanned it quickly. "Record company showcase, "he said. "Says 'Private Event.'"

Through the windshield, they could see more executives arriving, stepping out of sleek luxury cars in pressed suits.

Perry's lips curled into a wicked grin. "Let's give them something to remember."

Casey glanced up from her notebook, studying his expression. "What are you planning babe?"

Perry chuckled, his grin widening. "Art, baby. Pure art."

Backstage at the Whiskey, the dressing room was a flurry of activity. Perry stood in front of a cracked mirror, applying makeup with quick, deliberate strokes. His torn dress lay draped over a chair beside him. Casey stood behind him, fussing with his outfit, her camera dangling from her neck.

Dave, seated nearby, tuned his guitar while watching Perry with a raised eyebrow. "Are you sure about this?"

"About what?" Perry replied, dabbing at his eyeliner.

"All of… this, "Dave said, gesturing vaguely at Perry's ensemble and makeup.

"They want a show?" Perry said, meeting Dave's gaze in the mirror. "Let's show them… fucking everything." He turned to Casey. "More lipstick?"

The Whiskey's main room was packed wall to wall with industry professionals. They sipped expensive drinks and murmured to one another, their attention barely on the stage. Deals were being made in the shadows as music became an afterthought.

Then, the lights dimmed. A low hum of anticipation rippled through the room. Perry stepped onto the stage, his appearance stopping conversations mid-sentence. He was in full drag, his arms bare, the faint marks of needles visible even under the dim light. He locked eyes with an executive in the front row, a look of shock and discomfort flashing across the man's face.

"This one's called 'Whores, '" Perry announced into the microphone, his voice steady and defiant.

The band exploded into the song, their energy raw and untamed. Perry writhed on stage, his movements erratic but mesmerizing. Dave's guitar screamed, Eric's bass thundered, and Stephen's drums drove everything forward like a locomotive.

The room reputed. Some executives fled for the exits, unable to handle the intensity. Others stood frozen, unable to look away, their expressions a mixture of awe and disbelief.

Casey filmed everything, her camera capturing the raw, unfiltered energy of the performance.

By the time the song ended, half the room had emptied. Perry stood at the mic, breathing hard, sweat dripping from his painted face.

"Thank you for coming to our wedding, "he said, a sly grin tugging at his lips. He paused, letting the tension hang in the air. "Or perhaps it was a fucking funeral?"

With that, he turned and exited the stage, leaving the room in stunned silence as feedback wailed from the amps.

Backstage, the atmosphere was electric. The band was buzzing from the performance, their adrenaline still surging. Perry wiped off his makeup with a towel while Casey packed up her camera gear. The door opened, and a Warner Bros. A&R rep stepped inside, his tie loosened and his face unreadable.

"That was… interesting, "the rep said, his tone hesitant.

Perry leaned back in his chair, smirking. "Interesting enough to remember?"

The rep nodded, pulling out a business card. "Look, we need an answer, Perry. This back and forth bullshit, its… Warner would like to set up a meeting, soon. Or they're moving on"

"Of course they would, "Perry said, his smirk widening. What those cats doesn't fucking get, is that we, you know, the musicians…well, we need to be ready - musically."

The rep placed the card on a nearby table and exited, leaving the band to process the interaction. Eric turned to Perry, his voice tinged with frustration.

"What the hell are you doing?" he asked. "I thought we decided… that we're doing this!"

Perry leaned forward, his expression calm but firm. "I'm making these stubborn cats want it more, "he said. "We need them desperate before a deal is made."

Eric shook his head but said nothing. He grabbed a bottle of wine and a six-pack and left the room. Casey watched from the corner, her camera still in hand, capturing every moment.

The weeks following the Whiskey show passed in a chaotic haze, each band member retreating into their own rhythms and vices. For Perry, life seemed to oscillate between intense bursts of creativity and reckless indulgence. He spent most mornings surfing, carving into the waves with a focused energy that belied the chaos swirling around him. The beach became his sanctuary, a place where he could escape the demands of the band, the tension of looming decisions, and the pull of addiction.

When not in the water, Perry threw himself into a mix of writing lyrics and sketching ideas for sculptures. One afternoon, he sat on the porch of the Milton House with Casey, a notebook balanced on his lap, scribbling lines that came to him in fragmented bursts. Casey lounged beside him, her camera in hand, snapping candid photos of Perry as he worked.

"You know, "Casey mused, glancing at one of the Polaroids developing in her hand, "you look like a mad scientist when you're creating."

Perry grinned, the sun catching the salt still crusted in his hair. "Baby, that's the secret. All art is madness. Controlled chaos, you know?"

Casey leaned back in her chair, lighting a cigarette. "Just don't lose the control part."

Inside the house, Stephen and Eric had developed their own routine. The two spent long afternoons in the makeshift rehearsal space, getting hammered on Heineken and experimenting with new rhythms. Stephen had been pushing for a jazzier approach to some of their songs, and Eric, ever the perfectionist, worked tirelessly to blend his bass lines into the complex percussion.

Stephen sat behind his kit one evening, a cigarette dangling from his lips as he tapped out a complicated beat. "Try it again, Eric, "he said, nodding toward the bass player. "But swing it this time. Less precise."

Eric scowled but obliged, his fingers working the fret-board as he adjusted to the looser rhythm. The notes rolled out, rough at first but slowly falling into a hypnotic groove. Stephen grinned, pointing at him with a drumstick. "That's it, man. That's the shit."

In another corner of the house, Dave kept mostly to himself. When he wasn't at his girlfriends place he stayed holed-up in his "space." His guitar became an extension of his body, the only thing grounding him as he navigated the hazy, drug-fueled days. Heroin had its grip on him, but the creativity it unlocked was undeniable. He spent hours up in that room, noodling with riffs that ranged from hauntingly melodic to abrasively raw. A worn tape recorder on the floor captured everything, the hiss of the cassette tape barely audible over the sounds of his playing.

One afternoon, Eric poked his head into Dave's room, wrinkling his nose at the smoky air. "You ever think about opening a window, man? Smells like a goddamn opium den in here."

Dave, sprawled on the floor with his guitar, glanced up with a lazy grin. "What's the point? Inspiration doesn't need fresh air."

Eric shook his head, muttering something about "fucking degenerates" before disappearing back down the hallway.

It was during this chaotic period that the news came. One afternoon the phone rang. Stephen answered. It was Peter.

"I'm sorry Pete, can you fucking repeat that?!" He said excitedly in disbelief." "No Perry's not here. Hasn't been for days but we'll find him! And Pete, fucking thanks, man."

Perry had been surfing up and down the beaches for days, staying in hotels with Casey. Finally, he returned from surfing Venice beach one late afternoon, his wet-suit still clinging to his damp skin. He walked up to Wilton House, propped his surfboard against the wall by the front door and stepped inside, shaking saltwater from his hair. The faint smell of weed and stale beer hung in the air, a constant in the house.

He froze when he saw Dave and Stephen sitting on the couch, laughing, a rare sight considering how often they avoided each other's company. Dave looked up first, his expression somewhere between annoyance and relief.

"There the fuck you are! Everyone's been trying to reach your ass for days!" Dave said, leaning back and taking a drag from his cigarette.

Perry frowned, his brow furrowing in confusion. "What? Sorry, boys, surf was up. What's so urgent?"

Stephen stood, a grin spreading across his face. "Love and Rockets!" he announced, his excitement almost childlike.

Perry blinked, still not understanding. He tossed his wet-suit hood onto a nearby chair and headed toward the kitchen, muttering, "What about 'em?"

Stephen followed him, practically bouncing with excitement. "Dean and Peter pulled it off! We're going on tour with Love and Rockets!"

Perry froze mid-step, spinning around to face Stephen. "What?!"

Dave, still on the couch, laughed and exhaled smoke through his nose. "Yeah, man. It's happening. Looks like we're hitting the road."

Perry stood there, processing the information. His mind was already racing, thinking about what this meant for the band, for their momentum, and for their sanity. A tour with Love and Rockets was no small deal, it was the kind of opportunity that could propel them to the next level.

Stephen clapped him on the shoulder, his grin widening. "Big-time, man. This is it."

For the first time in weeks, a genuine smile broke across Perry's face. "Fuck, "he muttered, shaking his head. "I guess we better get our shit together."

The deal called for Jane's Addiction to be the "Special Guests"from November 7, 1987 through December 11, 1987 on love and Rockets' U.S. Tour. They would playing sold out halls, theaters and larger venues.

As the tour kicked-off, each member with their personal lives spiraling into chaos, the band still managed to deliver performances that left audiences awestruck. Each night, they walked the fine line between brilliance and implosion. Perry's onstage presence was magnetic, equal parts shaman and showman, drawing energy from the crowd like an electric current. Dave's guitar screamed and wailed with a rawness that spoke of pain and passion. Stephen and Eric, despite their quieter dispositions, locked into a rhythm section that was thunderous and hypnotic.

But behind the scenes, things were far from harmonious. The band's addictions became harder to hide. Perry and Dave's heroin use was increasing, with late-night binges bleeding into early morning rehearsals. Perry, ever the charmer, would sway into soundchecks late, his words slurring but his energy frenetic. Dave, while quieter about his struggles, would disappear for hours, leaving the rest of the band to wonder if he'd show up at all.

Stephen, ever the stabilizer, was doing his best to hold things together, but even he had moments of weakness. One night in Kansas City, after a particularly heated argument between Perry and Eric backstage, Stephen shocked everyone by accepting a hit of heroin from Dave. It was the first and only time he tried it, and the regret on his face the next morning was etched into every line of his body.

Eric, meanwhile, was retreating further into himself. He'd taken to writing in a leather-bound journal he carried everywhere, jotting down lyrics and thoughts while dropping acid in the solitude of his hotel room. Though his stoicism often masked his feelings, it was clear he was frustrated with the band's lack of discipline. He wanted greatness, but the chaos was starting to take its toll.

The Love and Rockets tour was a massive success on paper. The band played to thousands of new fans each night, their performances earning them a reputation as a group to watch. Industry insiders whispered about their unpredictable energy and dangerous allure. The press began taking notice, with glowing reviews in underground magazines and whispers in major publications.

But the cracks were starting to show. At one sold-out show in Chicago, Perry stumbled over lyrics, laughing it off as part of the act. The crowd didn't seem to mind, but Eric's glare from across the stage was ice cold. Dave, nodding off between songs, missed his cue during "Pigs in Zen, "forcing Perry to cover with an extended improvisation. Backstage, the tension was palpable, but no one wanted to confront the elephant in the room.

Casey, who had joined the tour as the band's unofficial photographer and Perry's partner, was barely keeping it together herself. Heroin had its claws in her as well, and she often spent shows slumped in a corner with her camera, capturing the chaos around her through a hazy lens. One night, after a performance in Boston, she disappeared entirely, only to be found hours later passed out in the in the tour bus - wrong tour bus. She was found in Love and Rockets' bus with a needle still in her arm. Perry's reaction was a mix of concern and detachment, his own addiction clouding his judgment.

The after-parties were legendary, a blur of drugs, alcohol, and debauchery. The camaraderie among the musicians was real, but so was the sense of impending doom.

By the time the tour wrapped on December 11th, the band was barely holding together. They had gained momentum, fans, and the attention of every major label, but the cost was beginning to outweigh the benefits. Perry, ever the visionary, saw the potential for what they could become, but even he couldn't ignore the fractures forming beneath the surface.

And, to make matters worse, they were set to sign a major record deal with Warner Bros. Records the following month.

As they piled into the bus after the final show, Dave slumped in the back, his guitar case leaning against him like a shield. Stephen sat silently, staring out the window, while Eric flipped through his journal, jotting down notes. Perry sat up front, his head leaning against the window, eyes closed but mind racing.

"We did it, "Perry muttered, almost to himself. "We fucking did it."

Casey, sitting beside him, lit a cigarette, her hands trembling. "Yeah, "she said softly, exhaling smoke. "But at what fucking cost, babe?" "Christ, you guys can barely stand to be around each other." She further mumbles, looking out the window, "fucking pathetic."

No one responded. The hum of the bus's engine was the only sound as they drove into the night.

Triple X and Stardom Awaits

The warehouse buzzed with an electric undercurrent, the air thick with anticipation and the smell of beer and cigarettes. Strings of Christmas lights hung haphazardly across the exposed beams, casting the space in a dim, surreal glow. The crowd was small, barely thirty people scattered across the industrial floor, but their eyes were fixed on the makeshift stage.

Perry stepped out, and the room collectively stiffened. He wore a flowing dress that shimmered faintly under the uneven lighting. His face was painted in vivid strokes of red and black, a chaotic yet deliberate design that gave him the air of a tribal shaman. The small crowd murmured, unsure whether to laugh or to lean in closer. He was already a spectacle.

He grabbed the mic, his voice cutting through the room with a raw edge. "This, "he said, a crooked smile spreading across his painted face, "is what revolution sounds like."

The band launched into "Pigs in Zen, "the baseline throbbing like a heartbeat, the guitars slicing through the air with serrated precision. The noise was controlled chaos, equal parts melody, and madness. Perry prowled the stage, arms flailing, his movements jagged and hypnotic.

At first, the crowd stood frozen, trying to process what they were witnessing. But then the rhythm grabbed hold. Bodies began moving, first tentatively, then with reckless abandon. A mosh pit erupted in the center of the room, a swirling mass of bodies slamming into each other, shouting, laughing, letting go.

From the side of the stage, Casey filmed it all. Her camera followed Perry's every move, capturing the raw energy that poured off him like heat. She glanced at Eric, who was locked into his bass groove, and then at Dave, who seemed to be at war with his guitar, wrenching out every note as though his life depended on it. Stephen's drumming was relentless, a thunderstorm of rhythm that seemed to shake the floor beneath them.

By the time the song ended, the crowd wasn't just transfixed, they were believers.

Later, as they packed up their gear, the warehouse was almost silent, save for the occasional clink of bottles and the faint hum of leftover amps. Casey set down her camera, grinning.

"Jesus Christ, Perry, "she said, shaking her head. "You looked like some kind of wild prophet out there."

Perry smirked, grabbing a beer off a nearby table. "That's because I am, Case. Stick with me, you'll see."

Eric leaned his bass against the wall, wiping the sweat from his face with his shirt. "They were into it, man. I wasn't sure at first, but… they were fucking into it."

Dave, sitting on a speaker case, lit a cigarette. "Yeah, well, let's not get cocky. Half of them were just trying to figure out what the hell you were wearing.

Perry turned to him, still smirking. "And the other half? They were being reborn."

Stephen laughed, throwing an empty beer can into the corner. "Whatever, man. Let's just get out of here before someone calls the cops."

The next few months passed in a blur of noise and neon.

In the cramped van, the band careened through the darkened streets of Los Angeles, heading to the next gig. Casey was behind the wheel, blasting music so loud the speakers crackled. Perry sat shotgun, doing lines of cocaine and handing the tray of it back to the two in the backseat, gesturing wildly as he recounted some half-remembered story.

"And then, get this, the guy just fucking drops the guitar in the middle of the set! Like, 'Yeah, I'm done here.' Who does that?"

Stephen cackled from the back. "Sounds like your kind of guy, Per."

In the corner, Eric was scribbling in a notebook, his bass propped awkwardly against his knees. Dave sat silently beside him, leaning against the window. He rolled up his sleeve, the dim light catching the sheen of the needle as he injected. No one noticed, or if they did, they said nothing.

At a dive club downtown, the band's set was feral, unrelenting. The crowd surged forward, a heaving wave of bodies. Kids climbed onto the tiny stage, throwing themselves into the pit as though gravity had no claim on them. Perry egged them on, his voice like gasoline thrown on a fire.

"Let's go!" he shouted between songs, sweat pouring down his face. "I want to see every single one of you lose your fucking minds tonight!"

And they did.

One night, they arrived at Zatar's Pyramid Club, lugging their gear through the cluttered back entrance. The green room was small and dingy, but they didn't care. Eric popped open a beer while Casey snapped photos of the band, catching them in candid moments, Dave laughing as Perry mimicked his guitar stance, Stephen leaning against the wall mid-cigarette.

"Alright, everyone, look at me!" Casey called out, camera poised.

Perry threw an arm around Eric's shoulders, grinning. "Take it now, Case. This is the picture they'll use when they call us legends."

Eric rolled his eyes but smiled anyway. "Yeah, sure, man. Legends. In this dump."

Perry winked at Casey. "Even legends have to start somewhere."

The moment everything shifted was at the venue, "Scream." As the van pulled up outside the venue, Eric nudged Dave, motioning upward. Dave followed his gaze, his mouth opening slightly as he read the marquee:

TONIGHT: JANE'S ADDICTION – SOLD OUT

For a moment, the noise in the van died down as the weight of the words settled over them. Perry broke the silence with a triumphant laugh, his voice ringing out like a victory cry.

"Well, boys, "he said, climbing out of the van. "Looks like we're in business."

Inside, the venue was packed wall-to-wall. The band's name was on everyone's lips, and the energy in the room felt like it could ignite the air. When they launched into the final notes of "Trip Away, "the place erupted. Perry knelt at the edge of the stage, extending the mic into the crowd, who screamed the lyrics back at him.

As the last chord faded, the band stood together at the front of the stage, sweat-soaked and grinning. They bowed, the roar of the audience washing over them. For a moment, they stood frozen, basking in it.

Backstage, they sat in the dim light, sipping beers and catching their breath. Casey hovered with her camera, capturing the exhaustion, the euphoria, the spark that had ignited something bigger than themselves.

They didn't say it out loud, but they all felt it: This was the beginning of something extraordinary.

The office at Triple X Records was suffocatingly-small, the walls lined with faded punk posters and a clutter of vinyl records. Afternoon sunlight filtered weakly through Venetian blinds, striping the room in alternating bands of light and shadow.

Perry leaned back in his chair, absently rolling the contract into a tube, his restless energy filling the space. Across the table, Eric was hunched forward, eyes sharp as he scanned the document.

Dave sat slumped to his right, one arm lazily hanging off the side of his chair. His other hand rubbed his face as if he were trying to shake off the drowsiness, or whatever haze he'd put himself into before arriving. He reeked faintly of stale cigarettes and the sweet, acrid tang of burnt foil. Stephen sat further down the line, arms crossed, looking as if he'd rather be anywhere else. His foot tapped an impatient rhythm against the scuffed hardwood floor.

Peter Heur cleared his throat, sliding a stack of contracts across the table. "Alright, gentlemen, "he began. "Here's the deal. As Perry and I discussed, it's straightforward. One record. Four grand to record it. And yes, I know you want it to be live."

Dean Naleway, seated beside him, added, "We're pressing forty-five thousand units to start. Vinyl and cassette. Marketing? We'll do what we can within budget. We'll manage you guys for now, get you real gigs, opening for some decent bands."

Eric leaned back in his chair, tossing the contract onto the table with a snort. "Forty-five thousand's a good start, "he muttered. "But let's be clear, we need someone who knows what the hell they're doing. Management-wise."

Dean shrugged. "You've got us for now. Once you blow up, and you will, you can shop around for someone bigger."

Stephen finally perked up, his arms uncrossing as he leaned forward. "Forty-five thousand? That's not bad at all. Perry?"

Perry stopped rolling his contract, his gaze drifting out the window as if he were weighing an invisible scale in his head. Then, with a quick burst of movement, he stood, extending his hand across the desk. "Let's do it."

The others followed his lead, standing to shake hands, except for Dave, who hadn't moved. Stephen sighed and leaned down to nudge him. "Come on, man. Time to go."

Dave groaned but stood, his movements sluggish. As they left, Eric walked alongside Perry, his voice low and deliberate. "This had better work, Perry. We're not screwing around here."

Perry didn't respond, but his smirk betrayed his confidence.

On January 26, 1987, The Roxy was alive with energy. This was it - the night their first record would come to fruition. The walls vibrated with the buzz of anticipation as the band crowded into the small green room backstage. Perry paced, a bottle of wine in hand, while Dave sat cross-legged in the corner, carefully tying off his arm. Stephen glanced at him, frowning but saying nothing. This was routine by now.

"Forty-five thousand copies of a live album, "Stephen said, breaking the silence. "Think we can sell that?"

Perry turned, lifting his bottle in a mock toast. "Abso-fuckin'-lutely boys!"

Dave, now leaning back against the wall, smirked. "Yeah. If Perry doesn't scare 'em all off first."

By the time they hit the stage, the crowd was ready to explode. Perry's voice sliced through the room as they opened the set with the mellow, "Slow Diver." By the time the band launched into "Pigs in Zen, "the audience was moving as one chaotic, writhing body. Perry climbed the speaker stacks, wine bottle still in hand, his voice a hypnotic growl.

The crowd loved it, but the band was already splintering at the seams. Eric, who dropped to tabs of acid and drank roughly a half bottle of vodka, locked eyes with Dave during the break between songs, his expression dark. Dave barely noticed, his focus inward as he adjusted his guitar strap with shaky hands.

Offstage, Perry slumped into a chair, sweat pouring down his face. Casey knelt beside him, handing him a glass of water." You okay?" she asked softly.

Perry nodded, exhaling slowly. "I'm not sure they're not ready for this, "he muttered. "Not yet." He grabbed a small vial of coke from his pocket and took a few snorts, then chugged a glass of wine

Casey tilted her head, watching him. "You sure you are?"

Perry didn't answer. He stood up, kissed her on the forehead, and went back out onstage.

Backstage at The Roxy, the atmosphere buzzed with a frenetic, chaotic energy. The show had been a triumph, a packed house vibrating with the raw, unpolished power of a band on the edge of something big. But behind the curtain, the dressing room was a maelstrom of debauchery, egos, and vices.

Perry lounged on a battered couch, a half-empty wine bottle dangling from his hand. His makeup was smeared from the intensity of the set, sweat glistening on his chest. Around him, women fluttered like moths to a flame, their laughter loud and syrupy sweet. "Did you see them out there?" Perry said to no one in particular, gesturing vaguely toward the stage. "We burned the fucking place down. They're not gonna forget that."

Eric leaned against the wall, detached from the noise. His eyes were hooded, and his movements were slow and deliberate as he tied off his arm and prepped a hit of heroin. It wasn't a secret, nothing was hidden in this room, but no one paid much attention. It was just another night in a scene where limits didn't exist.

In one corner, Dave sat sprawled on a chair, a girl perched on his lap and another on the floor between his legs, lighting his cigarette. His eyes were bloodshot, his speech lazy. "I'm telling you, "he drawled to anyone within earshot, "we're gonna take over this city. One show at a time."

Stephen sat in the corner, quiet as usual. Rebecca clung to his arm, a steadying presence amid the chaos. Stephen wasn't immune to temptation, but he wasn't eager to jump into the fire either. He sipped his beer and gave Perry a sidelong glance. "Same circus, different night, "he muttered.

But tonight wasn't just any night. The band's friends and peers had shown up in droves to witness the spectacle. Flea, Hillel Slovak, and Anthony Kiedis from the Red Hot Chili Peppers leaned against a wall, talking animatedly about the performance while passing a joint. Flea was wasted but wide-eyed with admiration. "Man, that fucking set, "he said to Perry during a brief pause in the chaos. "You're onto something special. You know that, right?"

Perry grinned, lifting his wine bottle in a mock toast. "Takes one to know one, brother."

From another corner, Slash and Izzy Stradlin of Guns N' Roses puffed on cigarettes, did rails of coke, their leather jackets glinting under the dim lights. "The fucking gig was something else, "Slash said, his voice low and gravelly. Izzy nodded, his eyes flicking toward Perry. "Guy's got balls, climbing those speakers. I thought he was gonna fall and break his fucking neck."

Even Henry Rollins had made an appearance, standing stiffly against the wall, observing the scene with a mixture of amusement and disdain. A couple of guys from Poison and Ratt milled around as well, looking slightly out of place but still nodding along with the energy of the room.

Casey hovered near the edge of the chaos, camera in hand. She'd wanted to document the night, to capture the moment they crossed into something bigger. But watching Perry, sweaty, manic, and surrounded by chaos, she felt an ache of disappointment. The night was supposed to feel like a victory, but it felt hollow. She slipped out the back door, her camera dangling limply at her side.

In the alley behind the venue, she climbed into the band's beat-up van and prepared a hit of heroin. Her hands were steady, mechanical, as she tied off her arm and injected herself. Moments later, she slumped against the seat, unconscious.

Inside, the celebration continued, fueled by wine, beer, and a smorgasbord of illicit substances. Perry was now shirtless, a girl on each arm, recounting some wild story about a fan who had tried to climb on stage. "I almost pulled him up!" Perry exclaimed, laughing. "But then he fucking fell back into the pit. Should've held on tighter!"

Dave leaned over from his corner, his expression half-amused, half-annoyed. "Yeah, well, don't forget about the rest of us out there, man. We're a band, not your backup act."

Stephen shook his head, sipping his beer. "He's riding the high, man. Let him have it."

But Perry was already onto another story, his energy boundless, his focus scattered.

As the night wore on, the band piled into a limo to head to the after-party thrown by Triple X Records at a venue further down the Strip. Perry was still animated, his words slurred but enthusiastic. "This is it, boys!" he shouted. "This is the beginning of the rest of our God-forsaken lives!"

Dave and Eric sat silently in the back, lost in their respective highs. Stephen stared out the window, his hand fidgeting with a cigarette he hadn't lit.

Rebecca leaned toward Stephen; her voice low. "Are you okay?"

Stephen nodded, though he didn't meet her eyes. "Yeah. Just… tired."

No one noticed Casey's absence.

The after party was a blur of noise and light, a surreal mix of industry suits, groupies, and scenesters. Perry was the star of the show, holding court with his wine bottle still in hand. He laughed too loud, hugged too hard, his energy a little too forced.

Dave disappeared into a shadowy corner with two women, while Eric found himself deep in conversation with one of the label reps, though his speech was starting to slur.

Stephen stayed close to Rebecca, nursing a beer and trying to keep his distance from the chaos. The effects of the heroin were starting to wear off, leaving him pale and shaky.

When they finally returned to the house in the early hours of the morning, Perry staggered out of the limo and into the living room. His manic energy was finally starting to wane.

"Where's Casey?" he mumbled.

No one answered.

In the van outside, Casey still hadn't moved.

In the months following their chaotic live recording at The Roxy, the band found themselves in a strange limbo. On the surface, the anticipation of their first record, which would come to be known as "Jane's Addiction, Triple X, "should have been thrilling. But the truth was far messier. Stephen and Eric had begun pulling away from the whirlwind, opting for quieter, more solitary pursuits. Stephen spent most of his time with his girlfriend, while Eric disappeared for hours, sometimes days, experimenting with acid and losing himself in endless journaling and songwriting.

Dave and Perry, however, were inseparable, but not in the ways that fostered creativity. Their shared habits, heroin, cocaine, and a relentless appetite for debauchery, kept them tethered. Nights bled into mornings without anyone knowing where one ended and the other began.

The post-show atmosphere at The El Cid Theater was a mixture of exhilaration and exhaustion. Perry stood in front of a cracked mirror, wiping off his elaborate stage makeup with a damp towel. His face was still glistening with sweat, but his energy hadn't dimmed. Casey sat cross-legged on the floor, packing up her camera gear, her head bent low as she scribbled notes in her ever-present sketchbook.

Dave leaned back on the couch, a lit cigarette dangling between his fingers, the adrenaline from the performance still coursing through him. "Hey man, did you see how many fucking major-label guys were out there?" His voice broke the silence. "There's more and more coming to each show."

Stephen, perched on the armrest of a chair, nodded. "I counted at least seven of those fuckers, "he said with a mix of amusement and skepticism. He popped the tab on another beer and took a long swig.

Eric, who had been sitting quietly in the corner, his journal balanced on his lap, looked up sharply. "Don't get excited just yet, kids, "he muttered, his tone pragmatic. "We need to think about this carefully, "

"Look, boys…" Perry interrupted, tossing the towel onto the counter, and turning to face them. His voice was calm but deliberate. "Warner has called Dean and myself several goddamn times this past month or so."

Dave sat up straighter, the cigarette falling from his lips onto the floor. "Wait. What the fuck, Perry?" His voice was rising, incredulous. "You don't think the rest of us should have been fucking told that Warner Bros. Records has been calling us?!"

"I didn't want it on everyone's mind, Dave, "Perry replied, unbothered by the sudden heat. He grabbed a bottle of wine and took a long sip before continuing. "Not until we got through our deal with Triple X. And honestly? I still don't think we're ready to sign with a major." His eyes shifted to Eric. "Eric?"

Eric let out a heavy sigh, shutting his journal and placing it on the table beside him. "Perry's right, guys. Triple X isn't big-time, that's for goddamn sure. But they've been good to us. They're putting out this record. Let's see where it goes for now."

"Exactly, "Perry said, cutting him off before anyone else could chime in. "Not yet. We keep doing this our way, for now."

As the room settled into a tense quiet, Casey's pencil scratched across the page of her sketchbook. She didn't look up as she muttered, almost to herself, "The beginning of the end."

Perry's head snapped toward her, his eyes narrowing. "What was that?" he asked, his tone sharp.

Casey didn't flinch, and her focus was still fixed on the page in front of her. "Nothing, "she said, her voice even.

She kept drawing, and Perry eventually looked away, but the words lingered in the air like a prophecy no one wanted to acknowledge.

Tension and a Masterpiece

The Warner Bros. Records office exuded polished authority; its sleek conference room bathed in sunlight streaming through panoramic windows overlooking Los Angeles. Perry, Casey, Eric, Dave, and Stephen sat on one side of a massive table, their moods ranging from reserved to visibly eager. On the other side, the Warner entourage entered, led by Mo Ostin himself. At first glance, the sixty-something executive, dressed casually and without pretense, seemed more approachable than his sharply suited lawyers. Yet there was no mistaking the power he held.

Mo settled into his chair with the ease of someone who had seen it all and began without ceremony. "Sorry to keep you waiting, "he said, scanning the band with keen eyes. "I've been in this business for forty years. Never heard anything quite like you."

"That's the point, "Perry replied, leaning back in his chair, calm but watchful.

Mo smiled faintly. "Let's cut the bullshit, "he said. "Complete creative control. Your artwork, your music, your vision." He paused, letting the words settle before delivering the part that made even his entourage shuffle uncomfortably. "And you're fuckin' lucky boys. Your manager is a hell of a deal-maker. $250,000 advance."

Dave and Stephen couldn't contain their excitement, hugging each other across the table. "Holy shit, man!" Stephen exclaimed. Dave, grinning ear to ear, gave Perry a thumbs-up, though his tired eyes betrayed the long night before. Eric nodded, smiling, his body language calm but inwardly reeling. Perry, however, didn't flinch. He simply leaned forward and met Mo's gaze.

"And the publishing?" Perry asked, his voice cool.

"Standard split, "Mo replied.

Perry's response was immediate. He rose to his feet, pushing his chair back with deliberate slowness. "No deal, "he said flatly.

The room fell silent. Dave froze mid-cheer. Stephen glanced nervously at Eric, who was gripping the edge of the table, his knuckles white. Casey, seated beside Perry, smirked, sensing the drama unfold like a script she'd already predicted.

"I want 62.5 percent, "Perry declared, his tone firm.

A ripple of disbelief ran through the room. Lawyers exchanged bewildered glances, rustling papers, while Mo stared at Perry like he'd just declared war. "That's an oddly specific number, "Mo finally said, his voice even.

"It's beautiful, isn't it?" Perry replied, his confidence unshaken.

A long pause followed as Mo studied him, and then, to the band's collective shock, he laughed. "You've got balls, kid, "Mo said, shaking his head. "Done."

The lawyers stammered in protest, but Mo shut them down with a curt wave of his hand. "Draw up the papers, "he ordered before standing and heading for the door. He stopped briefly, turning back to face Perry. "Just don't make me regret this."

"Oh, you will, "Perry said, a sly grin spreading across his face. "But you'll love every minute of it."

The band followed Mo's entourage into the hallway, a mix of triumph and confusion hanging over them.

Eric caught Perry's arm, pulling him aside. "What the hell was that about?" he hissed, his tone sharp.

"What?" Perry said, feigning innocence. "Getting what we deserve."

"62.5 percent? Where'd you even pull that from?" Eric pressed, his frustration clear.

"The Fibonacci sequence, "Perry replied, his grin widening. "The golden ratio. The mathematics of beauty. Everything perfect has it."

Eric stared at him, equal parts baffled and annoyed. "Or maybe you're just a fucking greedy little prick?" he muttered before walking ahead.

"Maybe, "Perry said softly, watching him go. "But someone has to protect this vision."

As Eric walks off down the hall, he yells, "This isn't over Perry! I'm not signing that bullshit."

Perry yells back, "Nothing's set in stone! Let's just make some fucking magic in the meantime….on their dime. Come on brother. We'll deal with all the fucking money crap later."

Eric stops, hands on hips and turns, looking very pissed off. "Oh I'm gonna make some music Perry, but I'm not agreeing to that bullshit." As he turns and continue to walk, "And I'm not your 'brother!'

Perry sighed, nodded his head and exhaled as he lonesomely continued walking, with a lot less confidence.

That night Perry and Dave sat on the beach, getting drunk on vodka, and shooting cocaine and heroin as they attempted to work on lyrics.

Warner and the band had agreed and decided on David Jerden, to produce their debut album.

Jerden developed his engineering and mixing skills at El Dorado Recording Studios in Hollywood, California, beginning in the late 1970s.t He engineered and mixed acclaimed and successful records by artists such as Talking Heads, David Byrne, Frank Zappa, Mick Jagger, The Rolling Stones and many others.

The recording studio was a state-of-the-art labyrinth of equipment, its walls lined with soundproofing panels and cables snaking along the floor. It smelled of cigarettes, coffee, and the tension of long hours. The band was midway through recording "Mountain Song, "with producer David Jerden sitting behind the mixing board, equal parts bemused and exasperated.

Dave stood in the recording booth, his guitar slung low, playing the song's iconic riff over and over. "One more take, "Jerden said through the mic.

"It was perfect, "Eric muttered, his tone clipped.

"It wasn't, "Perry snapped back, pacing the control room like a caged animal.

"Then you fucking do it, "Eric shot back, his voice rising.

Through the glass, Dave sighed, muttering, "Here we go again, "as he adjusted his stance. Stephen, tapping his drumsticks nervously, glanced between Perry and Eric, ready to intervene if things escalated.

Jerden leaned toward his assistant, whispering, "Get me some coffee. And something stronger. This is gonna be a long night."

The assistant nodded, hurrying out. Meanwhile, Dave started the riff again, but Perry waved his arms, interrupting. "No, no, no!" he shouted. "It needs to sound like… like sex and violence had a baby. And that baby grew up and killed its parents."

Through the talk-back, Dave stared at him, incredulous. "What the fuck does that even mean?"

And so, the studio sessions had turned into a war-zone, a nightly clash where exhaustion, inspiration, and egos collided under the dim glow of control room monitors. For Jerden, it was unlike anything he'd experienced in his already storied career. Tension was a given when working with artists, but Jane's Addiction brought it to new heights.

Perry was the epicenter of that tension, his energy relentless and consuming. He didn't just want the songs to sound good, he wanted them to bleed, to haunt, to shake the listener to their core. He prowled the studio like a restless animal, his bare feet slapping against the carpeted floor as he flitted between the console, the booth, and the scribbled notes on his lyric sheets. Nothing satisfied him for long. A riff might be good, but it wasn't *there* yet. A vocal take could be raw, but it wasn't raw enough.

"Again!" he'd bark into the talk-back mic, the word cracking like a whip, cutting through the air thick with cigarette smoke and the low hum of amps.

Jerden, perched in his producer's chair, had seen his share of obsessive musicians, but Perry was something else entirely. The man wasn't creating music so much as chasing it, some intangible, impossible-to-capture sound that existed only in his head. Jerden leaned back and rubbed his temples as Perry continued his pacing, muttering half-formed thoughts that alternated between poetic and incomprehensible.

In the corner of the control room, Jerden's assistant, a young woman with dark circles under her eyes and a permanent look of exasperation, leaned against the wall. She held a tray of coffee cups, their contents long gone cold, and a bottle of whiskey, now half-empty. With a weary sigh, she set it down on the cluttered console, not bothering to announce its arrival. Everyone in the room knew it was going to be another long night.

Eric Avery sat slouched on the couch, a cigarette dangling from his fingers, its ash threatening to drop onto the already-stained upholstery. For Eric, these sessions were torture. He had always approached music with precision, building songs like an architect, each note and rhythm serving its purpose in a carefully constructed whole. Perry, however, was pure "eccentric incarnate", a storm that tore through structure, dragging everything in its wake.

Their artistic differences had always been part of the band's DNA, but in the pressure-cooker environment of the studio, it had become a constant source of conflict. For every riff Eric played, Perry wanted something wilder, something that felt like it had been ripped from the depths of a primal scream.

"Make it sound like…" Perry waved his arms as he searched for the right metaphor. "Like you're making love and going to war at the same time!"

Eric groaned, leaning forward and burying his head in his hands. "You've got to be kidding me, "he muttered. "That's not even a real fucking direction, Perry."

Dave Navarro, still in the booth, adjusted his guitar strap and smirked, watching the tension unfold through the soundproof glass. He began idly picking out a few notes on his guitar, deliberately taking his time.

"It's close, "Perry continued, his tone almost pleading now. "But it's not there. I need it to… to hurt, you know? To mean something." He turned to Jerden for support, his eyes wide and unrelenting. "You hear it, right?"

As they began recording, "Pig in Zen" Stephen felt it needed something. Something with a "jazz" hook. He had idea to reach out to a good friend of the bands'. He called Perry that night.

"Alright, "Perry said one afternoon, pacing the studio barefoot, his movements quick and frantic. His hands moved as if he were conducting an invisible orchestra. "We've got this groove on 'Idiots Rule, ' but it's missing… something. Something dirty, something wild, something totally unexpected."

Eric leaned back in his chair, arms crossed, his bass resting against the wall behind him. "You mean like your entire fucking personality?" he deadpanned, earning a laugh from Stephen, who was tapping his drumsticks against his knee.

Perry ignored the jab, his mind already miles ahead. He snapped his fingers. "I know who can do it."

Dave lit a cigarette, exhaling a plume of smoke as he arched an eyebrow. "Oh, this should be good."

"Flea, "Perry said with a grin, his eyes gleaming with the spark of an idea.

"Flea? As in Chili Peppers - Flea ?" Eric asked, sitting forward in his chair.

"Yes! Flea, "Perry said, his voice rising with excitement. "He can play sax. And not just play, it's like the saxophone is having a fucking seizure when it's in his hands. That's exactly what this track needs."

Eric rolled his eyes. "The guy barely stands still when he plays bass. Now you want him in here with a saxophone? Jesus Christ."

Perry grinned wider. "That's the point. He's craziness in human form. It's perfect."

A few phone calls later, Flea arrived at the studio like a whirlwind. Dressed in cutoff shorts and a vintage t-shirt, he carried his saxophone case in one hand and an infectious grin on his face.

"Alright, motherfuckers, "he announced, stepping into the studio and throwing his arms wide. "Who called for some noise?"

Perry met him with a bear hug, laughing. "That would be me, Flea. We need you to bring your insanity to this track."

Flea looked around the room, sizing up the vibe. "What are we working with?"

Perry led him to the soundboard, hitting play on the rough mix of "Idiots Rule." The horns, arranged by Perry, were already there, but they felt too polished, too restrained. Flea listened, nodding along, his face breaking into a wide grin when the groove kicked in.

"Oh, hell yes, "he said, pulling out his sax and assembling it with quick, practiced movements. "Let me fuck this up for you."

When Flea started playing, it was like unleashing a storm inside the studio. The sax wailed and screeched, weaving its way through the track with a raw, untamed energy that perfectly matched the song's rebellious tone.

Perry stood behind the glass, his hands pressed against the console, his eyes wide with delight. "That's it!" he yelled into the talk-back mic. "Make it nasty, Flea! Don't hold back!"

Flea grinned through the glass and pushed harder, his saxophone screaming over the track, blending with Dave's scorching guitar and Stephen's pounding drums. The sound was chaotic and electrifying, exactly what the song needed to push it over the edge.

After the final take, Flea leaned against the wall, sweat dripping from his forehead, his chest heaving as he caught his breath. "That was fucking fun, "he said, grinning.

Perry burst into the room, practically vibrating with energy. "You just turned this song into a goddamn war cry, Flea. It's perfect."

Eric, who had been skeptical at first, couldn't help but nod in agreement. "Alright, I'll admit it, he nailed it."

Dave smirked, putting out his cigarette in a nearby ashtray. "Yeah, not bad for a guy who usually just jumps around shirtless."

Flea laughed, flipping Dave off. "Hey, jumping around shirtless is an art form, Navarro. Don't knock it."

The band spent the rest of the afternoon playing back the track, the room buzzing with excitement. "Idiots Rule" had taken on a life of its own, thanks in no small part to Flea's wild, unrestrained saxophone.

Jerden's eyebrow twitched, the pen in his hand tapping out an irregular rhythm against his clipboard. "I hear *something, *" he said dryly. "Whether it's genius or madness, I'm not sure."

As midnight came and went, the atmosphere in the studio grew heavier. The same riff had been played so many times that it now echoed in everyone's heads, a relentless loop that refused to be forgotten.

Finally, Eric snapped.

"Then you do it, "he growled, his voice thick with exhaustion and fury. He slammed his cigarette into the ashtray and stood abruptly, his movements sharp and erratic. His words cut through the room like a blade, hanging in the air as everyone froze.

Perry turned to him slowly, his face unreadable. The two men locked eyes, their shared vision overshadowed by months of tension and creative friction. They needed each other, everyone in the room knew it, but in that moment, their stubborn pride created an unbridgeable chasm between them.

"Go ahead, "Eric added, throwing out his arms in frustration. "You've got all the answers, right? Let's see it."

The silence that followed was deafening. Jerden shifted uncomfortably in his seat, glancing toward Dave, who was now leaning against the booth wall, clearly enjoying the show.

Perry didn't take the bait. Instead, he leaned against the mixing console and tilted his head, his expression calm, almost serene. "You're right, "he said quietly, his voice cutting through the tension like a razor. "I do have the answers. That's why you're here."

The arrogant tone of his words hit Eric like a blow. He opened his mouth to respond but thought better of it, his jaw clenching as he stormed out of the control room.

The door slammed shut, leaving the rest of the room in an uneasy silence.

Later that night, long after the session had ended, Perry found solace in Casey's apartment.

The small space was lit only by the faint glow of candles, their flickering flames casting long shadows across the walls. The air was heavy with the smell of incense and wax, a stark contrast to the sharp, industrial atmosphere of the studio. Casey moved languidly through the room, her presence both grounding and electric, her dark eyes watching Perry with an intensity that saw through his every defense.

Together, they sketched out ideas for the artwork that would become *Nothing's Shocking*. Perry's mind was alive with images, twisted, provocative, unforgettable. And Casey was the perfect partner to bring those ideas to life.

"What do you think about Siamese twins?" he asked, his voice low and contemplative.

Casey raised an eyebrow, intrigued. "Like conjoined?"

Perry nodded, his hands gesturing as he spoke. "Yeah, but… beautiful. Unsettling, but magnetic. They're sitting on a chair, and they're… on fire."

Casey didn't flinch. She reached for her sketchbook, her pencil moving swiftly across the page as she began to translate Perry's vision into something tangible.

The artwork they created that night would become as much a part of Jane's Addiction as the music itself. It was raw, provocative, and fearless, an extension of everything Perry wanted the band to be.

And as the first faint rays of dawn began to creep through the windows, Perry leaned back against the wall, his mind finally quiet, his vision finally clear.

Casey's artistic style was a force unto itself. Her sculptures were unapologetic ally raw, stripped of pretense, and layered with a vulnerability that made them impossible to look away from. Often rendered in jagged, unpolished forms, her pieces explored themes of love, pain, and the fragile nature of the human condition. Perry found himself both captivated and unsettled by her work. To him, Casey wasn't just a girlfriend, she was his mirror, his creative equal, and sometimes even his rival.

Her sculptures mirrored the duality of everything he wanted Jane's Addiction to embody: beauty and decay, sex and violence, chaos and control. She understood his need to provoke, to shock people into paying attention, and her art reflected that same defiant philosophy.

One night, as they worked on the sketches for the album cover, Casey glanced at him from across the room, her dark eyes sharp. Her fingers, smudged with charcoal, moved over the paper with quick, deliberate strokes. She exhaled slowly, as though bracing herself, and said, "They'll never let you use these. Not in a million years."

Perry sat cross-legged on the floor, his back resting against a pile of scattered canvases. He glanced at her over the rim of his glasses, a sly grin playing at the corners of his mouth.

"They will, "he said, his voice low and sure, his tone leaving no room for argument. "Or I'll burn the fucking master tapes."

Casey paused, her hand stilling over the paper as she studied him. She could see it in his eyes, he wasn't joking. Perry never made idle threats. If he felt the band's vision was being compromised, he would destroy it all without hesitation. To him, staying true to their art meant everything, even if it meant alienating everyone around him.

She leaned back against the wall, her expression torn between admiration and concern. "You'd really do it, wouldn't you?" she asked, though she already knew the answer.

Perry, who wasn't a smoker, reached for the cigarette in her hand and took a long drag - the glow of the ember briefly illuminated the faint track marks on his arm. He exhaled slowly, the smoke curling upward like a ghost. "What's the point of making art if it's not honest?" he said finally. His voice was calm, but there was an edge to it, something raw and unrelenting.

Casey nodded, but her gaze lingered on the marks on his arm. She knew Perry believed in the idea of altered states fueling creativity, he'd preached it to anyone who would listen, citing poets, musicians, and artists who had lived and died by the same philosophy. At first, she had been drawn to his passion, his willingness to throw himself completely into his art, no matter the cost. But now, as their heroin use had become more frequent, she was beginning to see the toll it was taking on both of them.

For Perry, the stress of finishing the album had driven him deeper into his addiction. He believed the drugs helped him tap into something primal, something that allowed him to create without fear or inhibition. But the highs were getting shorter, and the crashes were hitting harder. When he wasn't high, he became irritable, restless, and increasingly difficult to be around.

Casey wasn't immune, either. At first, she'd joined him in shooting up to escape the pressure of her own work, to silence the constant noise in her head that told her she wasn't good enough. But now, she needed it just to feel normal, just to keep her hands from trembling as she worked. The sickness that came when they were sober, the nausea, the sweating, the aches, only added to the stress, creating a vicious cycle they couldn't seem to break.

Their nights in her apartment had taken on a dreamlike quality, a haze of candlelight, turpentine, and the slow, rhythmic click of a lighter sparking to life. They would sit together on the floor, surrounded by sketches and sculptures, their conversations veering between the profound and the nonsensical as the drugs took hold.

"The fire needs to look alive, "Perry muttered one night, leaning over a sketch of the conjoined twins. His voice was distant, his pupils blown wide. He gestured toward the drawing, his movements slow and deliberate. "It needs to feel like it's moving. Like it's eating them alive, but they're still… beautiful."

Casey nodded, her own hand unsteady as she reached for her pencil. She could feel the dull ache in her stomach, the creeping nausea that reminded her she would need another hit soon. But for now, she focused on the drawing, her mind tethered to Perry's vision.

"You're driving yourself crazy, "she said softly, her voice carrying both affection and a quiet warning. She glanced at him out of the corner of her eye, taking in the way his hands trembled slightly as he poured another glass of wine.

Perry didn't look up from the sketch. "If it doesn't drive me crazy, it's not worth doing, "he said, his voice flat but resolute.

Casey sighed, her fingers tightening around the pencil. She understood him better than anyone, but even she couldn't ignore the toll his obsession was taking. The circles under his eyes were darker, his frame thinner. He was burning himself out, and she knew it. But what scared her more was that she couldn't pull him back.

"You know this is going to kill us, right?" she said finally, her voice quiet, almost fragile.

Perry paused, his hand hovering over the sketch. He looked up at her then, his gaze softening. For a moment, the fire in his eyes dimmed, replaced by something quieter, something almost like fear. "No, it's not, "he said, shaking his head. He leaned back against the wall, his fingers rubbing the bridge of his nose.

"Once the album's finished, "he continued, his voice low but certain, "we're going back on methadone. We'll kick. Before the tour starts. I promise."

Casey raised an eyebrow, skeptical but unwilling to call him on it. She had heard promises like this before, promises made in moments of clarity that crumbled under the weight of withdrawal. But something about the way he said it, the raw determination in his voice, made her want to believe him.

"You mean it?" she asked, her tone softer now, her gaze searching his.

Perry nodded, a faint, tired smile tugging at the corners of his mouth. "I mean it, "he said. "We're not going to be one of those bands. We're not going to burn out before we even get started."

Casey exhaled slowly, leaning back against the wall. She wanted to believe him. She needed to believe him. But as she looked at the faint sheen of sweat on his forehead, the jittery way his fingers tapped against his knee, she couldn't ignore the sinking feeling in her gut.

They sat in silence for a while after that, the weight of their unspoken doubts hanging in the air between them. Perry leaned his head against her shoulder, his breathing slow and steady as he began to drift off.

Casey closed her eyes, her hand brushing lightly against his hair. She wanted to believe that they could get clean, that they could create something beautiful without tearing themselves apart in the process. But as the faint hum of Jane's Addiction's unfinished tracks played on a loop in the background, she couldn't shake the fear that the fire they were chasing would consume them both

David Jerden's car screeched to a halt outside the studio, his face a storm of confusion and concern as he spotted the band spilling out of the building like a dam had broken. Perry led the charge, his stride loose, a bottle of wine in his hand. Dave was already halfway to the car, muttering under his breath, his shoulders hunched in frustration.

"What the hell's going on?" Jerden barked, slamming his car door as he stepped out.

Perry stopped mid-stride, turning back with a smirk that was more mask than emotion. "We're done, "he said, his voice flat. "Band's broken up. No record."

Dave cursed audibly as he yanked open the car door, sliding in with a force that shook the entire vehicle. Stephen lingered on the curb, one hand rubbing the back of his neck, looking like he wanted to say something but couldn't muster the energy. Instead, he let out a long sigh and followed Dave, the car door closing behind him with a muffled thud.

Jerden blinked, his mouth opening and closing as if the words Perry had just spoken physically hit him. "You're serious?" he finally asked, incredulity dripping from every syllable.

Perry shrugged, raising the bottle to his lips and taking a swig. "Dead fucking serious."

The casual dismissal sent Jerden into a tailspin of anger and disbelief. He didn't move, his hands tightening into fists at his sides as he watched Perry saunter toward his car like it was just another day.

"Perry, stop goddammit!" Jerden yelled, his voice cutting through the tense silence like a whip.

Perry hesitated, his back to Jerden, the bottle hanging loosely at his side. For a moment, it seemed like he might ignore the man entirely, but then he sighed, his shoulders slumping ever so slightly, and stopped in his tracks.

Jerden stalked closer, his face red with anger. "Emergency meeting. Tomorrow morning. My office!" he spat, his tone leaving no room for argument. "All of you. Execs will be there too. We're settling this once and for all."

Perry still didn't turn around, but his head tilted slightly, signaling he'd heard.

"And in the meantime, "Jerden continued, jabbing a finger toward Perry's back, "don't fucking speak to them. Don't do anything stupid. You hear me?"

The silence dragged on, heavy and brittle, before Perry finally muttered, "Yeah, whatever."

He started walking again, the sound of his boots on the pavement echoing in the night. Jerden stayed rooted in place, shaking his head in bitter frustration as he watched the retreating figure.

"Goddamn fucking artists, "he muttered under his breath, turning back to his car. He climbed in, gripping the wheel so tightly his knuckles turned white. Somewhere in the distance, the studio lights flickered, casting long, distorted shadows against the building, ghosts of a band that seemed to be unraveling at the seams.

The next day Perry, Stephen, Eric and finally Dave, stumbled into the conference room at Warner Bros., which was unusually cold. The band sat around an apparently, recently-polished table that seemed to swallow them whole. Perry leaned back in his chair at the head of the table, exuding his usual casual defiance. Across from him, Eric sat stiffly, his arms crossed, his face etched with simmering anger. Dave slouched in his chair, looking pale, tiered and strung-out, while Stephen leaned forward, rubbing his temples like a man caught in a migraine.

At one end of the table were two Label Execs, on the other was Jergen. The tension in the room was thick enough to cut with a knife, but the two label executives on the far side of the table were trying their best to appear neutral. Their body language betrayed them, though, fidgeting hands, tight lips, and shifting glances revealed their discomfort.

Perry leaned forward suddenly, breaking the silence. His voice was sharp, almost cutting. "I told you what I wanted. Fifty percent. I'm not gonna keep repeating myself, "he said, his tone brooking no argument.

Eric shot up straighter in his chair, his expression darkening. "And I told you it's bullshit. Fifty percent? Are you kidding me? That's not a band, Perry. That's a fucking dictatorship. And you know it."

Perry smirked, the kind of smirk that could set anyone's blood boiling. "Call it whatever you want, E. It's still my name on the songs."

Eric's hands clenched into fists on the table. "Our name is on the fucking album. The band is called 'Jane's Addiction, ' not 'Perry Farrell and Friends.'"

Dave stopped strumming, looking up with a resigned expression. "Look, Eric, I'm not saying it's fair, "he said flatly. "But he's not gonna budge. We all know that."

Eric turned on Dave, his voice rising with frustration. "So you're just gonna roll over? Let him take whatever he wants?"

Dave shrugged, his exhaustion evident. "What the fuck do you want me to do? We're weeks out from the release. You think this fight is gonna help anything?"

Stephen raised his hands in an attempt to mediate. "Alright, alright, calm the fuck down, "he said, his voice tinged with desperation. "Look, no one's happy about this, but the album's done. I mean, shit, guys, we're going on the road with Iggy-fucking-Pop and The Ramones! This is it! We're pulling this shit-show of an idea off! I just want to play, man. Make people happy. Wasn't that the whole fucking point of all this?"

Eric's head snapped toward Stephen, disbelief etched into his features. "Move forward? At what cost? This isn't just about the money. It's about the principle. You and I started this fucking thing together. Or have you already forgotten that? You're seriously okay with throwing that away?"

Perry cut in, his tone ice-cold. "I didn't throw anything away, Eric. I wrote the songs, I brought the vision. You wanna walk? Fine. It sure as hell isn't what I want, brother, but the door's right there."

The words hit like a slap, and Eric stood abruptly, his chair scraping loudly against the floor. "Fuck you, Perry, "he snarled, his voice dripping with venom.

Perry didn't flinch, his eyes locked on Eric like a predator waiting to strike.

"You're outvoted. Three to one. That's how this works. Democracy, right? You should appreciate that, "Perry said, his smirk returning like a dagger twisting in Eric's gut.

Eric's face flushed, his anger bubbling over. He glanced at Dave and Stephen, who both avoided his gaze. Their guilt was written all over their faces, but neither spoke up.

"You're all just letting him get away with it, "Eric said, his voice quieter now, tinged with bitterness. "You fucking know this is wrong."

Without another word, he stormed out of the room, slamming the door behind him. The sound echoed like a gunshot, leaving a heavy silence in its wake.

Stephen let out a long breath, leaning back in his chair. "That could've gone better, "he said quietly.

Dave shook his head, setting his guitar down. "Could've gone worse."

Perry, for once, looked unsettled. He leaned over the table, rubbing his temples before leaning back in his chair. "It went exactly how it needed to, "he muttered.

The two label executives, who had been watching the exchange like spectators at a car crash, finally moved. One of them, an older man with thinning hair, stood up and shook his head in frustration.

"Christ, you kids, "he muttered. "Okay, now that we've sorted out all the bullshit, we have a major fucking issue to discuss."

He tossed a proof of the album's cover art onto the table. It was a photograph of a sculpture, a Siamese twin female figure with flaming heads, designed by Perry and Casey. The image was striking, beautiful, and unapologetic-ally provocative.

"We can't put this in stores, fellas, "the executive said, exasperated. "I mean, what the hell are you thinking? Children buy rock albums. You think their parents are going to fork over money for a record with fucking breasts on the cover? Much less allow it in their suburban, 'Christian' homes?"

Perry smirked, leaning back in his chair. "That's exactly who I'm thinking of. The ones suffocating in suburban perfection."

The executive stared at him, dumbfounded, before turning to Dave and Stephen, as if hoping for backup. Both of them shrugged, their expressions saying, "He's not wrong."

The executive threw up his hands in frustration. "We'll lose retailers. Walmart, K-Mart, "

"Good, "Perry interrupted, his smirk widening. "Art isn't meant for fluorescent lights."

The executive glared at him, then turned and stormed out, slamming the door on his way. The room fell silent again, the tension thick but oddly victorious.

Finally, another executive, younger and less jaded, cleared his throat. "There's another issue, guys, "he said hesitantly.

Dave groaned, leaning back in his chair. "Jesus Christ, what the fuck now?"

"The video, "the executive said, shuffling papers nervously. "For, uh, 'Mountain Song'? MTV refuses to air it."

Stephen snorted. "So? Who gives a rat's-ass?"

The executive's patience snapped. "Your fucking record label does. You know, the people who paid for it?!"

Perry, who had been staring at the ceiling, finally spoke up. "So we put the video out ourselves, "he said, his tone calm but decisive. "On VHS tape. Your Warner Bros., aren't you? So make a short film out of it. Get it in the fucking video rental stores. And for sale in retail shops. You'll make your money back and then some."

The executive blinked, caught off guard. "Dammit, "he muttered, nodding slowly. "Okay. I'll see what we can do."

Nothings Shocking

The summer of 1988 hit Los Angeles like a goddamn furnace, an unrelenting heatwave that made the asphalt shimmer and the smog hang heavy over the city, and on August 28, 1988, *Nothing's Shocking* is released, to massive critical acclaim. But inside Tower Records on Sunset Boulevard, the air was thick with something hotter than the weather: controversy.

The staff at the iconic store were busy following corporate orders, wrapping Jane's Addiction's *Nothing's Shocking* in plain brown paper. The decision, they were told, wasn't up for debate. The album's cover, a conjoined nude sculpture of Perry's girlfriend Casey Niccoli, their heads engulfed in flames, was deemed too "explicit" for public display. To Perry, this was fucking perfect.

The band hit the road immediately, opening for Piggy Pop, a dream come true for all of them. This was the big time. Not only were they sharing the stage with one of their idols, but they were also playing to larger, more enthusiastic crowds than ever before. Word-of-mouth about *Nothing's Shocking* spread like wildfire, fueled by both its critical acclaim and the controversy surrounding its artwork and limited availability. But behind the scenes, the chaos of addiction and tension loomed large.

One night, early in the tour, Dave and Stephen were in a dimly lit hotel room. Stephen sat cross-legged on the bed, flipping through a Rolling Stone magazine, while Dave crouched at the desk, nervously fiddling with something out of Stephen's line of sight. The faint glow of the TV filled the room with flickering light.

Onscreen, an MTV News Break suddenly aired, the voice of a female VJ cutting through the silence.

"A hard rock band from Los Angeles that calls themselves 'Jane's Addiction', currently on the road opening for Iggy Pop, released their highly anticipated debut album *Nothing's Shocking* last week to high critical praise, "the VJ announced. "The first single 'Mountain Song' has generated significant buzz, though MTV is unable to air its music video due to regulations. Meanwhile, record stores have reportedly been wrapping copies of the album in brown paper due to its controversial cover art depicting frontal nudity. Jane's Addiction can be seen touring with Iggy Pop and The Ramones across the country through the end of the year and next spring. This has been an MTV News Update."

Stephen set the magazine down and glanced at the screen, shaking his head. Cracking a beer, "Man… all this press, and they're still censoring us."

Dave didn't look up, his focus elsewhere. "Yeah, well… we'll sell more records because of this bullshit. People want what they can't have."

Stephen sighed, watching Dave for a moment. "You good, man? You've been been hitting the needle hard lately. Do I need to concerned?"

Dave paused, then gave a small, distracted nod. "I'm fine Stephen"

The tension in the room was thick, unspoken but palpable. Stephen exhaled deeply, grabbing the remote and turning off the TV. He stood up and stretched, rubbing the back of his neck. "Whatever, man. Just… don't let all this get to you."

Dave nodded again, barely registering Stephen's words. As Stephen left the room to join the others downstairs, Dave leaned back in the chair, running his hands through his hair. The growing pressure of fame and expectation pressed down on them all, threatening to crack the fragile bond they had built.

In another room down the hall, Perry sat with Casey, the two of them sprawled on the floor amid notebooks, sketches, and scraps of lyrics. Perry was scribbling frantically, the creative rush pouring out of him like a torrent. Casey watched him with a mix of admiration and concern, her camera resting beside her.

"So a while back you asked me. so now I'm asking you: Ever think this shit is all happening way too fucking fast?" she asked, her voice soft.

Perry paused, tapping his pen against the paper. "Fast? Yeah, it's fast. But this is…its our world now, baby. Right?"

Casey frowned, but said nothing, watching as Perry returned to his writing.

The band was riding high on success, but beneath the surface, cracks were forming, cracks that, if ignored, could shatter everything they had worked so hard to create.

"Man, this is exactly what Perry wanted, "Dave Navarro would later recall, leaning back in the control room of Radio Tokyo Studios, his feet propped up on the console, a lit cigarette dangling between his fingers. "The more they tried to hide it, the more kids wanted to know what the fuck was inside. It was genius."

Inside that plain brown wrapping was more than just a provocative image, it was a declaration. Perry Farrell's artwork was as confrontational as the music itself. The nude sculpture of Casey wasn't pornographic, despite what the suits at Walmart seemed to think. It was haunting and surreal, an unsettling collision of beauty and destruction. The conjoined twins rocked silently in their chair, their fiery heads casting shadows across an imagined world.

"It wasn't just about shock value, "Perry explained years later during a local T.V. interview, stretched out on a ratty couch backstage, a glass of red wine held loosely in his hand. His voice carried that familiar mix of mischief and conviction, the tone of someone who knew exactly how to rattle cages. "It was art, man. Raw, unapologetic art. You're supposed to feel something when you see it. You're supposed to be uncomfortable. That's what art is fucking for."

But middle America didn't see it that way.

The reaction from conservative America was swift and hysterical. Walmart, the retail behemoth that controlled a massive chunk of the country's album sales, took one look at the cover and promptly lost their shit. Their executives decreed that *Nothing's Shocking* would not grace their shelves, no matter what kind of packaging it came in. Other big chains followed suit, sending a clear message: Jane's Addiction wasn't welcome in polite society.

The outrage rippled outwards, carried by conservative radio hosts and Sunday morning preachers who clutched their pearls at the "moral decay" of rock music. "Sick, "they called it. "Degenerate."

Eric was less of pessimist and sardonic observer, and found the whole situation hilariously ironic. During a soundcheck at the Roxy, he leaned against his bass amp and smirked, shaking his head. "We're being censored by people who probably couldn't tell you the difference between Beethoven and Chuck Berry, "he said, his voice dripping with disdain. "These suits are deciding what's too shocking for America? That's what's fucking shocking."

The backlash only fueled Perry's fire. He wasn't interested in catering to the Walmart's of the world. For him, the controversy wasn't just a byproduct of the art, it was the art.

However, The refusal to stock *Nothing's Shocking* was a logistical nightmare for Warner Bros., Jane's Addiction's label. Without Walmart and the other big retail chains, the album was effectively shut out of the mainstream market. But for the band, that only added to its allure.

"You can't find the damn thing in half the country, "Dave Navarro said, grinning as he adjusted his guitar strap before a sold-out show at the . "But that just made people want it more. It turned the album into this forbidden thing. Like, 'Why the fuck can't I buy this?'"

Perry, of course, leaned into the controversy. During interviews, he refused to backpedal or apologize for the album's artwork. "If they're so scared of a naked woman with flames on her head, "he told a journalist from Spin with a devilish grin, "what the fuck are they gonna do when they actually hear the music?"

The music itself was incendiary, a raw blend of punk, funk, and metal that defied categorization. Songs like "Ocean Size" and "Ted, Just Admit It…" weren't just tracks, they were declarations. Perry's lyrics didn't just flirt with taboo, they stared it dead in the eyes and dared it to blink. And the album's centerpiece, "Mountain Song, "was an anthem of unrelenting power, Navarro's blistering riffs colliding with Avery's steady, hypnotic bass-line.

For Perry, *Nothing's Shocking* wasn't just an album, it was a cultural flash-bang, a wake-up call for a generation he felt had grown numb. The title itself was a challenge, a sneer at a world where shock and outrage had become commodities. "The only reason nothing's shocking anymore, "Perry said during a chaotic radio interview, "is because everyone's too afraid to take risks. They're too afraid to feel anything. That's the real fucking tragedy."

Despite the backlash, or maybe because of it, *Nothing's Shocking* found its audience. In the underground clubs of Los Angeles, kids lined up to buy tickets to see Jane's Addiction live, their excitement buzzing in the overheated air. For every Walmart that banned the album, there was a kid with a fake ID walking into Tower Records, peeling off the brown wrapping, and discovering the wild, unfiltered world Perry had created.

And the band, for all their dysfunction, delivered. On stage, they were a force of nature. Perry stalked the stage like a shaman, his voice climbing to impossible heights as he threw himself into each song with reckless abandon. Dave Navarro shredded his guitar with an intensity that left the crowd breathless, while Eric Avery's bass-lines held everything together, a steady heartbeat in the storm. Stephen Perkins, the youngest of the group, pounded the drums like his life depended on it, his rhythms tight and tribal.

"You couldn't ignore it, "one fan would later say, recalling a sold-out show at the Palladium. "You couldn't fucking ignore them. Jane's Addiction wasn't just a band, they were an experience."

Even as the band celebrated the small victories, the growing crowds, the underground buzz, the unspoken tension simmering beneath the surface, especially due to Perry's drive to shock and provoke, was starting to wear on the group. The endless battles over the music, the artwork, the costs of the live shows, it was taking its toll.

But for now, in the fall of 1988, none of that mattered. Jane's Addiction was on fire, and the world was starting to feel the heat.

MTV, the almighty arbiter of musical taste in the late 1980's, proved just as squeamish as the retail chains. The banning of "Mountain Song" was pure hypocrisy. This was the same channel that had no problem airing a parade of spandex-clad hair metal bands, stripper poles, and coke-fueled excess. But Perry Farrell standing shirtless under dim lights, singing about addiction and freedom, was apparently too much for their fragile sensibilities.

"They were fine with tits and ass as long as they came with Aqua Net and fake smiles, "Perry said later, grinning as he knocked back a shot of tequila during an interview. "But give them something real, something with a little grit, and they freak the fuck out. That's the hypocrisy, man. They don't want art, they want a product."

Stephen Perkins had a different take. Sitting on a stool during a break from a marathon drumming session, he laughed it off. "The whole thing is like gasoline on a fire, "he said, twirling a drumstick between his fingers. "Every time someone tries to shut us down or cover us up, ten more kids show up at the next show. They wanna know what all the fuss is about. It's fucking awesome." And those kids kept coming.

The band's live shows during this period became the epicenter of the controversy, a visceral, undeniable experience that couldn't be contained by brown paper wrappers or corporate gatekeepers. Night after night, Jane's Addiction proved that the power of *Nothing's Shocking* wasn't in its packaging or promotion, it was in the fucking music.

"Mountain Song" hit the crowd like a bomb. Navarro's guitar ripped through the air, sharp and relentless, while Eric's bass-lines thundered beneath it, holding everything together. Perry prowled the stage like a man possessed, his wiry frame illuminated by harsh spotlights, his voice rising to a manic scream that seemed to tear through the crowd's collective chest.

"Jane Says" was the moment when chaos gave way to catharsis. The crowd, sweaty and bruised, transformed into a choir. Thousands of voices joined Perry in telling Jane's story, a bittersweet tale of addiction and hope that resonated with a generation searching for something to believe in.

Once the Iggy Pop tour ended and before starting the tour with The Ramones, Jane's Addiction would spend the winter of '88 / '89 honing their live performance and skills, by doing multiple night "residencies" at notable clubs and venues all over L.A. and a small headlining tour across the U.S. in major cities, growing their following, one crazy, in-your-face show at a time.

The Scream wasn't just a club, it was a fucking sanctuary. Housed in an old Korean church in downtown Los Angeles, The Scream had become ground zero for Jane's Addiction's growing cult. Its faded wooden pews and stained-glass windows bore silent witness to a new kind of worship, one built on tribal rhythms, distorted guitars, and the kind of primal energy that felt both sacred and profane.

Michael Stewart, the club's owner, watched the scene unfold night after night. "The line starts forming around four in the afternoon, "he said, leaning against the bar during a rare quiet moment. "You've got kids with mohawks standing next to art school types, next to metal-heads, next to punks. By showtime, it's wrapped around three city blocks. It's like everyone who doesn't belong anywhere else shows up here."

Inside, the atmosphere was electric, chemical, spiritual, volatile. The old wooden floors groaned under the weight of hundreds of bodies, all moving in unison, pulsing with the energy of the music. The walls, once painted white, were now covered in graffiti, the scrawled messages of kids desperate to leave their mark on something bigger than themselves.

Casey Niccoli, watching from the edge of the stage one night, described it as "an underground revolution." She lit a cigarette, her gaze scanning the crowd as she spoke. "These kids come clutching their copies of *Nothing's Shocking* like they're carrying sacred texts. And in a way, they are. The brown paper wrapper just makes it more mysterious, more powerful. It's like they're holding something the world doesn't want them to see, and that makes it feel… important. The shows themselves were transcendent.

When the band launched into "Up the Beach, "the entire building seemed to shift. Stephen's tribal drums and Eric's deep, hypnotic bass-line filled the space, a sonic wave that moved through the crowd like a force of nature.

"You see these kids in the front row, "Dave Navarro said, adjusting his guitar strings before a soundcheck one night. "They know every fucking word, every riff. But it isn't just about the music. They're looking for something bigger. Something real in a plastic fucking world."

The pit during "Pigs in Zen" was legendary, a swirling, chaotic mass of bodies and sweat, all moving to the primal rhythm laid down by Stephen and Eric. Perry stood above it all, arms outstretched, conducting the insanity like a deranged prophet.

"It's beautiful violence, "Stephen said, catching his breath after a particularly brutal set. "Like a tribe finding itself through rhythm and noise. You don't just play a Jane's Addiction show, you survive it."

Meanwhile, in the sterile offices of Warner Bros. Records, executives were scratching their heads over the sales reports.

The numbers didn't make sense. Here was an album being refused by major retailers, with videos banned by MTV, and yet somehow, sales were climbing week after week. The controversy had become currency.

"These suits can't understand it, "Eric said, rolling his eyes during an interview at Radio Tokyo Studios. "They keep trying to figure out how to market us, while we're already selling out shows across the country. The kids get it. They don't need some fucking marketing campaign to tell them what's real."

The brown paper wrapping had become a symbol of rebellion. Across suburban bedrooms and inner-city apartments, kids sat cross-legged on their floors, peeling back the paper like it was some kind of sacred ritual. The cover, a fiery, conjoined monument to Perry's vision, stared back at them, unapologetic and bold.

"They tried to hide it, "Perry said later, during an interview on KROQ, the premier L.A. alternative station, his voice tinged with satisfaction. "But all they did was make it louder. It's fucking beautiful. They think they're protecting their kids from something dangerous, but the kids know better. They know we're telling the truth."

The truth was in the grooves of the vinyl. It was in the raw sexuality of "Mountain Song, "the jagged vulnerability of "Ted, Just Admit It…, "and the tribal pulse of "Up the Beach." It was in Perry's snarling voice, Eric's steady heartbeat bass-lines, Dave's razor-sharp riffs, and Stephen's relentless drums.

But the truth wasn't just in the music, it was in the reaction. Jane's Addiction wasn't a band to be neatly packaged or sold. They were a fucking movement, a primal scream against the sanitized rebellion the mainstream tried to sell. And the kids who showed up night after night, their fists raised and their voices hoarse, weren't just fans, they were believers.

Rock Stars

Warner Bros. Records found themselves in an unprecedented situation. They had a product, a fucking explosive one, that was thriving despite every traditional marketing channel being slammed shut in their faces. Walmart wouldn't stock it. MTV wouldn't play it. Retailers didn't want it on their shelves unless it was wrapped up like some kind of porno mag.

And yet, *Nothing's Shocking* was selling.

It wasn't just selling, it was building momentum. The album was spreading like a goddamn wildfire, the controversy fueling its growth instead of stifling it. Perry Farrell and Jane's Addiction had accidentally created a new paradigm: a world where censorship wasn't a roadblock, but free advertising. Where every refusal, every ban, every pearl-clutching reaction only added to the mystique.

No marketing exec could have predicted it, and no one in the boardrooms of Warner Bros. knew how to replicate it. But the band didn't give a shit about replicating anything. They were too busy living it.

"Look, "Perry said one night, perched on his amp after another sweat-soaked show at the Roxy. His shirt was off, his chest streaked with drying sweat, and his voice carried the scratchy edge of someone who'd just spent the last hour screaming his fucking heart out. His eyes were wide and wild, glinting in the dim backstage light.

"We're not setting out to piss people off, "he said, gesturing vaguely with his glass of wine."We're just making the fucking album we have to make. All this other shit, the controversy, the wrapped albums, the banned videos? That's just proof that we're striking a nerve. And isn't that what real art is supposed to do? Make you feel something real?"

Dave Navarro leaned back against the wall, cradling his guitar. He smirked, watching Perry with a mix of amusement and admiration. "You're pretty good at pissing people off, though, "he said dryly, flicking his cigarette into a half-empty beer can.

Perry grinned, his face lighting up like a kid who'd just gotten away with something. "Yeah, well. Sometimes people need a good kick in the ass."

In the end, *Nothing's Shocking* was becoming more than just an album. It was a fucking statement.

The brown paper wrappers, the censored videos, the angry letters to the editor, all of it only added to the mystique. Every kid who tore away that plain packaging wasn't just opening an album; they were opening a door. Inside, they found something raw and real in a world full of cheap imitations.

In cramped record stores across America, teenagers huddled together, passing the album around like contraband. The brown paper would fall away to reveal Casey Niccoli's sculptured form, conjoined and ablaze, staring back at them like a challenge. Then they'd drop the needle, and the real revelation would begin.

From the opening notes of "Up the Beach, "the album wrapped around you like a fucking tidal wave. Eric Avery's deep, hypnotic bass-lines pulled you under, while Stephen Perkins' tribal drumming pounded like the heartbeat of something ancient. Dave Navarro's guitar slashed and soared, raw and electric, and then there was Perry, howling, pleading, snarling. His voice didn't just tell stories; it dragged you into them, kicking and screaming.

By the time "Mountain Song" roared through the speakers, there was no going back.

"The power of the album isn't in the cover, or the controversy, "Eric said during an interview with a college radio station in Chicago. His tone was calm, but there was a sharp edge to it, as if he was daring the interviewer to disagree. "It's in the songs. It's in the way they hit you, right in the fucking gut."

While hair metal bands posed and punk bands spat, Jane's Addiction invented a genre.

Nothing's Shocking wasn't just an album title, it was a challenge. A defiant sneer at a culture that had grown numb, too comfortable with its own boundaries. Perry wasn't just saying "nothing's shocking anymore." He was asking, Why the fuck not?

The songs on the album weren't safe. They didn't play by the rules. They didn't wrap themselves up in neat little packages with easy-to-digest messages. "Ted, Just Admit It…" tore open the ugliness of voyeurism and violence, throwing it in your face with Perry's haunting refrain: "Nothing's shocking."

"Jane Says" was raw and painfully vulnerable, a song about a woman trying to claw her way out of addiction, her hope as fragile as the steel drum Perkins played beneath it. And then there was "Pigs in Zen, "a snarling, feral declaration of defiance, Perry's voice slicing through Navarro's riffs like a razor.

"This wasn't about rebellion for the sake of rebellion, "Dave explained in an interview years later. "It was about cutting through the bullshit. It was about showing people the truth, whether they wanted to see it or not."

"They don't get it, "Eric said, rolling his eyes during a post-show interview at a dive bar in Detroit. "They're sitting there scratching their heads, trying to figure out what marketing trick we pulled. Meanwhile, the kids already know. They fucking know."

The kids did know. They didn't need a TV commercial or a flashy magazine spread to tell them what was real. All they needed was a copy of the album, that brown paper wrapper, and the first crackle of the needle hitting the vinyl.

Casey, leaning against the bar at The Scream one night, summed it up best: "The brown wrapper just makes it more powerful. It's like they're holding something the world doesn't want them to see. And when they rip it open, it's like finding something forbidden. Something sacred."

In bedrooms and basements across America, *Nothing's Shocking* became more than music. It became a fucking movement. Kids played it on repeat, its raw energy seeping into their bones. They scribbled Perry's lyrics in the margins of their notebooks, etched the band's name onto their backpacks. At shows, they screamed along with every word, their voices cracking with emotion.

Perry would later say, "We weren't trying to be anyone's saviors. We were just telling the truth. And maybe that's all people really need, someone willing to say what's real."

The controversy would fade. The brown paper wrappers would crumble away. But the music, raw, defiant, fucking glorious, would endure. And in the end, that's what mattered.

Behind the growing success of *Nothing's Shocking*, cracks within Jane's Addiction are ever-widening. For all the controversy surrounding the album and its raw, unfiltered power, the band itself is teetering on the edge.

The summer of 1989 was a blur of chaos and sound. Jane's Addiction was at the peak of their early fame, playing larger venues, mesmerizing audiences with raw, unhinged energy. But behind the curtain, the band teetered on the brink, their addictions eating away at them. For Eric Avery, the drugs that once seemed to fuel the creative fire were now extinguishing it.

Touring internationally had turned the simple act of scoring heroin into an exhausting, humiliating grind. In Los Angeles, it was easy, he knew the spots, the people, the routines. On the road, it was a scavenger hunt in strange cities, trying to make connections where none existed. He hated himself for it, but he hated the sickness more. When the withdrawal came, it was like his body had declared war on him, skin crawling, bones aching, and a gnawing pit in his stomach that wouldn't let up.

On a humid night in London, the band stumbled off stage after a show that had left them and the crowd in pieces. Backstage, Perry wiped his face with a towel, still buzzing from the performance, but his sharp eyes immediately caught Eric slumped in a chair, pale and trembling. He walked over, leaning against the edge of a table.

"E, you look like shit, "Perry said, more concerned than mocking.

Eric exhaled, his hand shaking as he set his bass aside. "Thanks, man. Really needed to hear that. Asshole"

"No, seriously." Perry knelt in closer, lowering his voice. "You're dope sick, aren't you?"

Eric didn't answer right away. He wiped sweat from his face, his jaw tight. "Yeah, "he muttered. "But I'll get through it."

Perry tilted his head, studying him. "You want me to find something? I'll ask around. Could make a few calls, get you sorted out."

Eric's eyes snapped up to Perry, his expression sharp. "No."

"Don't be fucking stupid, man, "Perry insisted, his tone calm but insistent. "You don't have to suffer through this. I know the right people. I can get us both straightened out."

"I said no." Eric's voice was firm now. "I'm done, Perry. Done with this shit."

Perry blinked, genuinely taken aback. "What do you mean, done?"

Eric leaned back, staring at the ceiling for a moment before looking back at Perry. "I mean I'm not doing it anymore. I'm not you. I'm not letting this… fucking shit control me. Not again. Not after tonight."

Perry looked skeptical, his mouth twitching into a half-smirk. "You've said that before, man."

Eric shook his head. "Not like this. That last shot last night. That's it. I'm gonna suffer through this." Holding his stomach, he leans over in pain, exhales, "I'm done."

Perry crossed his arms, leaning back against the table. "You really think you can just… stop?"

Eric nodded, the conviction in his voice solidifying as he spoke. "Yeah. Because this isn't about survival anymore, Perry. It's not even about the music. It's about holding on to the one thing I've got left, myself. This shit isn't adding to the creativity, it's killing it. It's killing me."

Perry tilted his head, an odd look passing over his face. He looked as though he wanted to say something but stopped himself, finally nodding. "Alright, E. If that's what you want… I hope you can stick to it. Truly I do, brother."

Eric stood, still shaky but more resolved than he'd ever been. "I will."

That night, the band headed back to their hotel. Perry sat in a corner of the van, staring out the window in silence, while Dave and Stephen traded jokes to pass the time. Eric sat quietly, his head resting against the glass, already fighting the internal war he knew was coming. But this time, he welcomed it.

By the time they reached the hotel, Eric collapsed onto his bed, staring up at the ceiling as waves of nausea and aching overtook him. His mind buzzed with memories of the band's early days, the hope and chaos that had brought them together. He thought about the dreams they'd had when they started, about the fire that had driven them to create something bigger than themselves. Somewhere along the way, he'd lost sight of that. He wasn't going to let it slip away completely.

The next morning, Stephen knocked on his door, holding two cups of coffee. "You alive in there?" he joked, stepping inside.

"Barely, "Eric muttered, sitting up. He took the coffee, his hands still unsteady. "Thanks."

Stephen sat down across from him, sipping his own. "You serious about what you said last night? About quitting?"

Eric nodded, his voice quieter now. "Yeah. I can't do it anymore, man. It's not fucking worth it."

Stephen nodded, his usual joking demeanor softening. "Good. I don't wanna lose you, buddy." He gives a laugh, "I can't handle being in this traveling circus with those other two. Not without you."

Eric gave him a small, tired smile. "You won't."

And from that day on, he stuck to his word. That last shot on August 29, 1989, was his final one. The road ahead wasn't easy, but for the first time in a long time, Eric felt like he was moving toward something instead of away from it. He was ready to reclaim the parts of himself he thought he'd lost forever.

Perry, the restless visionary who once swore he'd kick heroin after finishing the record, is nowhere near sobriety. If anything, the relentless pressure of touring, interviews, and the weight of his own expectations have driven him deeper into the habit. The highs are shorter, the crashes more brutal, and the sickness that comes when he's not using is unbearable.

"Every time I try to stop, "Perry admits one night backstage, pacing with a wine glass in hand, his restless energy spilling out in rapid bursts. "It feels like the fucking world is collapsing. And when everyone's pulling you in a hundred different directions, labels, press, fans, it's easy to convince yourself you need it just to stay upright. But, man… this shit…this shit can own you when you let it"

Dave Navarro isn't faring much better. At first, Dave stayed distant, watching Perry's spirals with a mix of concern and fascination. But the grind of the tour, the relentless routine of life on the road, and the pressure to always deliver have pulled him in, too. Heroin quiets the noise in Dave's head. It makes it all bearable. For him. its always made life in general, bearable.

It doesn't take much for Perry and Dave to become each other's worst enemies and closest allies.

"They're like gasoline and a fucking match, "Eric Avery mutters during a soundcheck, shaking his head as he watches Perry stumble into the venue late, his hair disheveled and his jaw grinding slightly. "When Perry's not pushing Dave over the edge, Dave's dragging Perry down with him. It's toxic, man. And the worst part? They don't even fucking see it. They think they're fine as long as the music's good."

Perry and Dave's addictions are starting to bleed into everything. They still deliver onstage, Perry prowls like a madman, and Dave's guitar shreds the air with raw, blistering power, but backstage, things are falling apart.

The band has split into two camps. On one side are Eric Avery and Stephen Perkins, the rhythm section and the self-proclaimed "sane ones." They keep their heads down, focusing on the music and trying to hold everything together. On the other side are Perry and Dave, spiraling further into addiction, their behavior unpredictable and their tempers increasingly short.

"It's like living with two different bands, "Stephen says to his drum roadie one afternoon, adjusting his drum kit before a show. "There's the band that plays music, and then there's the band that's constantly fucking fighting or completely wrecked. And somehow, we're both of those things at the same time."

Eric's frustration is boiling over. Always the most grounded of the group, he believes in structure and discipline, treating the band like the job it is. Perry and Dave's unreliability drives him insane.

"We're holding this thing together with duct tape, "Eric snaps one night after Perry and Dave disappear during load-in. He paces the green room, running his hands through his hair. "I'm done babysitting these assholes. It's like they don't even give a shit anymore."

Stephen shrugs, keeping his voice calm. "They care. They just don't know how to handle the pressure."

"They're not handling shit, "Eric fires back. "We're the ones handling it. We're the ones who have to clean up their fucking mess."

The tension explodes one night after a show at The Aragon Ballroom in Chicago. Backstage, the room is thick with the tang of weed smoke and the sour stench of spilled wine. Perry paces like a caged animal, holding an empty glass and muttering under his breath. His movements are sharp, restless, his energy erratic. Dave is slouched in a chair, his eyes glassy and half-lidded, his guitar propped against his leg.

"You two need to get your shit together, dude" Eric says, his voice sharp as he leans against the wall. His arms are crossed, his expression tight with anger. "This daily, fucked up routine isn't sustainable. I'm fucking done covering for you."

Perry stops pacing, turning to face him, his eyes narrowing. "Don't fucking start with me, man, "he snaps, his voice low and threatening. "You think this is easy? You think carrying this whole fucking band is a walk in the park?"

"Carrying it?" Eric's voice rises, his anger bubbling over. "Are you fucking kidding me? You're dragging us down, Perry. You and Dave, you're like two fucking anchors, and we're the ones trying to keep this thing afloat."

"Maybe because you're babysitting two fucking junkies, "Dave mutters, smirking faintly from his chair. His voice is lazy, dripping with sarcasm. "What do you want, a gold star?"

"Shut the fuck up, Dave, "Eric shoots back, pointing a finger at him. "You're just as bad as he is."

Stephen steps between them, raising his hands in an attempt to de-escalate. "Guys, come on, "he says, his voice calm but firm. "This isn't the time for this shit."

Perry glares at Eric for a long moment before storming out of the room, slamming the door behind him.

Eric exhales sharply, running a hand over his face. "I can't do this much longer, man, "he mutters to Stephen, his voice weary. "This is gonna fucking break us."

And yet, despite everything, the addiction, the fights, the chaos, the music keeps pulling them back.

For all their differences, Jane's Addiction shares one unshakable bond: the music. When they're onstage, when the first notes of "Up the Beach" fill the room, the tension melts away. They're no longer Perry and Eric, or Dave and Stephen, they're Jane's Addiction.

"The music is bigger than us, "Stephen says quietly, sitting at the edge of the stage after a show, speaking with a local radio host. "No matter how fucked up things get offstage, when we play, it's like none of that shit matters."

For Perry and Dave, the music is both a refuge and an excuse. As long as the shows are good, they can convince themselves that they're fine. But the cracks are beginning to show.

During a soundcheck in New York, Perry stumbles into the venue an hour late, his jaw tight, his body jittery. He mumbles something about "traffic" as he pours himself a glass of wine from a bottle he swiped off a catering table.

Dave is already there, leaning against his amp with a vacant expression, his guitar hanging loose at his side.

Eric watches them both, his disgust written all over his face. "You're a fucking mess, "he says bluntly, shaking his head.

Perry smirks, sipping his wine. "Don't worry about me, "he says, his voice light but with an edge of defiance. "I've got this under control."

But everyone in the room knows he doesn't, and by the last leg of their *Nothing's Shocking,* headlining tour, the band is barely holding it together. The performances remain electric, the crowds growing larger and more fervent with every show. But behind the scenes, complete collapse

"We all knew it couldn't last forever, "Stephen would later admit to *SPIN* Magazine. "Not the way we were going. But at the time, it didn't matter. We had the music. And for us, that was enough."

Nothing's Shocking isn't just an album. It's a moment in time, a raw, chaotic burst of creativity and rebellion that burns bright, even as it threatens to destroy the people who created it.

And as the tour rages on, Perry's voice and Dave's guitar carry them forward, even as their addictions threaten to pull them apart.

Starting a Ritual

By late 1989, Jane's Addiction was deep in the creative process, of writing and recording what would become *Ritual de lo Habitual.* For weeks, the band had cycled in and out of the studio, pushing themselves to exhaustion, fraying nerves, and occasionally descending into outright conflict. Days bled into nights under the dim glow of the studio lights, and though the music they were creating was extraordinary, it came at a cost.

But Perry Farrell wasn't just thinking about the album. He had a new obsession: a film. He called it, "Gift."

The idea had been swirling in his mind for months, taking shape in moments of clarity between the chaos of recording sessions. It wasn't just a tour film or a behind-the-scenes documentary. Perry envisioned something much bigger, a raw, unflinching look at the band's creative process, their life on tour, and the intensity of his relationship with Casey. It would be part performance art, part confessional, a swirling mix of beauty, pain, and the truth of their world, no matter how uncomfortable that truth might be.

"We're not just making an album, "Perry told the band one night as they sat around the studio. His voice carried a manic energy, his words spilling out faster than he could organize them. "This is about showing people who we really are, onstage, offstage, everything. Not the polished bullshit they want us to give them. The real fucking deal. The music, the chaos, the love, the drugs, the art. All of it."

Eric, as always, looked skeptical. "You really think people are going to sit through a movie about us shooting up and fighting in between sets?" he asked, folding his arms across his chest.

"It's not about people sitting through it, "Perry shot back. "It's about making them feel it. You don't get it, man. This isn't about making people comfortable. It's about waking them the fuck up."

Casey sat quietly nearby, her sketchbook balanced on her knees, listening as Perry outlined his vision. She wasn't surprised by his ambition, Perry was always chasing something bigger, always pushing to turn his life into art. And though she knew the project would pull him deeper into his own obsessions, she couldn't help but admire his determination.

Eventually, Perry took his vision to Warner Bros. Records. The meeting wasn't an easy one. Perry walked into the boardroom with his management team trailing behind him, looking every bit the part of a rock star, lean, intense, and exuding an energy that couldn't be ignored. The executives, on the other hand, looked wary. They'd seen this kind of pitch before: big ideas, bigger risks, and a potential disaster if it didn't work.

"This isn't going to be some sugarcoated tour documentary, "Perry began, leaning forward in his chair, his voice calm but charged with intensity. "It's going to be raw. Real. You're going to see everything. The recording sessions, the fights, the shows, the ugly shit people don't want to talk about. You're going to see what it takes to make art. And yeah, that means the heroin, the chaos, all of it."

One of the executives cleared his throat, looking uncomfortable. "So, you're asking us to fund a film that... highlights addiction?"

Perry didn't flinch. "I'm asking you to fund a film that shows the fucking truth. You want to sell this band? You want to sell this album? Then show people who we really are. Don't hide it. Fuck man, embrace it."

The room fell into tense silence as the executives exchanged uncertain glances. Perry leaned back, crossing his arms. "Look, you guys want another pop-rock bullshit movie, go make it. But that's not us. This film isn't just about the band, it's about art. It's about showing people the beauty in the mess. You either get that, or you don't."

After a long pause, Warner Bros. caved. Reluctantly, they advanced Perry $300, 000 to produce *Gift*. It was a risk they weren't entirely comfortable with, but Perry's conviction was impossible to ignore.

The project quickly became another layer of tension in an already fractured environment. The band was struggling to keep it together as the recording sessions for *Ritual de lo Habitual* grew increasingly volatile. Perry's creative vision was as consuming as ever, and his heroin use was creeping further into the foreground, while Eric, his main song-writing partner, was completely sober. This combination created a toxic, conflicting environment, to say the least.

For Casey, the film was becoming a double-edged sword. On one hand, she saw it as a chance to capture something meaningful, a way to turn their struggles into something beautiful. But on the other hand, it felt like yet another weight pressing down on an already fragile relationship.

Perry's obsession with *Gift* often left her feeling like she was losing him to his ambition. He was constantly darting between ideas, one minute focused on the album, the next talking about scenes for the film. And though Casey tried to keep up, she was battling her own demons. The drugs, the stress, the constant whirlwind of their lives, it was all becoming too much.

"You're spreading yourself too thin, "she told Perry one night in the studio, her voice quiet but firm.

He looked up from his notebook, where he'd been sketching out ideas for the next day's recording session. "What the hell does that mean?"

"It means you can't do everything at once, "she said, setting her sketchbook down. "You're trying to make an album, a movie, tour plans… and then there's us."

Perry sighed, running a hand through his messy hair. "I can't stop, Casey. You know that. If I stop, everything falls apart."

She stared at him for a long moment, her expression unreadable. "Or maybe it's already falling apart, "she said softly, her words hanging in the air like a challenge.

Even within the band, the tension was impossible to ignore. Eric and Stephen watched from the sidelines as Perry and Casey's struggles spilled over into the studio. It wasn't just the drugs or the film or the pressure of making *Ritual de lo Habitual*. It was everything.

"Every day was a fucking circus, "Eric later recalled. "Perry's running around with a million ideas, Casey's upset, Dave's either high or trying to keep Perry grounded, it was nuts. A total, unadulterated goddamn mess "

But even amid the mess, the music kept pulling them back. No matter how fractured they were, no matter how close they came to falling apart, the music always came first.

"It didn't matter how fucked up things got, Stephen said in a 1998 interview with Rolling Stone, "When we played, it was like the rest of the world disappeared. The music was the only thing holding us together."

Gift would eventually become a controversial and provocative project, just as Perry intended. But for now, it was simply another layer of tension in a band that was already teetering on the edge.

And as the sessions for *Ritual de lo Habitual* continued, the lines between creation and destruction blurred even further.

They'd been at it for weeks now, but tonight, a strange intensity filled the room, a tension that buzzed just below the surface, making everyone feel on edge. The session had been brutal, even by their standards. The band was spent, half their equipment packed, shoulders slumped in exhaustion. They were more than ready to call it a night.

Perry, however, sat on the edge of the studio couch, eyes unfocused, looking almost as if he were in a trance. His face, hollowed by days without sleep, held an intensity that no one else could quite understand. The others recognized that look by now, the one that meant something was brewing in him, something restless and unyielding. He'd been silent for the past hour, drifting in and out of his own mind, barely engaging as the band tried to wind down.

Without warning, he sat up, eyes flashing with sudden urgency. "We're recording 'Three Days', "he announced, his voice low but commanding. "All of it. Right fucking now."

The others froze, exchanging wary glances. They were beyond done for the day, their bodies aching, their minds frayed. None of them had any interest in launching into an unplanned eleven-minute track, especially not after a session that had already taken everything out of them.

But Perry was relentless. When he got that look, it was clear he wouldn't take 'no' for an answer.

"You're serious?" Dave muttered, his tone somewhere between disbelief and irritation.

"Damn right I'm serious, "Perry shot back, his voice sharp and unyielding. "This isn't tomorrow's song. It's tonight's. If you don't want to be here, don't let the fucking door hit you on the way out. Any of you!"

Dave rolled his eyes, halfheartedly swearing as he unzipped his guitar case again. The rest followed, each member moving with a mix of frustration and reluctant understanding. They knew by now that when Perry had a vision, it was best to get out of his way and let him chase it. No matter how strange or inconvenient, his impulses usually led to something extraordinary.

They settled back into their places, moving sluggishly as they unpacked their gear, the weight of exhaustion pressing on all of them. The room was silent except for the low hum of amps warming up and the faint rustle of cables being uncoiled. The dim light from the overhead fixtures cast long shadows across the walls, giving the studio a cavernous, almost haunted feel.

Stephen adjusted his drum kit without a word, his jaw tight. He glanced at Eric, who was tuning his bass with mechanical precision, his lips pressed into a thin line of frustration. Dave knelt by his pedal-board, his movements sharp and deliberate, muttering under his breath about Perry's tendency to push them past the breaking point.

But Perry didn't seem to notice, or, more likely, he didn't care. He stood in the middle of the room, his hands gripping the mic stand like it was a lifeline, his hollowed eyes scanning the space as if he were looking for something just out of reach.

The tension In the room was almost suffocating, but as the first notes of Eric's bass-line began to rumble through the speakers, everything shifted.

The riff was slow and hypnotic, a dark and steady pulse that seemed to anchor the room in place. Stephen's drums joined in next, tribal and deliberate, each beat reverberating through the studio like the distant echo of a storm.

Dave stayed quiet for a moment, his fingers hovering over the strings of his guitar as he watched Perry. There was something in the way Perry gripped the microphone, the way his body leaned into the rhythm, that told Dave this wasn't just another song to him.

With a resigned sigh, Dave dropped his pick against the strings, letting a jagged, ethereal melody float into the mix. The sound sliced through the low thrum of bass and drums, adding a sharpness that made the air feel electric.

Then Perry began to sing. "Three days was the morning…"

His voice was raw, frayed at the edges, but there was a depth to it that stopped everyone in their tracks. He wasn't just delivering lyrics; he was pulling something out of himself, something deeply personal and painful.

The words sliced the air, laced with longing and regret. The song wasn't just a memory, it was a resurrection. For Perry, it was a way to relive a weekend that had been equal parts beautiful and devastating: three days spent with Casey and a close friend in a whirlwind of love, intimacy, and excess. That friend was gone now, lost to the same addiction that was slowly pulling Perry under.

But it wasn't just about loss. It was about connection, about the fleeting moments of closeness that feel infinite while they last but are gone before you can hold on to them. Perry wanted the song to capture that feeling, the way love and grief can exist side by side, tangled together in a way that makes them impossible to separate.

His voice climbed and fell, each word dripping with emotion, his body swaying as he leaned into the mic.

"Erotic Jesus, lays with his Marys / Loves his Marys…"

The band followed his lead, their frustration melting away as the music swallowed them whole. Stephen's drumming grew more forceful, each beat driving the song forward like a heartbeat on the edge of collapse. Eric's bass-line thrummed with an almost meditative quality, grounding the chaos while Dave's guitar wailed above it all, jagged and raw, like a scream trying to claw its way free.

The room became a vortex of sound, the tension that had hung over them now transformed into something primal and alive.

Perry closed his eyes, gripping the mic stand even tighter as his voice cracked and soared, pushing past its limits.

For Casey, watching from the corner of the room, it was like seeing a part of him she hadn't seen before. She knew the story behind the song, had lived it with him, but seeing him pour it out like this, completely unguarded, was something else entirely. She set her sketchbook down, her eyes fixed on him as his voice broke again, this time carrying an edge of anger that hadn't been there before.

By the time they reached the chaotic, frenzied peak of the song, the air in the studio felt electric, almost unbearable. The music swirled around them, each member completely consumed by the moment.

Stephen's drumming was relentless now, thunderous and raw, his arms a blur as he pounded out a rhythm that felt more like a ritual than a beat. Dave's guitar screamed through the mix, his fingers moving furiously over the fret board, each note jagged and cutting. Eric's bass held everything together, his steady, hypnotic groove the only thing keeping the song from spinning out of control.

And then there was Perry, his voice ripping through the storm, a jagged, broken wail that seemed to come from somewhere deep inside him.

"True love was… discovered!"

The final words hit like a wave, crashing over the band and pulling them under. Perry dropped to his knees, clutching the mic as though it were the only thing tethering him to the ground. He was drenched in sweat, his hair plastered to his face, but he didn't stop. He couldn't stop.

The song finally unraveled into silence, the last notes fading into the walls of the studio. No one moved.

Perry stayed on the floor, his chest heaving as he tried to catch his breath. Dave set his guitar down gently, his hands trembling slightly from the intensity of what they'd just played. Eric leaned against the wall, his bass still slung over his shoulder, his expression unreadable. Stephen wiped sweat from his face with a towel, his grin faint but genuine.

"That, "Dave said finally, his voice hoarse, "was fucking insane."

Perry looked up at him, a faint smile tugging at the corners of his mouth. "That's the point, "he said quietly, his voice raw and unsteady.

Eric sighed, shaking his head. "We're gonna feel that one tomorrow."

"Yeah, "Stephen added, dropping onto a chair and cracking his knuckles. "But we fucking nailed it."

Perry stood slowly; his movements unsteady as he leaned on the mic stand for support. "That's it, "he said simply, his voice soft but firm. "That's the take, boys. The only take we'll ever fucking need." No one argued.

That first take of "Three Days, "was recorded live in the studio on that fateful night. would end up on the album without mixing or overdubbing, and go on to become one of Jane's Addiction's most iconic tracks, a cornerstone of *Ritual de lo Habitual* and a haunting reminder of the band's ability to transform chaos into something transcendent. But for the band, that night wasn't about the legacy of the song. It was about the moment, the raw, messy, beautiful moment when everything came together.

And as they packed up their instruments, their exhaustion momentarily forgotten, they all knew they had just created something unforgettable.

The eccentricities that defined Jane's Addiction made the recording sessions for *Ritual de lo Habitual* not just about making music anymore; they were about survival. Each song was a battleground, a fight to extract meaning from the negativity that was surrounding them. But the closer they got to capturing it, the more it felt like they were losing themselves in the process.

Perry leaned against Casey as they walked out into the cool night air, their footsteps echoing in the empty parking lot. His body felt drained, his mind a haze of exhaustion and adrenaline, but somewhere deep inside, there was a flicker of satisfaction. Whatever part of himself he had sacrificed tonight, it had been worth it. He had captured the truth, no matter how much it hurt.

"Hey baby, you okay? You want to get some food or something?" Casey asked, breaking the silence. Her voice was calm, careful, as if trying not to shatter the fragile shell that seemed to surround him.

Perry shook his head, his voice low. "No. I just… I need to sit with it for a while, Case."

Casey didn't push. She had learned when to give him space, even if it left her feeling helpless. She watched him as they sat in the car, his head tilted back against the seat, his eyes closed. He looked older than he had that morning, the weight of the night etched into the lines of his face.

Back in the studio, the rest of the band lingered, silently packing up their gear. The energy in the room was heavy, a strange mixture of awe and exhaustion.

"That was something else, "Stephen muttered, breaking their silence. His drumsticks twirled absently in his hand as he leaned against the wall, sweat still damp on his brow.

Dave shrugged, lighting a joint with trembling hands. "Yeah, but at what cost?" he said, his voice quieter than usual. He didn't sound angry, just drained, like the night had taken more out of him than he'd expected.

Eric sat in the corner, his bass leaning against his knee, staring at the floor. He didn't say anything, but his jaw was tight, his shoulders tense. He had seen this coming for a while now, the way Perry was pushing himself, pushing all of them, toward some impossible ideal. Eric admired Perry's vision, even believed in it on some level, but he also knew it was unsustainable.

"You think he's okay?" Stephen asked, looking between Dave and Eric.

Dave took a long drag, exhaling slowly before answering. "Define 'okay.'"

Eric finally looked up, his expression grim. "He's not okay, "he said simply. "But he never is. That's the fucking point, isn't it? He has to tear himself apart to make this shit. It's what he does. And we just…" He trailed off, shaking his head.

"We just keep going, "Dave finished, his voice flat.

The three of them sat in silence for a moment, the faint hum of the studio equipment the only sound. They all knew they couldn't stop Perry. They couldn't slow him down, couldn't convince him to take care of himself. All they could do was hold on and hope they didn't get pulled under with him.

Perry barely spoke on the drive back to Casey's apartment. He stared out the window, watching the city blur past, his thoughts racing. He could still feel the session pressing down on him, the memory of those final moments in the booth when the music had swallowed him whole.

By the time they reached the apartment, Casey was exhausted, but Perry seemed restless, his energy shifting into something anxious and jittery. He paced the small living room, lighting a joint and letting the smoke curl around him as he muttered half-formed ideas under his breath.

Casey watched him from the couch, her arms wrapped around her knees. She loved him, but nights like this scared her. There was something unrelenting about his drive, something that felt like it could consume him, and her, if she wasn't careful.

"You need to sleep, "she said softly, her voice cutting through his muttering.

He paused, turning to look at her. He looked like he might argue for a moment, but then he sighed, running a hand through his hair. "Yeah, "he said, his voice heavy. "Maybe."

But he didn't move. He just stood there, staring at the floor, the joint burning down to nothing between his fingers.

Casey stood and walked over to him, taking the joint from his hand, and stubbing it out in the ashtray. "Come on, "she said gently, taking his hand and leading him toward the bedroom. He followed her without protest, his steps slow and unsteady.

As they lay in bed, Casey watched him as his breathing evened out, his body finally giving in to the exhaustion. She wanted to believe that things would get better, that they could find some kind of balance, but deep down, she knew the truth. Perry wasn't built for balance. He was a storm, constantly swirling, constantly pulling everything around him into his orbit.

And she wasn't sure how much longer she could weather it.

The next morning, Perry was back in the studio as if nothing had happened. His energy had returned, his voice sharp and animated as he rattled off Ideas for the next track. The previous night's session was already a distant memory, filed away in the growing list of sacrifices he'd made for the music.

But the night lingered like a shadow for the rest of the band. They could feel it in the air, in the way they avoided each other's eyes, in the unspoken tension that seemed to hang over every note they played.

Ritual de lo Habitual was shaping up to be a masterpiece, but it was also becoming something else: a reckoning.

And as they pushed forward, each of them wondered how much more they could give before there was nothing left to hold them together.

Here We Go Again

By mid-1990, *Ritual de lo Habitual* was ready for release, but the band's biggest battle wasn't in the studio, it was at the negotiating table. Perry Farrell had poured his heart, soul, and vision into the album, and that vision included a controversial cover: a handmade sculpture he and Casey had created. The centerpiece was a depiction of Perry, Casey, and their late friend Xiola Blue, a visual representation of "Three Days, "the album's emotional anchor. It was provocative, deeply personal, and, predictably, a problem for Warner Bros. Records.

The last thing Warner Bros. wanted was a repeat of the *Nothing's Shocking* fiasco, where chain stores like Walmart and Kmart had outright banned the album because of its nudity. With *Ritual de lo Habitual*, Warner hoped to avoid similar headaches, but the cover Perry presented had executives bracing themselves for another storm.

The band sat in the Warner Bros. conference room, a long, sterile table separating them from the suits on the other side. Perry leaned back in his chair, legs crossed, a faint smirk playing on his lips as he watched the executives squirm. Casey sat beside him, quiet but resolute, her hands folded over a copy of the artwork. Dave Navarro twirled a pen between his fingers, looking disinterested, while Stephen Perkins tapped a steady rhythm on the edge of the table, trying to mask his frustration. Eric Avery, as usual, sat with his arms crossed, his expression unreadable.

The head of Warner's marketing team, a balding man in a crisp suit, cleared his throat and slid a folder across the table. "Look, "he began, his tone diplomatic but firm. "We understand the artistic vision here, but… the nudity, the imagery, it's going to create problems for us with retailers. Major chains won't carry it. We're talking millions in lost sales."

Perry tilted his head, his smirk widening. "Yeah? And?"

The man hesitated, clearly not expecting such a blunt response. "And… we're asking you to consider an alternate cover. Something less… provocative."

Casey couldn't hold back anymore. She leaned forward; her voice sharp. "Less provocative? The whole point is that it's provocative. It's art. It's supposed to challenge people, make them uncomfortable."

"That's not how Walmart sees it, "another executive cut in, his voice tinged with annoyance. "They see it as pornography. And they're not the only ones."

Perry's smirk disappeared, replaced by a flash of anger. He sat up straighter, leaning forward. "'Pornography?' Are you serious? This is a fucking sculpture. It's no different than what you'd see in a museum."

"Except it's not in a museum, "the marketing head shot back, his frustration slipping through. "It's on the cover of an album that's going to be sold in stores across the country. Parents are going to see it. Kids are going to see it. And we're going to be the ones fielding the complaints."

"Good, "Perry said, his voice cold. "Let them complain. Maybe it'll force them to have a conversation they've been avoiding."

Eric finally spoke, his tone measured but firm. "Look, we get it. You're worried about sales. But we signed with Warner because you promised us artistic freedom. This is part of the art. It's not just a cover, it's the fucking heart of the album."

The room fell silent for a moment, the weight of Eric's words hanging heavy in the air.

The head of Warner Bros., a graying man with tired eyes, sighed and leaned forward, clasping his hands together on the table. "What if we compromise?" he suggested, his voice calm but tired. "We'll print the cover you want, but we'll also release an alternate version, something neutral, for the stores that refuse to carry the original. That way, everyone gets what they want."

Perry narrowed his eyes, studying the man. "An alternate version?" he repeated, his voice dripping with disdain.

The executive nodded. "Yes. Something simple. Just the band's name and the album title, along with a statement defending the First Amendment. We've drafted something." He gestured to one of his assistants, who slid a piece of paper across the table.

Perry picked it up, skimming the text. His expression softened slightly as he read the opening line: "Congress shall make no law respecting an establishment of religion, or prohibiting the free exercise thereof; or abridging the freedom of speech, or of the press; or the right of the people to peaceably assemble, and to petition the Government for a redress of grievances."

A faint smile tugged at the corner of his mouth. "The Constitution, huh?"

"We thought it would be… appropriate, "the executive said carefully.

Perry glanced at Casey, who gave him a slight nod. "Alright, "he said finally, tossing the paper back onto the table. "You can print your boring-ass version. But the real cover goes out too. No watered-down edits, no cropping, no bullshit." He then leans back in his chair and firmly says, "OH, and I'm writing my 'two-cents' on the sleeve. You cats fucking owe me that… for agreeing to this complete horseshit!"

He abruptly gets up, turns and walks out the door.

The executives exchanged glances, then nodded in agreement.

Later, in the car ride back to the studio, the tension began to lift. Perry stared out the window, the city lights blurring into streaks of color. "It's not the win I wanted, "he admitted, his voice low. "But it's something. And it'll piss off the right people, which is good enough for me."

Casey leaned her head against his shoulder, her voice soft. "It's better than letting them bury it. At least the cover will be out there."

Dave, sitting in the backseat, chuckled. "Yeah, but you know the First Amendment version's gonna end up in half the stores anyway. Welcome to corporate America."

"Let them print it, "Perry said, a defiant edge creeping back into his voice. "They're proving our point for us. Censorship's just a fancy word for fear."

That night, while a rare California rainstorm poured down, Perry, high on heroin and drunk on two bottles of fine red wine, wrote the liner notes for the inner sleeve of the album jacket.

The rain drummed against the windows of Casey's apartment, a steady rhythm that filled the room and muffled the sounds of the city outside. The sky was deep and bruised, clouds swallowing the light and leaving only reflections of neon on the slick, black streets below. Inside, the air was thick with the heady scent of wine, wax, and the faint metallic trace of burned foil.

Perry sat cross-legged on the floor, his back against the couch, a half-empty bottle of Cabernet beside him, the other bottle drained and lying on its side. A flickering candle on the coffee table cast distorted shadows across the cluttered room, Casey's sketches scattered haphazardly, ashtrays overflowing with spent cigarettes, and Perry's notebook, its pages wrinkled and streaked with smudges. He was high, drifting in and out of a haze that softened the edges of reality but couldn't quiet his mind. His pen moved feverishly over the page, scribbling half-legible sentences and fragmented thoughts that spilled out faster than he could organize them.

Casey sat on the couch behind him, her knees pulled to her chest, watching him in silence. She had seen him like this before, lost in his own storm, chasing something only he could see. The rain outside seemed to mirror his energy, chaotic yet rhythmic, relentless but strangely beautiful.

"Do you even know what you're writing?" she asked softly, her voice cutting through the low hum of the room.

Perry smirked but didn't look up. "Do I ever?" he muttered, tapping the pen against the page as though trying to coax out the next line. "But it's not about knowing. It's about feeling. That's the whole fucking point."

Casey exhaled quietly, her eyes drifting to the notebook in his lap. She couldn't make out the words from where she sat, but she didn't need to. Whatever he was writing, it wasn't for anyone but him, not yet, anyway.

"You're going to piss them off again, you know, "she said, a faint smile tugging at her lips.

"Good, "Perry shot back without hesitation, his grin widening. He set the pen down for a moment and reached for the wine, taking a long, deliberate sip before continuing. "They deserve to be pissed off. All of them. The suits, the stores, the assholes calling this art 'pornography.' They don't get it, Casey. They don't fucking get it."

"And what exactly don't they get?" she asked, leaning forward, resting her elbows on her knees.

Perry paused, staring at the candle's flame, his expression suddenly serious. "That this album… this whole fucking thing… it's not for them. It's for the people who are drowning. The ones who can't fucking breathe. It's for the ones like us."

Casey's smile faded as his words hung in the air. She knew exactly what he meant.

Perry turned back to his notebook, his pen moving faster now, his handwriting growing more erratic. He wrote about freedom, rebellion, love, death, and the fragile beauty of it all. The words flowed out of him in bursts, sometimes stopping mid-sentence before picking up again in jagged fragments. He wasn't trying to make sense; he was trying to capture a feeling, something raw and unfiltered that he couldn't put into music but needed to say.

By the time the rain began to ease, the notebook was filled with lines, some scrawled hastily, others circled or crossed out. Perry leaned back, exhaling slowly as he dropped the pen onto the floor beside him.

"Done?" Casey asked, her voice soft.

He nodded, his head resting against the couch, his eyes half-lidded. "For now."

Casey stood and walked over to him, picking up the notebook carefully. She glanced at the last page, the lines messy but unmistakably his:

"The paper these words are written on also contains the music of Jane's Addiction. The music is original, the cover is not. The original cover is as colorful as the music. It is a daydream of the music, made tangible. It will take effort to get, it is being sold, but we are

having difficulties. There is an invisible force, the same one you have heard faintly buzzing all your life. This time it buzzes much louder. I myself have felt its pain. When I looked down at the spot where it hurt, I saw a very small mosquito. A bug so old, it was known to Confucius as the "intellectual mosquito." He sucks off of you and he sucks off of me.

Sometimes to realize you were well someone must come along and hurt you.

I have grown to become proud of myself. I have aligned with all those who have been stung by suppression. As heirs to this planet, we must maintain, honor and enjoy the gift of freedom. A cause to validate everyone's life? Indeed.

The world looks at America because we are the beautiful!

Hitler's syphilis-ridden dreams almost came true. How could it happen? By taking control of the media. An entire country was led by a lunatic? We must protect our First Amendment before sick dreams become law. Nobody made fun of Hitler?!"

She read the words twice, her fingers brushing over the ink. "This is… intense, "she murmured, her voice a mix of admiration and concern.

Perry opened his eyes, a faint smirk tugging at the corner of his mouth. "Good, "he said simply. "It's supposed to be."

She set the notebook down on the table and returned to the couch, watching as he closed his eyes again, his breathing slowing. The candle flickered, casting long shadows across the room as the rain finally tapered off into silence.

For a moment, Casey thought about blowing out the candle and urging him to go to bed. But she didn't. She just sat there, watching him, knowing that nights like this were part of who he was, part of who they were.

And as Perry drifted into a restless sleep, the notebook sat open on the table, the words glowing faintly in the flickering light, a reflection of the chaos and beauty that defined him.

When *Ritual de lo Habitual* hit the shelves on August 21, 1990, the controversy exploded almost immediately. Conservative groups across the country condemned the album, calling the cover "immoral" and "obscene." Major retailers like Walmart and Kmart refused to carry the original version, opting for the alternate "Amendment Version" instead.

But the backlash only fueled the album's mystique. Fans flocked to independent record stores to get their hands on the uncensored cover, treating it like a badge of rebellion. To them, the sculpture wasn't just art, it was a statement, a challenge to a society that seemed more offended by nudity than violence.

"Every time they try to shut us up, "Perry said in a later interview, "they just make us louder. The controversy isn't the problem, it's the proof we're doing something right."

And with *Ritual de lo Habitual* rapidly climbing the charts, the band proved once again that true art couldn't be silenced.

The album was acclaimed by music critics, similar to the band's previous album. "The gigantic swerve and swagger of 'Stop', the Chili Pepper-ish taunts of 'Ain't No Right', 'Of Course''s raga rocking and, above all, the epic 'Three Days', where guitarist David Navarro gets to pile the layers shoulder high, prove to be the stuff of true compulsion, "wrote Peter Kane in Q. "Enigmatic, audacious and unpredictable to the last."

Ritual de lo Habitual was certified "Gold" (500, 000 copies sold) by November, 1990. It sold more units in its first six weeks than *Nothing's Shocking* did in its entire run, to date.

The journey of "alternative music" to the mainstream music scene had now begun. The industry was taking notice… and there was no looking back.

Chaos Begins.

MTV Studios felt like a hall of mirrors for fame, a chaotic maze plastered with posters of celebrities, neon lights, and the buzzing sound of a hundred people talking all at once. The studio was alive, pulsing like some strange organism, packed with production assistants barking orders, VJs pacing in practiced anticipation, and cameramen setting up rigs as if they were gearing up for battle.

Perry Farrell slouched in a director's chair, looking perfectly at home in the madness. His eyes danced with that untamed spark he wore whenever he was about to throw a wrench into the works. A makeup artist hovered over him, dabbing at his face, trying to keep up with his constant fidgeting. Perry had no patience for sitting still. The whole charade of "media grooming" felt like a joke, and he made no effort to hide it. He smirked at his reflection in the compact mirror she held, amused by the absurdity of the ritual.

Across the room, a monitor silently played the "Been Caught Stealing" video on a loop. Perry grinned at the sight of himself in a shopping cart, his infectious, devil-may-care expression beaming back at him. The video was a ridiculous, silly snapshot of rebellion, exactly what he wanted it to be. And judging by the response, it had struck a chord.

He shifted his gaze to Kurt Loder, MTV's straight-shooting, no-bullshit journalist, who had just taken his seat across from him. Loder, as calm and composed as ever, seemed prepared to dig deeper than the usual puff-piece nonsense MTV interviews were known for. Perry could see it in his eyes, the guy was ready to push. Perry welcomed it. He thrived on confrontation, on the chance to unsettle people and make them squirm. This was a game he played better than most, and he was more than happy to indulge.

"Three months since the release, "Loder began, his voice steady and measured, as if he were reciting facts from a well-researched script. "Gold record. 'Been Caught Stealing' is MTV's most requested video…"

Perry didn't let him finish. Leaning forward, he cut in with a flash of excitement, his voice sharp and alive. The sudden movement startled the makeup artist, who jerked back, startled. Perry didn't even notice. "You know why it's connecting?" he asked, his tone low and conspiratorial, a smirk tugging at the corners of his mouth. He didn't give Loder time to respond. "Because it's fucking real. Everybody's stealing something. Their boss's time. Their parents' dreams. Hell, their own goddamn life."

Loder blinked, momentarily thrown off by the intensity of Perry's response. That flicker of discomfort, the momentary crack in the journalist's calm facade, was something Perry lived for. He wanted people to feel off-balance, to confront truths they didn't want to admit, and he could tell he'd already gotten under Loder's skin.

Regaining his composure, Loder cleared his throat and leaned back slightly, re-centering himself. "The album's called 'Ritual de lo Habitual, '" he said, his voice even again, but with a faint edge of curiosity. "What's the ritual?"

Perry's grin widened, his eyes narrowing with a mischievous glint. He tilted his head slightly, as if sizing Loder up, deciding how far he wanted to go. "Living, "he said, his voice deliberate, almost reverent. "Dying. Getting high. Making love. Making art. It's all ritual." He paused, letting the weight of the words hang in the air before adding, "All habit. All addiction."

The words landed like a challenge, daring Loder to dig deeper. Perry wasn't just spouting some artsy bullshit for the sake of sounding profound. To him, these weren't just poetic musings, no, they were the raw, unvarnished truth. Life itself was one endless ritual, a cycle of highs and lows, of creation and destruction, of reaching for something meaningful only to watch it slip through your fingers. And that truth, as messy and uncomfortable as it was, bled through every note of the album.

Loder studied him for a moment, a flicker of intrigue crossing his face. Perry could tell he was trying to decide whether to press further or let the moment speak for itself.

"Habit and addiction, "Loder finally said, repeating Perry's words like he was testing them out. "You talk about that a lot. It's all over the album. You're not exactly shy about your own struggles, either."

Perry's grin softened into something more serious. He leaned back in his chair, one arm draped lazily over the side, his fingers tapping against the fabric. "Why would I be shy?" he asked, his voice low and steady. "It's the truth, man. And people can smell bullshit a mile away. If you're not willing to bleed for your art, then what the fuck are you doing?"

Loder nodded slightly, as if he understood where Perry was coming from, even if he didn't entirely agree. "But doesn't that kind of honesty come with a price?" he pressed. "It's all part of the story, but it's not exactly sustainable, is it?"

Perry's expression darkened for just a moment, a flash of something raw and unguarded crossing his face. But then the smirk returned, and he shrugged, the moment gone as quickly as it had appeared. "Nothing worth doing is sustainable, "he said simply. "If it doesn't burn you out, it's not worth it."

Outside the studio, the world was catching fire with *Ritual de lo Habitual*. The album was climbing the charts despite, or perhaps because of, the controversies surrounding it.

"They're scared of a fucking sculpture, "he'd said in an earlier interview, shaking his head in disbelief. "Meanwhile, they're out there selling violent video games to twelve-year-olds. It's a joke."

The censorship only fueled the album's mystique. Fans sought out the original version, eager to own what they saw as a symbol of rebellion. And songs like "Three Days" and "Stop!" were gaining traction on the airwaves, pulling more people into the band's orbit with their hypnotic, explosive sound.

But even as the album's success grew, the tensions within the band were rapidly deepening. Perry and Dave were still in the throes of their addictions, enabling each other in a toxic cycle that left them both erratic and unreliable. Eric and Stephen, increasingly frustrated, tried to keep things grounded, but the rift between the two camps was widening by the day.

Back in the MTV studio, none of that tension was visible. Perry thrived in the spotlight, his charisma and unpredictability drawing people in like moths to a flame. But beneath the surface, the strain of holding everything together was starting to show. For now, though, Perry was in his element.

"You ever worry about the future?" Loder asked, his voice cutting through the buzz of the studio.

Perry's grin returned, sharp and defiant. "No point in worrying about the future, "he said. "It's gonna come whether you like it or not. Might as well burn as bright as you can while you're here."

Loder nodded, a faint smile tugging at the corner of his mouth. He knew better than to push further. Perry had already said everything he needed to.

140

Bitter Success.

Backstage at the Aragon Ballroom was a scene of barely-contained emotions. The air was filled with sweat and smoke, an oppressive cloud of energy and nerves, tinged with the faint scent of incense that Perry insisted on burning before every show. It was his own twisted kind of ritual, an odd mix of mysticism and mania that the band had grown used to over the years.

Stephen sat cross-legged on the floor in a meditative pose, his drumsticks resting across his lap. He breathed deeply, eyes closed, trying to center himself amid the madness. Around him, roadies darted in and out of the room, their hurried movements making the small space feel even tighter.

Across the room, Dave hunched over his guitar, his fingers moving with precise, methodical motions as he tuned each string. He was locked in his own pre-show ritual, his face impassive but focused, his thoughts clearly elsewhere. Eric, on the other hand, perched in a corner with a worn paperback in his hands. He wasn't reading, his eyes kept flicking up every few seconds, restless, uneasy, as though he were bracing himself for something to break.

Then Perry burst into the room, Casey trailing behind him. He moved like a lightning bolt, all energy and unpredictability, half his face painted in streaks of black and white, his corset laced so tightly it looked like it might snap. His grin twisted his mouth as he threw his arms out dramatically.

"Fucking four thousand out there!" he shouted, his voice booming. It wasn't just an announcement; it was a challenge.

Stephen cracked one eye open but didn't move, his breath still deep and even. Dave didn't look up, his fingers continuing to pluck at the strings of his guitar, though a faint smirk tugged at the corner of his mouth. Eric sighed, snapping his book shut with a soft thud.

"Congrats, "Eric said dryly, not even looking at Perry. "You counted to four thousand."

Perry ignored the jab, already rifling through his bag in the corner. He pulled out his work kit, placing it on the makeup table with deliberate care. It was a ritual as much as any other part of the pre-show routine, and no one had the energy to stop him.

But Eric's voice cut through the room, sharp and pointed. "Really? You're gonna do that shit now?"

Perry didn't bother looking at him, his hands moving with the steady precision of someone who had done this countless times. "You want the good version or the half-ass version?" he shot back, his tone half-joking, half-dead serious.

Eric leaned forward in his chair, his arms resting on his knees, his expression dark. "I want the version that doesn't fucking die on stage."

Perry finally glanced at him, a smirk curling his lips. "Relax, mom, "he said, his voice dripping with sarcasm. "Nobody's fucking dying tonight." He turned back to his kit, unbothered, as if Eric's concern was background noise.

From across the room, Dave's gaze flicked up, his hands still on his guitar. He watched Perry with a mixture of curiosity and dread, his expression unreadable. Dave knew that ritual, that pull, it was the same one he fought every day. For now, he kept his distance, though the hunger in his eyes betrayed him.

"Fifteen minutes!" the tour manager's voice bellowed from down the hallway, snapping everyone back to reality.

Stephen unfolded his legs, standing and stretching with a quiet groan. "Better put your shit together, "he muttered, grabbing his drumsticks, and twirling them absently.

Perry finished tying off, his hands moving fast now. He wiped a small trickle of blood from his arm with the edge of his palm and smeared it across his painted cheek in a slow, deliberate motion. "War paint, "he murmured, his voice low and reverent.

Casey stood off to the side, her arms crossed tightly over her chest, her face a mask of conflicting emotions. She had seen this ritual too many times, the way Perry seemed to both sharpen himself and destroy himself in equal measure before stepping on stage. She wanted to say something, to stop him, but she knew how this would go. It always went the same way.

"Perry…" she started, her voice soft, almost pleading.

He turned to her, his eyes gleaming with manic energy, his grin as wide and wild as ever. "What?" he asked, his voice light, playful, but with an edge that warned her not to press.

She hesitated, her shoulders slumping slightly. "Just… don't overdo it, "she said finally, knowing it was a pointless request.

He laughed, the sound sharp and short, as he adjusted the corset around his waist. "Overdo it?" he repeated, his tone incredulous. "Casey, that's the whole point."

Eric, unable to hold back any longer, slammed his book down on the table beside him, his voice cutting through the room. "You know, one of these days you're gonna push too far, and we're all gonna have to pick up the fucking pieces."

Perry whirled on him, his grin fading into a hard, dangerous look. "You don't get it, do you?" he snapped. "This, this right here, is why they're out there. Because I don't hold back. Because I give them everything. You want safe? You're in the wrong fucking band."

Eric stood, his jaw tightening as he took a step forward. "Yeah? Well, maybe I'm tired of watching you destroy yourself and taking the rest of us with you."

"Guys, "Stephen said, stepping between them, his voice calm but firm. "Not now."

Perry laughed again, this time softer, darker, as he backed off. "Don't worry about me, Eric, "he said, his tone dripping with sarcasm. "I'm not the one hiding in the corner with a book while the rest of us are out there bleeding for this shit."

"Fuck you, Perry, "Eric muttered, turning away, his fists clenching at his sides.

"Ten minutes!" the tour manager shouted again, his voice closer this time.

Dave, breaking the tension, set his guitar down and stood, stretching his arms over his head. "Alright, boys, let's save the fistfight for after the encore, "he said with a smirk, trying to diffuse the situation.

Perry's grin returned, sharp and feral, as he grabbed the microphone stand leaning against the wall. "You're right, "he said, his voice light again. "It's showtime."

As the band moved toward the stage, and the roar of the crowd got louder, the tension in the room lingered, thick and heavy, like the scent of incense Perry had burned earlier.

For the others, it was another night in the chaos that was Jane's Addiction. But for Perry, it was a ritual, a way to burn bright, even if it left him and everyone around him scorched in the process.

The "Ritual de lo Habitual Tour" swept across America like a hurricane, leaving behind the stunned faces of crowds who couldn't believe what they'd just witnessed. Outside concert arenas, marquees flashed in bold, blinding letters: JANE'S ADDICTION – SOLD OUT. The words blazed against the night, symbols of the band's sudden, overwhelming success, a chaotic ascent that few had predicted. Each sign, glowing bright against the dark, felt like an omen, one that promised brilliance and destruction in equal measure.

Perry loved it, every damn second of it. To him, the signs, the crowds, the manic energy in the air were proof of everything he'd been pushing toward. It was validation of every dark lyric, every boundary he'd crossed. Night after night, he stood at the edge of the stage, the spotlight a harsh white halo against his painted face, his silhouette cutting sharp against the lights. But for Perry, the stage itself was never enough. He'd climb the speaker stacks, scaling them with reckless abandon as the crowd gasped below, hands reaching up like he was some untouchable deity. Security would scramble beneath him, panicked, but Perry would only laugh, that wild, defiant laughter that echoed across the venue, daring anyone to pull him down.

Backstage, the insanity didn't stop. The tour was a circus of late-night parties, endless alcohol, every drug imaginable and a parade of new faces that blended into one another, as the days blurred. But the holes in the foundation were starting to show, and grow.

"Do you ever fucking stop?" Eric's voice cut through the backstage haze one night, sharp and angry, as Perry swayed slightly, a nearly empty bottle of red wine dangling from his fingers.

Perry turned, the grin never leaving his face. "Why the fuck would I want to stop?" he shot back, his tone teasing but with a hard-edge underneath. "This is it, Eric. Look around. It doesn't get better than this."

Eric stepped closer; his voice low but tense. "Maybe for you. But for the rest of us? We're barely holding it together."

Perry tilted his head, his grin faltering just slightly. He took a long swig from the bottle, his eyes scanning Eric's face. "Oh, don't give me that sanctimonious bullshit, "he said, his voice cutting. "You think you're above it all? You're here, aren't you? You're just as deep in this as I am."

Eric's jaw tightened, but he didn't reply. He knew arguing with Perry was like trying to stop a tidal wave, it was impossible, and you'd only drown in the attempt.

On stage, the tension was less obvious. To the crowd, they were unstoppable. Jane's Addiction wasn't just playing music, they were conjuring something primal, something that felt alive. The music was raw, chaotic, and hypnotic, pulling the audience into their world whether they wanted to be there or not.

"Perry's like a fucking cult leader out there, "Dave said in an interview with Rolling Stone, a cigarette balanced between his fingers as he leaned back in his chair. "The way they look at him, it's not normal. He could tell them to burn the whole place down, and I swear to God, they'd do it."

For Dave, the tour was a blur of highs and lows, both literal and figurative. His heroin use was creeping back into the picture, quietly at first, but gaining momentum as the weeks wore on. The late nights, the pressure, the constant roar of the crowd, it all demanded something from him that he couldn't quite find in the music alone anymore.

One night after a show, Dave and Perry sat in the green room, the remnants of the night scattered around them: empty bottles, crumpled cigarette packs, a half-eaten tray of cold catering food. The rest of the band had left, leaving the two of them alone in the dim, smoke-filled space.

Perry leaned back in his chair, staring at the ceiling. "You ever think about how long this can last?" he asked suddenly, his voice distant.

Dave, hunched over his guitar, didn't look up. "What do you mean?"

"This, "Perry said, gesturing vaguely around the room. "The band. The shows. The madness. You think we'll still be doing this when we're fucking old and gray? You know, like the 'Stones' or something?

Dave snorted, shaking his head. "I can barely think about next week, man. You're asking me about decades?" He paused, lighting a cigarette, his hands shaking slightly. "But no. I don't think it's gonna last. Nothing this fucked up ever does."

Perry laughed, a short, sharp sound. "Yeah, "he said softly. "That's probably true."

There was a long silence between them, the kind that only happens when two people are thinking the same thing but are too afraid to say it out loud.

"Does it bother you?" Dave asked finally, his voice quiet.

Perry shrugged, his grin returning, but it didn't reach his eyes. "Why would it? Things that burn bright don't last. That's the whole fucking point."

Dave looked at him, his expression unreadable, then turned back to his guitar, plucking out a few aimless notes.

Outside the venues, the controversy around *Ritual de lo Habitual* continued to swirl. Conservative groups protested at certain stops in the "Bible-belt, "waving signs and chanting slogans about morality and decency. Some shows were delayed, others canceled altogether due to pressure from local authorities. But for every protester, there were hundreds of fans who came out in defiance, their passion only fueled by the backlash.

MTV News covered the spectacle with urgency, as if they couldn't keep up with the band's furious ascent. Clip after clip aired on heavy rotation, Perry's manic grin as he howled into the mic, Dave's eyes glazed as he ripped through his guitar, Stephen pounding his drums with relentless force, and Eric, intense, weaving his bass-lines like dark magic.

One reporter described the band as "a beautiful disaster, "a phrase that stuck with Perry. He liked it, liked the way it captured the messy, unpredictable energy that defined Jane's Addiction.

"We're not here to play nice, "Perry said in an interview backstage in Nashville, "We're not here to make people comfortable. If you want that, go listen to the fucking Eagles. This? This is Jane's Addiction. And it's exactly what the world needs right now."

In the control room, the MTV execs could hardly believe it themselves.

"Are we glamorizing this?" one of them muttered, running a hand through his hair.

"Glamorizing?" laughed another. "Hell, they're glamorizing themselves. We're just broadcasting the fireworks."

The camera feed flashed back to Jane's Addiction, playing to a sea of screaming fans. Each performance was like watching the world tilt slightly on its axis, charged with something wild and raw, teetering between triumph and chaos.

Magazine covers started to flood the newsstands, each one trying to capture that dangerous allure. Perry's face was everywhere, eyes rimmed in thick, smudged black liner, staring out at the world with a gaze that was both inviting and menacing, a challenge and a promise wrapped in one. *SPIN* had him grinning wickedly, his face tilted just so, with the caption: "The Man Who Wants to Set Rock on Fire."

One afternoon in the dressing room, Perry tossed a copy of *Rolling Stone* onto the table, the page open to his own face, shadowed and skeletal, with the headline "The Madman of Jane's Addiction." He snorted as he sat back, propping his boots up on the table.

"Guess I'm the 'madman' now, "he muttered, reaching for a glass of red wine.

Dave, sprawled out on the couch, barely looked up. "They're just jealous you've got more fun than they do, "he said with a smirk. "Bastards wouldn't know 'mad' if it hit 'em in the face."

Stephen laughed, shaking his head as he flipped through another magazine with their faces on it. "You gotta admit, Perry... you do look a little unhinged here, "he said, tapping his finger on the page. "I mean, look at your eyes, man."

"Maybe 'cause I am, "Perry replied, lighting a joint, his eyes gleaming with amusement.

Eric was less impressed. He threw his copy of Alternative Press down, the cover showing Perry's face lit in stark, surreal lighting, looking like some unholy creature from another realm.

"Enough with the damn photos already, "Eric muttered, voice tight. "It's like they're trying to make us out as... as demons or some shit."

Perry leaned in, eyes sharp. "Isn't that the whole point? They love it. They're scared, but they fucking love it. And they should be scared, we're scared. This is something else, man. Bigger than all of us."

Eric didn't respond, just shook his head, but there was something in his gaze, an edge of excitement hidden behind the cynicism.

In every interview, Perry would ramp it up even more. Reporters sat across from him, unable to figure out whether he was serious or just winding them up. And Perry loved it, played into it, leaned into every question with a grin that said he could burn down the entire room and walk away laughing.

One reporter asked, "What's the endgame, Perry? You're burning bright, but at what cost? You ever worry you'll burn out?"

Perry just laughed, leaning back in his chair. "Endgame? There is no fucking endgame, man. You think I'm doing this for the future?" He shook his head, exhaling smoke. "I'm doing this because it matters now. I don't care if I go out in flames. Hell, that'd be a fitting way to go, don't you think?"

In the break room afterward, Eric couldn't help but roll his eyes. "You know that stuff's going to bite you in the fuckin ass eventually, right?!" He continued, "And if it bites you in the ass, it bites us all." He calms down, exhales and looks directly at Perry and Dave, "More importantly, I don't want to see my friends kill themselves. Okay?!"

"Let it, "Perry replied, shrugging. "It's part of the gig. You think they'd be this obsessed if we played nice? The world doesn't need another goddamn nice band, Eric. They need a reason to feel alive." He leaned in closer, a dangerous edge to his voice. "And if that means they watch us tear ourselves apart, so be it."

Dave chuckled darkly from the corner. "That's what I love about you, Perry, you never make it fucking easy."

"Easy for the weak guys, "Perry replied, his eyes gleaming with the thrill of it all.

By then, the world was captivated by the sheer madness of it, the beautiful recklessness of a band that seemed hell-bent on running full-speed toward the cliff's edge. Each cover, each headline, each breathless MTV clip was just another shot of gasoline on the fire. And for Perry, that was all he wanted: to be the one lighting the match.

But the highs came with shadows, with cracks forming beneath the surface that no one could ignore. Dave, brilliant and intense on stage, began nodding off during interviews, his head slumping forward, eyes glassy and unfocused. The late nights, the drugs, the relentless pressure to keep up with Perry's vision, it was starting to show. Perry, ever the front man, took over seamlessly, weaving stories that danced between myth and reality, his words blurring lines and bending truth to his will. To the outside world, it looked like Perry had everything under control. But to those who knew him, it was clear that something was unraveling.

Eric and Perry, once inseparable in their creative vision, began moving in separate circles. After shows, they'd leave in different limos, check into different hotels. Their interactions grew tense, each encounter laced with the weight of things left unsaid, of half-spoken arguments and resentment that simmered just below the surface. Fame, with its relentless demands and unforgiving light, was pushing them apart, its pressure wearing down the fragile bond that had once held them together.

Each time they parted ways after a show, their faces worn and drained, it felt like another step away from the unity they'd once shared, another step toward a fracture they couldn't repair.

Old Tensions Resurface.

The relentless grind was getting to all of them, but for Stephen, the toll was etched a little deeper. He had always been the quiet one, the solid anchor amidst the destructiveness, the drummer who let his rhythms do the talking. But now, as the band seemed to unravel a little more each day, his usual calm was fraying at the edges.

Late nights on the road, sleep slipping away with every passing hour, Stephen found himself gripping his drumsticks like they were the only thing holding him together. He'd sit in the green room, his eyes hollow, watching Perry and Eric tear into each other like enemies rather than bandmates. Each argument was worse than the last, escalating from annoyed jabs to vicious accusations, each one dredging up past grudges and buried resentment.

"Could you both just, "Stephen would start, voice low, trying to cut through the tension.

But it never worked. Perry would just scoff, his eyes wild, practically daring Eric to throw another punch, verbal or otherwise. "Oh, so you're on his side now too, huh, Stephen?"

"I'm not on anyone's fucking side, "Stephen would reply, voice tight with frustration. "I'm on the side of getting this band through one damn rehearsal without it turning into a bloodbath."

Eric would mutter something under his breath, something cutting, and Perry would jump on it, accusing him of sabotaging the band, of never really believing in the vision. Each jab would land with a little more force, digging deeper, turning rehearsals and meetings into battlegrounds. Stephen would just sit there, head in his hands, his fingers digging into his skull. He'd clench his fists, a desperate attempt to keep himself from storming out or screaming. It felt like he was caught in the middle of a war, his two closest friends tearing each other apart, and he had to keep them both from falling over the edge.

During one particularly brutal rehearsal for the next American leg of the tour, Perry and Eric went at it again, this time over a song arrangement that Perry wanted to change at the last minute. Eric's face twisted in irritation; his voice laced with sarcasm.

"Of course, let's just throw structure out the window, "Eric sneered, his tone dripping with contempt. "Let's go with whatever wild-ass idea you come up with this time."

Perry smirked, leaning back, his voice taunting. "Hey, structure is your thing, man. I'm just here to make something real. Sorry if that's too much for you to handle."

Stephen's patience snapped. "Will you both just shut the hell up for one second?" His voice came out harsher than he'd intended, the words slicing through the room like a knife.

Perry and Eric turned, both looking a little taken aback. Stephen rarely raised his voice, rarely called them out, but now the quiet drummer, the one who was supposed to be the steady rock, looked like he was ready to throw his drumsticks across the room.

"Do you two even hear yourselves?" Stephen demanded, his voice low, simmering with anger. "We're supposed to be a fucking band guys! You both say you care about the music, but all I hear is a couple of egos tearing each other apart."

Perry rolled his eyes, crossing his arms. "Oh, come on, Stephen. Don't act like you're above it all."

"I'm not above shit, "Stephen shot back, eyes blazing. "I'm right here in the middle, trying to keep this whole thing from going up in flames because you two can't get out of each other's way."

There was a silence, thick and heavy. Perry and Eric exchanged a look, a rare moment where neither of them had anything to say. Stephen took a deep breath, feeling a little of the tension ease from his shoulders, but he could still feel the weight pressing down, the sense that they were all teetering on the edge.

Dave broke the silence with a low chuckle from his corner, where he'd been idly strumming his guitar through the whole ordeal. "Jesus Christ, Stephen. When did you grow a pair?" His tone was light, teasing, but there was an edge of admiration there.

Stephen shot him a withering look, but before he could respond, Perry let out a long, exaggerated sigh, his grin creeping back as he leaned against the wall. "Fine. You want structure, Eric? You want me to play by the fucking rules?" He gestured toward the drum kit. "Stephen here's the referee now guys. He calls the shots. We all good with that?"

Eric didn't respond immediately, his eyes narrowing as he stared Perry down. But then he shrugged, his lips curling into a bitter smile. "Yeah, sure. Why not? Let's see how long this one lasts."

Stephen rubbed his temples, muttering under his breath, "Oh, for fuck's sake."

The rehearsal limped forward after that, tension still hanging in the air like a storm cloud, but at least they got through the set-list without another explosion. Stephen's shoulders ached from the effort of holding everything together, but he couldn't let himself fall apart, not now, not when it felt like the band was hanging by a thread.

Later that night, long after the rehearsal had ended, Stephen sat alone in the empty studio, his drumsticks resting across his lap. The room was silent except for the faint hum of the overhead lights, the echoes of the earlier chaos still ringing in his ears. He stared at his kit, the one thing in his world that made sense, that didn't demand anything from him except rhythm and focus.

He thought about Perry's grin, Eric's glare, Dave's laughter. The band had always been like this, a mess of egos and energy, held together by the music and little else. But lately, it felt like the cracks were getting bigger, harder to ignore.

Stephen tapped out a soft beat on his thighs, his mind drifting. He didn't know how long they could keep going like this, how long they could survive the pressure, the drugs, the fights. But for now, they had the tour, the music, the shows that somehow made it all worth it. For now, they were still Jane's Addiction. And for now, that would have to be enough.

Burning the Candle

The photo shoot wrapped up in a strained, uneasy silence. The band scattered as soon as the final shot was taken, each member retreating to their own corner of the world as quickly as possible. Perry stayed behind, lounging in the chair while the photographer packed up, his smirk lingering like a scar across his face. Casey stayed too, leaning against the wall with her camera in hand, watching him carefully.

"You really know how to make a room uncomfortable babe, "Casey said finally, her tone flat but tinged with amusement.

Perry glanced at her, his smirk deepening. "What's the point of comfort, Case? It's boring. Makes people lazy."

"Yeah, well, there's uncomfortable, and then there's… whatever that was, "she replied, gesturing vaguely toward the now-empty set.

Perry shrugged, reaching for a bottle of wine sitting nearby. "They wanted Jane's Addiction. They got goddamn Jane's Addiction." He took a long swig, his eyes drifting to the mirror where his reflection stared back at him, half-smeared makeup and wild eyes. "We're not here to be easy, you know? Let them choke on it a bit, ya know?"

Casey didn't respond immediately. She lifted her Polaroid and snapped another picture of him before the moment could slip away. The photo slid out with its familiar mechanical whir, and she let it develop in her hands, watching as the image of Perry emerged, a grinning figure on the edge of something unspoken, something dangerous.

"Sometimes I wonder if you really believe the shit you say, "she said quietly, not looking up from the Polaroid.

Perry turned toward her, his grin fading slightly, replaced by something harder to pin down. "What do you mean?"

Casey met his gaze, her expression steady. "I mean, all this talk about burning it down, about pushing things to the edge. Do you actually believe that, or is it just another show?

He stared at her for a long moment, his eyes narrowing slightly, as though weighing whether to let her in or brush her off. Finally, he stood, crossing the room to stand in front of her.

"Case, "he said softly, his voice dropping into something almost vulnerable, "this isn't a show. This is survival. You think I'm doing this for fun?" He gestured toward the empty set, toward the broken band, toward himself. "This is the only way I know how to fucking stay alive. If I stop, if I pull back, it all comes crashing down."

Her eyes softened, but there was still a flicker of doubt in her expression. "And what happens when there's nothing left to burn?"

Perry's grin returned, but it was smaller now, almost resigned. "Then I'll find something else to set on fire."

By the time the band hit the stage that night, the tension had barely dissipated. The venue, a packed amphitheater just outside the city, pulsed with restless energy. Fans screamed, bodies pressed tightly together as the opening notes of "Stop!" Ripped through the air. Perry prowled the stage like a man possessed, his voice slicing through the roar of the crowd as Dave's guitar thundered behind him.

But even in the middle of all the "greatness" on display, the cracks were visible. Eric played with a sharp precision that felt almost detached, his face expressionless as he anchored the sound. Stephen's drumming was tight, methodical, but there was a stiffness to his movements, a tension that mirrored everything else around them. Dave, usually locked into his own world on stage, seemed distracted, his riffs occasionally missing the sharp edge that defined their sound.

Perry, oblivious, or pretending to be, threw himself into the performance with reckless abandon. He climbed the speakers, dangling from the edge as the crowd screamed beneath him. He tore his shirt off, exposing his sweat-drenched torso painted in smeared colors, his body a canvas of chaos and control.

As always, Casey watched with her camera in hand, snapping photos of the man she loved as he teetered on the brink. She saw the way his movements grew increasingly erratic, the way his eyes darted around like he was searching for something he couldn't quite find. And for a moment, she wondered if this was it, the moment where it all came crashing down.

But Perry never fell. He never stumbled. He stayed on that edge, balanced precariously between brilliance and destruction, pulling everyone along for the ride.

After the show, the band gathered backstage, their energy depleted but still buzzing from the high of the performance. Perry was sprawled on a couch, a bottle of wine in his hand, his face glowing with the remnants of adrenaline. Eric sat on the other side of the room, silent, his bass propped against the wall beside him. Stephen paced near the door, his hands shoved into his pockets, while Dave slumped in a chair, his head resting against the wall, eyes half-closed.

"Well, that was… something, "Stephen muttered, breaking the silence.

Perry grinned, lifting the bottle in a mock toast. "You're welcome."

Eric snorted, his eyes narrowing as he looked at Perry. "You think this is sustainable? The theatrics, the constant bullshit? You really think this band will NOT survive if you keep pulling stunts like that?"

Perry's grin didn't falter. He took a long sip of wine before replying. "This band survives because of those stunts, Eric. You think anyone out there gives a shit about four guys standing still and playing nice?"

Eric's jaw tightened, his hands clenching into fists at his sides. "It's not just about the fucking show, Perry. It's about the music. And if you burn yourself out, or take us down with you, then what's the point?"

The room went silent, the weight of Eric's words hanging heavy in the air. Perry's grin faded slightly, his expression hardening.

"You don't get it, "he said quietly, his voice low and sharp. "This is the music. Every scream, every leap, every risk, that's the fucking point. If you can't see that, maybe you're the one who doesn't belong here."

Stephen stepped forward, raising his hands in a gesture of peace. "All right, enough, "he said firmly. "We're all exhausted. Let's just… call it a night."

Eric stood, grabbing his bag without another word and walking out. Perry watched him go, a flicker of something unreadable crossing his face before he leaned back into the couch, raising the bottle to his lips.

Casey lowered her camera, the weight of everything she'd seen pressing down on her chest. She knew they couldn't keep going like this, not without something breaking. But as she looked at Perry, his face still lit with defiance, she wondered if he even cared at all, at this point.

Perry sat cross-legged in the middle of his apartment, surrounded by a sprawl of notebooks, clippings, and sketches, his eyes wild, driven, lit by the strange glow of inspiration that only surfaced at odd hours. It was early morning, long past midnight, but well before dawn, and he hadn't slept. The floor around him was a storm of scrawled notes and frantic diagrams, the kind of thoughts that only took shape in the sleepless haze of night.

At the center of it all, in his erratic handwriting, was a single word that he'd circled so many times it had started to bleed through the page: LOLLAPALOOZA. It was an idea he couldn't shake, one that had burned its way into his mind months ago, lurking just out of reach until tonight. He'd been feeding on cold coffee, weed, and sheer adrenaline, and now the idea was finally taking shape.

Around the word, like the limbs of some mythical beast, he'd jotted words in hurried strokes: Music + Art + Politics + Freaks + Revolution. He wanted it all, the music that broke rules, the art that defied norms, the unapologetic weirdness of those who didn't fit into society's clean-cut mold. It was the world he knew, the world he'd cultivated and grown into. But now he wanted to give it a stage.

Casey stirred on the couch, muttering something incoherent. She'd stayed up with him as long as she could, listening to him ramble, but eventually, exhaustion had won out. She shifted beneath a blanket as Perry, pacing now, muttered to himself about logistics and execution.

The next morning, Perry called his agents, Ted Gardner, Marc Geiger, and Don Muller, to pitch the idea. The three of them met him later that day in a small office above a club on Sunset. Perry entered the room like a whirlwind, dumping his chaotic mess of notes, sketches, and scribbles onto the table.

Geiger, a veteran booking agent with sharp features and a keen sense for spotting trends, raised an eyebrow. "So, what's this about, Perry? Some kind of manifesto?"

"It's more than a manifesto, "Perry replied, eyes gleaming. "It's a movement. Picture this: a traveling festival. Music, art, activism. We're not just putting on shows, we're creating a world, man. Something bigger than just music. Something that fucking means something."

Ted Gardner, Perry's longtime agent and manager, leaned back in his chair, rubbing his beard thoughtfully. "You're talking about a festival on wheels?"

"Exactly, "Perry said, gesturing wildly. "Not just one city, not just one crowd. We take it everywhere. We bring the underground to the surface. A place where people who don't fit in can come together, celebrate, and feel seen."

Don Muller, ever the pragmatist, frowned slightly. "That's a lot of logistics, Perry. Travel, venues, bands, sponsors. Do you have a plan, or are we just running on passion right now?"

Perry grinned. "Passion is the plan. But you're the guys who make it real, right? You tell me what it takes, and we make it happen."

Marc Geiger leaned forward, his interest clearly piqued. "You're onto something, "he admitted, his voice cautious but intrigued. "This alternative scene, it's exploding. Kids are looking for something real, something that doesn't come out of a major label's boardroom. This could be that."

"Not could be, "Perry corrected, his voice firm. "It will be."

Ted exchanged a glance with Marc and Don before turning back to Perry. "You're serious about this?"

Perry slammed his hand on the table, the force startling everyone. "Do I look like I'm joking? This is it, man. This is the fucking revolution we've been talking about. I want every kid out there who's ever felt like an outsider to see this and know they belong somewhere. But I need you guys to help me sell it to Warner."

The room fell silent as the three agents processed what Perry was asking. Finally, Ted nodded. "Okay. Let's do it."

The following week, Perry, Casey, and his agents sat in a Warner Bros. boardroom. The polished table gleamed under fluorescent lights, and the room reeked of corporate sterility. Across the table sat a group of executives, their suits immaculate, their expressions carefully neutral.

Perry, on the other hand, looked like he'd just rolled out of bed. His hair stuck out in wild tufts, and his shirt was half-buttoned. Casey, seated beside him, held her Polaroid camera, snapping candid shots as the meeting began.

"Multiple stages, "Perry said, jabbing a finger at the roughly sketched map he'd slapped onto the polished table. "Art installations, political action tents, weird shit you'd never see at a regular concert." He looked up at the room, eyes bright and unrelenting. "It's a traveling circus of the mind, man. We're bringing the music, but we're bringing everything else too, the art, the politics, the whole culture of the fringe. This isn't just a tour. This is the kind of shit people will remember."

Marc leaned forward, arms crossed, his sharp features locked on Perry with a mix of intrigue and seriousness, "Perry, we're asking Warner to fund the logistics of something this… sprawling. Multiple stages, political activism, and now apparently, puppet shows, too? We're talking about moving this machine from city to city. Do you have any clue how much that costs?"

Perry knew Marc was setting him up for the forthcoming objections from the execs, and now he could passionately rebuttal. He didn't miss a beat, his voice sharp and defiant. "Fuck logistics. You're thinking too damn small." He jabbed his finger at the map again, as if trying to shake the suits out of their corporate mindset. "This isn't about spreadsheets and bottom lines. This is about creating a movement. It's not safe. It's not predictable. That's the whole point." He let the weight of his words settle before he launched into his next thought, his energy crackling like a live wire.

"I'm talking something bigger than any concert, bigger than any tour. I want people to leave with their minds blown, questioning everything they know. This is the Alternative Nation, right here." He tapped the map again for emphasis, then spun around to pace, unable to stay still as his vision spilled out in a fevered rush.

Ted adjusted his glasses and sat back, arms crossed as he watched the room's temperature shift. He was used to Perry's theatrics by now, but even he felt the gravity of what was being proposed. "Okay, "Ted said carefully, his gravelly voice cutting through Perry's relentless pacing. "Let's talk about talent. Who's on the bill?"

Perry turned on his heel, grinning like a predator ready to pounce. "We bring in Nine Inch Nails to give it that industrial edge, something raw and real. Ice-T, he's got the street knowledge; he'll give them something to think about. Siouxsie Sioux? She's goth royalty. The goth kids will lose their minds. Rollins… that guy's pure punk credibility, and he's got a voice no one questions. And Living Colour. They'll blow people's minds with sheer talent." He paused, letting the names hang in the air like an invocation. "Everyone's gonna see themselves in this lineup, even if they didn't think they fit in anywhere before."

An older Warner executive, his face lined with years of industry wear and tear, raised a skeptical eyebrow. "Nine Inch Nails? Ice-T? Perry, this is like trying to cram five different genres into one tent. Aren't you worried about mixing these crowds?"

Perry shot him a withering look, his voice dripping with conviction. "You don't get it. The kids don't give a fuck about genre. Not anymore. They're not looking for labels; they're looking for something real. Something that speaks to them." He leaned forward, palms flat on the table. "You've got punks, goths, metal-heads, hip-hop heads, freaks. They're all the same tribe, they just don't know it yet. We're gonna show them."

Marc tapped a pen against his notepad, considering. "And Jane's Addiction? Where do you fit in this lineup?"

Perry froze for half a second, then straightened, his wild energy settling into something darker, more deliberate. He locked eyes with Marc, then let his gaze sweep the room, daring anyone to look away. "Jane's Addiction brings the farewell, "he said finally, each word slow, deliberate, laced with finality.

A heavy silence fell over the room. Ted stiffened in his chair, his eyes narrowing. Marc leaned back, his face unreadable. The younger Warner executives exchanged uneasy glances, while Don Muller tilted his head, his expression somewhere between disbelief and fascination.

"You're ending the band?" Don asked, breaking the silence, his voice sharp with incredulity. "Now? In the middle of all this?"

Perry's grin returned, softer now but no less intense. "Not ending. Sacrificing, "he corrected, his tone almost reverent. "We're going to burn it as an offering. A ritual to birth something bigger. This is more than Jane's Addiction. This is the fucking future."

The older Warner exec shook his head, his jaw tightening. "You're insane, "he muttered.

Perry laughed, leaning back in his chair. "You're damn right I am. But that's why it'll work."

Ted cleared his throat, pulling the attention back to logistics. "Let's not get ahead of ourselves. What about the venues? Are we talking arenas, amphitheaters, or something else entirely?"

"Anywhere that can hold the madness, "Perry replied, gesturing wildly. "We'll take over fields, parking lots, abandoned airstrips if we have to. This thing will adapt to wherever it lands. No two stops will be the same."

A younger agent with slicked-back hair leaned forward, resting his elbows on the table. "So let me get this straight: you're pitching a traveling festival with no set format, no guaranteed structure, and a farewell performance at every stop?"

"That's exactly what I'm pitching, "Perry said, his grin widening. "And you know what? It's gonna work because it's everything they're not expecting."

The older exec opened his mouth to argue again, but Marc Geiger cut him off. "He's right, "Marc said, his voice firm. "The timing is perfect. The kids are starving for this. Perry's vision is crazy, sure, but it's exactly the kind of crazy that works. You're not just selling tickets here, you're selling a moment. A cultural shift."

Perry clapped his hands together, his excitement boiling over. "Exactly! This isn't just a festival. It's the event. The circus. The revolution."

The Warner execs exchanged glances, their skepticism starting to soften under the sheer force of Perry's conviction. Finally, the graying man with wire-rimmed glasses leaned forward, twitting his fingers. "Ok Perry, so why are you talking with us? Warner is your record label, although apparently it seems, not for long. We're not concert promoters." He sighs, leans back, "so I'm not sure what our part in this is."

Perry looks at Marc, who gives him a nod.

Marc, "We need Warner to back us. To help sell this to the individual promoters in all the cities. To help seal what will be, multiple deals.

The execs all look at each other , waiting for someone to speak.

Marc quickly sees the exchange and continues, "Yes, you are Jane's label. And if this idea works, which it will, well…think of the boost in record sales for Jane's and by the way, Ice-T? Your other act in this lineup."

The older executive sat forward, thinking and twiddling his thumbs for what seemed like an eternity. Finally, "We're going to need hard numbers. Sponsors. Logistics. This isn't something Warner can go to bat with if there isn't a clear plan."

Marc nodded, already scribbling notes. "We'll get you numbers. But you need to understand, this is a leap. You back this, and you're taking a chance on, God-forbid, Warner being involved with something that could redefine live music forever, "he said sarcastically with a grin.

The exec hesitated, his eyes scanning the room. Perry held his breath, his whole body vibrating with tension.

Finally, the older man nodded. "All right, Perry. You got your shot. We'll see what we can do." He stands up and before Perry could speak,

"Get us those numbers…and Perry, don't screw it up kid."

Perry's grin turned feral. "Oh, you just wait. This is gonna blow the roof off everything."

Casey snapped a Polaroid as the meeting broke up, a candid shot of Perry, wild-eyed and triumphant, standing amid the suits and agents who had just agreed to fund his revolution. It wasn't just the birth of a festival. It was the beginning of an era.

The announcement spread like wildfire, sparking excitement across the country. News outlets picked it up, newspapers ran full-page spreads with headlines that screamed, "Perry Farrell's Lollapalooza: Festival of Rebellion" and "The Birth of Alternative Nation." Each article painted the festival as something bigger than a concert, a movement that promised to disrupt the mainstream, to create a space for the voices on the fringes.

MTV News ran segment after segment, each clip featuring a shot of Perry leaning into the microphone at press conferences, eyes gleaming with the fire of his vision. "This isn't just a tour, "he told the reporters, voice full of that dangerous edge that dared anyone to question him. "This is a revolution. This is for the people who don't fit, who don't give a damn about fitting in. This is about tearing down walls, bringing awareness to what we're doing to this planet-our home. It's about giving artists of all types a voice and a space. It's about burning every fucking rule."

Magazines splashed his image across their covers.

Lollapalooza and…

The first day of Lollapalooza was a blazing testament to Perry's vision, a fever dream come to life under the relentless desert sun. The Mesa Arizona Amphitheater buzzed with life, a sprawling carnival of sound, activism, and culture that had never been seen before. The air crackled with a restless energy, fueled by the pulse of music and the sense that something new, something monumental, was happening here.

Booths lined the grounds, staffed by passionate volunteers from organizations like Greenpeace, PETA, and even the Save the Sharks Foundation. Their displays drew curious festival-goers in with bold signs, hand-painted banners, and pamphlets filled with urgent calls to action. Nearby, vendors hawked an eclectic mix of wares: handmade jewelry that glinted in the sun, flowing tie-dye clothing, and earthy scents wafting from incense stalls. The smell of sizzling ethnic foods mingled with the dry heat, creating a sensory overload that set the stage for the chaos to come.

The crowd Itself was a living, breathing mosaic, punk kids with spiked hair mingling with goths draped in black, Deadheads twirling in tie-dye next to suburban teens wearing fresh band T-shirts they'd just bought at the merch tent. It was a scene pulled straight from Perry's imagination: a world without boundaries, where every outcast and rebel could find their place. The music hit like a bolt of lightning.

Onstage, Nine Inch Nails detonated like a time bomb, their raw industrial edge gripping the crowd in a visceral frenzy. Trent Reznor prowled the stage like a caged animal, his screams cutting through the desert air as the band tore through a blistering set. The ground seemed to shake beneath the stomping, writhing masses, the music reverberating in their chests like a second heartbeat. Sweat-soaked bodies pressed together in the pit, a chaotic, thrashing sea of fists and screams, unified by the primal energy of the music.

Backstage, Perry watched from the wings, his face alight with the thrill of it all. He turned to Ted Gardner, his manager, a manic grin spreading across his face. "This is it, "he said, his voice hoarse from shouting over the music. "This is fucking - it!"

Ted gave him a wary look, nodding, but kept his eyes on the stage. He'd heard Perry say it a hundred times, but today, watching the crowd erupt for every beat, every scream, he had to admit, Perry might actually be right.

As the sun climbed higher, Ice-T and Body Count took the stage, and the amphitheater erupted once again. Ice-T commanded the crowd like a general leading his army, his voice booming as he introduced songs that blended searing riffs with politically charged lyrics. What could have been an uncomfortable mix, a predominantly white, suburban crowd and a Black front man singing about systemic injustice, turned into something unexpected: unity. The audience shouted along with every word, fists raised in solidarity. When Ice launched into "Cop Killer, "the crowd lost it, roaring so loudly it seemed to drown out the desert wind.

Backstage, Perry paced like a restless lion, his energy spilling out in every direction. "Do you see this shit?" he exclaimed, grabbing Marc Geiger's arm. "This is exactly what I was talking about. They don't even know they're a tribe yet, but they will."

Marc chuckled, shaking his head. "Yeah, Perry, you're a fucking genius. Now, stop pacing. You're making me nervous."

By late afternoon, the heat began to wane, giving way to the fiery hues of an Arizona sunset. Living Colour hit the stage, their technical prowess a sharp contrast to the raw aggression that came before them. Vernon Reid's guitar screamed as the band tore through their hits, blending rock, funk, and soul into something that felt almost transcendent. The crowd, drenched in sweat but still hungry for more, roared as they closed their set with "Cult of Personality, "the anthem's iconic opening riff igniting a wave of cheers that echoed through the amphitheater.

In the fading light, the atmosphere shifted. The chaos of the day settled into something deeper, more primal.

Siouxsie and the Banshees emerged, bathed in soft blue lights that cast eerie shadows across the stage. Siouxsie stood regal, almost otherworldly, her commanding presence pulling the crowd into a hypnotic trance. The goth icon's haunting voice wrapped around the audience like a spell, her every movement slow, deliberate, as if she were conducting a séance. They closed their set with "Israel, "a song so grand and sweeping it brought a hush over the amphitheater. For the first time all day, the crowd wasn't screaming or moshing, they were swaying, enraptured by the moment.

Backstage, Perry leaned against a stack of speakers, his face softening as he watched the performance. "She's like a goddess, "he murmured, half to himself. Casey stood beside him, snapping a Polaroid, the flash briefly illuminating their faces.

"She's everything, "Casey replied, lowering the camera and watching Siouxsie with the same reverence.

As Siouxsie's final note faded into the night, the crowd erupted into applause, their cheers breaking the spell. Backstage, the band filtered into the green room, the energy a mix of exhilaration and exhaustion. Perry clapped Ice-T on the back as he passed, the two exchanging a grin. "You killed it out there, man, "Perry said, his voice full of genuine admiration.

"You're putting together something special here, "Ice replied, nodding toward the stage. "This? This is bigger than music."

Perry smiled, a flash of pride breaking through his manic energy. "It's a fucking movement."

As the crew reset the stage for Jane's Addiction, the energy in the amphitheater shifted again. The fans pressed closer, their anticipation palpable. This was what they had come for, the band that had started it all. Perry could feel it too, that electric charge building in the air, the sense that this wasn't just another show.

In the wings, Dave strapped on his guitar, his fingers trembling slightly as he adjusted the strap. Eric tuned his bass in silence, his expression unreadable, while Stephen twirled his drumsticks, his face set in quiet focus. Perry paced, his painted face shadowed in the dim backstage light, his energy coiled like a spring ready to snap.

"Ready?" Ted Gardner asked, stepping into the wings.

Perry grinned, wild and unrestrained. "Always."

The stage lights dimmed, and the amphitheater roared as the opening notes of "Up the Beach" rolled out over the desert air. The sound was immense, raw, and almost otherworldly as the crowd surged forward, bodies pressed together, their voices rising in an ecstatic wave.

Perry stood at the center of the stage, a bottle of wine in hand, his painted face illuminated by the piercing white spotlight. He moved with serpentine grace, his every gesture commanding attention as he crooned the ethereal opening lines.

Next came "Whores, "and the amphitheater exploded. The energy was relentless, Perry's voice tearing through the night as Dave's guitar snarled, Eric's bass thudded like a heartbeat, and Stephen's drums pounded with primal precision. The band sounded tight, their chemistry undeniable as they fed off the audience's raw energy. It was the kind of show that reminded everyone why Jane's Addiction had become a force of nature in the first place.

But halfway through the set, cracks began to show. Perry felt it first, a subtle shift, like a ripple under the surface. It was in the way Dave's guitar began to slip, his timing just off enough to throw the balance of the song into disarray. Perry glanced over, his movements sharp, his expression tightening as he noticed the glaze in Dave's eyes, the way his hands trembled as they gripped the guitar.

Dave had been struggling all day. Mesa had been a dry spell for him, he couldn't score heroin, no matter how many frantic phone calls he made or how many shifty locals he approached. By the time they hit soundcheck, the withdrawal was clawing at him with brutal intensity. Desperate to dull the edges, he'd started drinking, knocking back shot after shot in the green room. But alcohol wasn't heroin, and now, halfway through the set, it was wearing off.

As they launched into "Ted, Just Admit It…, "Dave stumbled. His guitar wailed out an off-key note, jagged and jarring, cutting through the song like a knife. Perry spun around, glaring at him, his frustration barely concealed as he tried to hold the performance together.

"The fuck was that?" Perry snarled into the mic between lyrics, his voice sharp enough to make even the front rows notice something was wrong.

Dave swayed, his guitar strap sliding down his shoulder as he tried to recover, his playing erratic and uneven. Sweat dripped from his forehead, his face pale and drawn, the effort to stay upright visible in every shaky movement.

Perry killed the mic during a brief instrumental break and stormed across the stage toward Dave, his jaw clenched. "You're fucking up!" he hissed, his voice low but venomous, his painted face inches from Dave's.

Dave glared back, his eyes glassy, his voice slurred. "I'm fine. Fuck off, "he muttered, swaying on his feet.

"You're not fine, "Perry shot back, his tone filled with barely restrained fury. "Don't ruin this."

Dave shrugged him off, staggering back a step, his guitar dangling uselessly from his shoulder. "I said I'm fine, "he repeated, his voice rising as defiance mixed with desperation.

Stephen's drumming faltered for a brief moment, the tension onstage rippling through the music. Eric shot a glance at Perry, his face a mask of frustration, but he kept playing, his bass-lines steady, trying to keep the song from completely falling apart.

Dave stumbled forward, his foot catching on a monitor. He ripped the guitar strap from his shoulder and tossed the instrument aside, the sound of it hitting the stage reverberating through the amphitheater. The crowd murmured, their cheers faltering as confusion began to ripple through the sea of faces.

Perry stood frozen for a beat, his fists clenched at his sides, his eyes blazing with rage. Then he turned to the mic, forcing a manic grin as he addressed the audience. "Looks like we're having a little technical difficulty!" he shouted, his voice dripping with sarcasm. "Hang tight, my beautiful freaks. We'll be right back!"

The words hit the crowd like a slap, and a collective groan of disappointment rippled through them as Perry stormed offstage. Behind him, Dave stumbled toward the wings, ignoring the roadie who tried to steady him.

Backstage, the tension was explosive. Perry rounded on Dave the moment they were out of sight of the crowd, his voice a low growl that carried the weight of barely contained fury. "What the fuck is your problem?"

Dave collapsed onto a worn-out couch, his head in his hands. "I told you, I'm fine, "he mumbled, his voice thick and unsteady.

"You're not fucking fine!" Perry snapped, pacing in front of him like a caged animal. "You're drunk, you're sick, and you're screwing everything up out there. Do you even care?"

Dave's head snapped up, his eyes blazing with anger and pain. "Do you think I like this? You think I wanna feel like this? Fuck you, Perry. You don't know shit."

"I know you're fucking blowing it, "Perry shot back, his voice cutting like a whip. "We're out there giving everything we've got, and you can't even keep it together for one goddamn set!"

Eric and Stephen entered the room, their expressions grim. Eric crossed his arms, his jaw tight as he addressed Dave. "You need to pull your shit together, "he said, his tone even but laced with frustration.

Stephen held up a hand. "Look, we can't do this right now. The crowd's waiting. We need to get back out there and finish the set. Then we deal with this."

Before anyone could respond, Ice-T stepped into the room, his presence commanding, his gaze sharp. He blocked Perry's path, his arms crossed over his chest, and fixed him with a steady stare. "Man, you really gonna let your ego torch everything you've built?" His voice was calm but carried an unmistakable weight.

Perry bristled, glaring back. "He's not even here! Look at him!" He gestured wildly at Dave, who slumped against the wall, his head hanging.

Meanwhile, Siouxsie stepped forward, placing a firm hand on Dave's arm. "Love, you're better than this, "she said softly, her voice calm but resolute. Her piercing eyes locked on his, and for a moment, he seemed to falter, something breaking through the haze of his anger and withdrawal.

Dave shook his head, his voice cracking. "I'm trying, "he muttered. "I'm just sick but, fuck, I'm trying."

"You're not bloody fine, you little shite" Siouxsie continued, her tone unyielding but laced with empathy. "Neither of you fucking wankers are. But those kids out there?" She nodded toward the stage. "Most of those little shites saved up every bloody penny they could for your little experiment here. God only knows. But you owe them more than this bullshit."

Ice-T turned his gaze to Dave, then back to Perry. "Y'all got something special, something most people never even get close to. Why the fuck y'all think we're all here? Don't fuck it all up over stupid, white-boy pride."

The room fell silent, the weight of his words sinking in. Dave pushed himself to his feet, his legs unsteady. Perry watched him for a moment before extending his hand. Dave hesitated, then grasped it, their arms locking in a brief moment of understanding that said more than words ever could.

"You good?" Perry asked quietly, his voice stripped of its usual edge.

Dave shook his head, a weak smile flickering across his lips. "No. But I will be."

"Good, "Perry said with a faint smirk. "Let's finish this."

They turned toward the stage together, their steps slow but purposeful.

As Dave strummed the opening chords, his hands steady once more, the crowd erupted, their cheers rising into the desert air, filling the night with a sound that felt like redemption. For a few hours, the fractures, the fights, the addictions, they all faded into the background, swallowed by the music, drowned out by the sheer, unrestrained chaos that was Jane's Addiction.

And somewhere, in the shadowed wings, Ice-T and Siouxsie watched, arms crossed, smiles tugging at the corners of their mouths. They'd seen bands come and go, had watched artists burn bright and burn out. But tonight, as the music swelled and the crowd surged, they knew they were witnessing something rare, something that couldn't be bought, controlled, or manufactured.

Siouxsie turned to Ice, her voice a quiet murmur. "Think they'll make it?"

Ice shook his head, a rueful smile playing on his lips. "Tonight? Yeah. After that…" He trailed off, his gaze distant, thoughtful. "Who the fuck knows."

The crowd's roar grew louder, the energy building to a fever pitch as Perry, Dave, Eric, and Stephen played like it was the last show they'd ever perform. And maybe, in some way, it was.

We're Done.

The summer of 1991 spread across America like a fever, an endless, throbbing pulse that seemed to fuel every city Jane's Addiction set foot in. Lollapalooza had taken on a life of its own, far bigger than Perry had ever envisioned. What had started as a dream, a "carnival of the damned, "as he'd once called it, was now an unstoppable beast, roaring through town after town, leaving behind a wake of reverberating energy.

Each night, the crowds grew, swelling until they were practically spilling out of every venue. Each city was a new tidal wave of fans who came not just to watch but to immerse themselves, body and soul, in something they'd only ever dreamed of, a space where they could let loose, scream, be seen. Every beat, every note, every scream from Perry was a lifeline, a raw, blazing truth that cut through their lives, leaving them changed. Backstage, the band felt it too. The weight of it. The rush. The mounting pressure.

"I'm telling you, "Perry said, leaning back on a folding chair, watching the crowd start to surge from behind the curtain. "They're here for more than just music. This… this is something else. This is a fucking pilgrimage." His eyes gleamed, wild and intense, that familiar fire sparking to life.

Eric looked skeptical, sipping from a bottle of water. "A pilgrimage? Man, they're here to see you throw yourself off the speakers and scream your lungs out."

Perry laughed, but his grin stayed sharp, defiant. "Oh, come on, man. You think this is just about music for these people? Look at them!" He pointed toward the thrumming crowd. "They're here because they want something that's fucking real. They're searching for something… salvation, maybe." He shrugged, lighting a cigarette. "Or at least an escape from whatever bullshit they're leaving behind."

Dave, tuning his guitar nearby, chimed in, "Well, then let's give 'em a good fucking escape." He let out a low chuckle, shaking his head. "I swear, this thing is like… It's like a goddamn monster that keeps growing every night."

Perry grinned wider, "Exactly. And I want it to grow until it's so big it can't be ignored. I want every goddamn person in this country to know what's happening here. Not just see it. Feel it. Live it….hell, shit-it!"

Stephen, steady as always, cracked his knuckles, looking out at the crowd. "Well, Perry, looks like you're getting your wish. But you sure you're ready for what that means?"

Perry's eyes glinted, the challenge of it making his blood race. "I was born ready for this, man. We all were. This is our time."

As the opening chords echoed through the venue and the crowd let out an ear-splitting scream, Perry stepped toward the stage, turning back to his band with a wicked smile, and said,

"Boys! Let's give 'em something to remember."

Rolling Stone photographers documented everything, their lenses capturing the sweat-soaked nights, the fleeting moments backstage, the faces in the crowd as they were swept up in the sheer intensity of it all. And MTV News wasn't far behind, broadcasting the rise of the

"Alternative Nation" to homes across America. Every night, cameras captured the band's unfiltered energy, feeding the myth of Jane's Addiction to a hungry audience.

In the quiet moments between shows, Perry and Ice-T shared conversations that seemed to echo a revolution yet to come. They spoke of change, of dismantling the status quo, of art as a weapon against complacency. Their words were measured, serious, a stark contrast to the chaos that consumed their nights.

Meanwhile, Siouxsie took Casey under her wing, teaching her the art of stage makeup. Together, they worked in front of mirrors smeared with lipstick and sweat, Siouxsie's steady hands showing Casey how to create eyes that pierced the crowd and lips that carried a silent threat. Casey's eyes shone with admiration, soaking up every bit of wisdom Siouxsie offered.

Trent Reznor of Nine Inch Nails watched Jane's Addiction from the wings every night, his gaze fixed on Perry as if witnessing something sacred. Perry's stage presence, his ability to command a crowd, was magnetic, a lesson in power that Trent absorbed in silence, night after night.

But even as the crowds grew, the band itself began to fracture. Dave Navarro grew more strung out, the toll of the tour etched into the lines of his face, his movements becoming slow, erratic. Eric and Perry performed back-to-back, each lost in their own world, never looking at one another, their shared vision splintering into pieces.

One dawn, on the long stretch of highway between cities, Perry sat alone on the tour bus, his eyes fixed on the fading night as the world rolled by in shadows and faint light. His thoughts drifted, lost in the bittersweet feeling that accompanied the end of something profound. Henry Rollins joined him, his expression intense, his presence grounding.

"You know what you've started here?" Henry asked, his voice low, his gaze fixed on Perry.

Perry took a swig of wine, his eyes distant. "Feels like a funeral. Wasn't supposed to be this way. I wanted a celebration… looks like we ruined the best thing that ever happened to us."

Henry studied him, a flicker of understanding passing between them. "No, "he replied firmly, a spark of defiance in his voice. "A fucking renaissance."

Through the window, the first rays of sunrise bled across the sky, casting a golden glow over the endless stretch of highway.

In Chicago, Perry preached to the crowd about political action, his voice rising above the din, calling for change with the fervor of a man possessed. In Dallas, Dave barely made it through the set, his hands shaking, his eyes clouded with the weight of something dark and unspoken. In Detroit, Eric smashed his bass in frustration, the instrument splintering into pieces as he let his anger erupt in a moment that felt both cathartic and final. In New York, the band performed flawlessly, each note crisp, perfect, yet there was a distance between them, a feeling of separation that lingered despite their unity on stage.

Backstage in New York, Casey filmed as a swarm of interview crews buzzed around the band, their cameras and microphones capturing the exhaustion that had begun to seep into every aspect of their lives. Stephen took on most of the questions, his voice calm, steady, carrying the weight of his role as mediator.

One interviewer, sensing something unspoken, leaned forward, his tone gentle yet probing. "There are rumors this is Jane's Addiction's last tour…"

Perry appeared from nowhere, his eyes distant, his expression unreadable. "Nothing lasts, "he replied, his voice carrying a quiet finality. "That's what makes it beautiful."

Without waiting for a reaction, he turned and walked away, his silhouette slipping into the shadows as the camera followed, lingering until Casey lowered it. She whispered to the camera, her voice carrying a sorrow that spoke of truths only she could see. "He's grieving already."

September 16, 1991. The final night. It was supposed to be just another show, the last gasp of their Ritual de lo Habitual Tour, a tour that had become more like an odyssey, dragging them all to their limits. But tonight, felt different, charged, like the air was vibrating, too thick to breathe. It was a fever dream come to life; every second stretched so tight it was ready to snap.

The crowd was a writhing mass, voices blending into one deafening roar, bodies pressed together, everyone reaching out for that one last piece of Jane's Addiction, of the band that had redefined everything they thought they knew about music. This wasn't just another night. It was the end of something vital, the end of a band that had been a lifeline for so many and a powder keg of chaos, beauty, and raw emotion.

On stage, Dave played like he was tearing himself apart. His fingers raced across the strings, his eyes glassy, the tracks of fresh tears shining under the stage lights. Each chord was a release, every note felt desperate, like he was pouring every last piece of himself into the sound. He was almost frantic, his hands trembling as he fought to hold back the flood of emotion that threatened to break him open. There was a pain there, something raw and unguarded that had been buried under the layers of persona and rock star bravado. Tonight, it was all laid bare.

Across the stage, Eric finally turned, something he rarely did, his gaze meeting Perry's for the first time in what felt like forever. There was no anger, no resentment, none of the shit that had been eating away at them for years. Just a moment of understanding, a silent truce in the middle of their battlefield. They didn't need words; they never had. Everything they felt, everything they'd been through, was there in that look. They'd built this, together, brick by brick, riff by riff, and now they were here, watching it all burn down.

Stephen sat behind them, the quiet force that kept it all from falling apart, even now. His steady, relentless beat was like an anchor, grounding them, keeping them from drifting off completely. He was the pulse, the heartbeat that drove the music forward, even as everything around him spun out of control. There was a calm in his face, a focus that said he knew what his role was, and he would see it through, even if he was the only one holding it together. With each hit, each rhythm, he kept them tethered, refusing to let them drown in the chaos.

They played like it was the last time they'd ever set foot on a stage together. Every note, every scream from Perry, every beat was soaked in the weight of everything they'd been through, all the fights, the fucked-up nights, the addictions, the raw, ugly moments, and the times when it had felt like nothing else mattered. The music was their goodbye, their final, defiant statement, and the crowd felt it, understood it in a way that went beyond words.

As the last song built to its climax, Perry stepped to the edge of the stage, arms spread wide, his eyes closed, feeling the roar of the crowd like a wave crashing over him. He didn't need to see them; he could feel them, every single soul, connected in that moment. This was his church, his ritual, his final offering.

And when it ended, there was a silence that hung heavy in the air, the crowd unsure if it was truly over, if this was the end. But the band knew. They stood together, four men who'd started this journey as something more than a band and ended it as something far stranger, far deeper. They gave each other a look, something that held both gratitude and pain, a silent acknowledgment of everything they'd shared and everything they'd lost along the way.

But they would hit the stage again, for an encore, something they normally don't do. The crowd swayed like an ocean beneath them, a sea of faces, arms raised, their energy feeding back to the stage in waves, as the opening percussion began to "Ted, just admit it."' The song rises and falls, filling the space with a haunting beauty. Perry looked out over the crowd between verses, his voice carrying on the wind, the words drifting into the night:

"TVs got them images, TVs got them all…" he sang, his voice soft, reflective.

The final lyrics hung in the air, suspended, a heartbeat that stretched beyond time, "sex is violent!"

Perry approached the mic one last time as the opening drum beats of 'Trip Away' began, loud and visceral, filling every corner of the venue. He paused, then with a defiant grin, he stripped off his pants, standing fully nude before the crowd, a final, unapologetic farewell.

"Trip awayyyyy…" he called out, his voice echoing into the night, carrying a sense of liberation, of release.

As they finished the last song, Perry's voice dropped to a whisper. "Goodnight, "he said, the word soft, final.

Through the speakers, Lou Reed's 'Rock & Roll' began to play, a fitting end, a song that spoke of rebellion, of a life lived on the edge. One by one, the band members excited separately. Stephen hugged everyone, his arms strong, grounding, a quiet pillar amid the chaos. Eric gave Perry a nod, a gesture that held years of unspoken words. And Dave disappeared into the darkness, his silhouette fading into the night.

Hours later, in a Hawaiian hotel room bathed in the early light of dawn, Perry stood on the balcony, his gaze fixed on the horizon where the ocean met the sky. The waves rolled in below, dawn surfers riding the crest, their silhouettes moving with the rhythm of the water.

Casey joined him, two plane tickets to Thailand in her hand, her expression soft, contemplative.

"Ready?" she asked, her voice barely a whisper, carrying a mixture of excitement and sadness.

Perry looked out at the ocean, his face thoughtful, a faint smile playing on his lips. "You know what Icarus's real mistake was?"

Casey looked at him, her brows raised, a knowing smile on her face. "Flying too close to the sun?"

He shook his head, his gaze still distant. "No. Landing."

She took his hand, and together they stood, watching the sun rise over the ocean, its light spreading across the water, casting everything in shades of gold and rose. A Hawaiian rainbow formed behind them, arching over the sea, a fleeting moment of beauty.

Perry broke the silence, his voice soft, filled with a quiet pride. "We changed everything."

Casey nodded, her hand squeezing his. "And destroyed it."

He smiled, a bittersweet expression that held both joy and regret. "Same thing."

They turned, walking away from the camera, hand in hand, leaving behind the rising sun, the waves, and the rainbow that lingered over the ocean, a final mark on the journey they'd taken together.

PART TWO

Confusion.

Down on the Strip, in a nondescript rehearsal space, Dave sat on the edge of an amplifier, his guitar balanced on his lap. His fingers dragged lazily over the strings, the melody dark and aimless, like his mind was only half paying attention. His face was a mixture of exhaustion and quiet frustration, the kind of look that came from too much time in his own head.

Stephen leaned against the wall, his drumsticks tapping out a restless, uneven rhythm against his thigh. He'd been standing there for the past ten minutes, watching Dave noodle with his guitar, waiting for the right moment to speak. The weight of what he had to say sat heavy on his chest, and the silence between them only made it worse. Finally, he pushed off the wall, his movements abrupt, breaking the quiet.

"Dave, "Stephen started, his voice tight, unsure.

Dave glanced up, his fingers pausing mid-note. "What?"

Stephen hesitated, spinning one of the drumsticks in his hand, avoiding Dave's gaze for a moment before finally looking him in the eye. "Mike Muir hit me up, "he said, his tone casual but edged with discomfort.

Dave raised an eyebrow, the name registering immediately. "From Suicidal?"

"Yeah, "Stephen said, his tone measured. "He wants me to drum for Infectious Grooves, you know, that side project he's putting together."

Dave leaned back slightly, resting his guitar against his leg. "What'd you tell him?"

Stephen sighed, running a hand through his hair. "I told him I'd think about it."

Dave tilted his head, his eyes narrowing slightly. "And now you're telling me because…?"

"Because I'm gonna fucking do it, "Stephen admitted, the words spilling out in a rush, as though saying them fast would make them easier to hear.

Dave didn't react right away. He just stared at Stephen, his expression unreadable. "So, what? You're leaving?"

Stephen quickly shook his head, his voice firm. "No, it's not like that. It's just… a side gig, you know? It's not like I'm bailing on Jane's. Although, not sure there's a 'Jane's' left."

Dave snorted, the sound sharp and humorless. "Side gig, huh? Yeah, because Perry's gonna take that real fucking well. Even if Jane's is 'done' or what the fuck - ever. 'Oh, hey Perry, just so you know, I'm gonna fuck off and play with Suicidal for a bit, but don't worry, it's just for fun.' Yup, that'll go over great."

Stephen let out a frustrated breath, his shoulders slumping. "Look, man, I'm not trying to cause shit. But what's the alternative? Pretend everything's fine? You and I both know Eric's checked the fuck out. He's done. He barely speaks to anyone anymore. Half the time, I don't even know if he's coming to rehearsals until he walks through the door."

Dave frowned, his fingers tightening around his guitar. "Eric's just… he's in his head, man. He's always been like that."

Stephen shook his head, his voice rising slightly. "No, Dave. This is different. He's not just in his head, he's fucking done. He's counting the days until this is over. Lollapalooza was supposed to be the 'farewell' tour, remember? There's nothing on the horizon for Jane's. No next album, no next tour. We all agreed to this, didn't we?"

Dave's jaw tightened, his knuckles whitening as he gripped the neck of his guitar. "Yeah, we agreed. Doesn't mean it has to be the fucking end. I still think we have some magic left."

"Maybe not for you, "Stephen shot back, his frustration bubbling to the surface. "But for Eric? For Perry? It sure as hell feels like the end. Perry's already got one foot out the door, chasing his next big idea. And you… you're in no shape to hold this thing together on your own."

Dave glared at him, his eyes flashing with anger. "What the fuck's that supposed to mean?"

"It means you're falling apart, Dave!" Stephen snapped, his voice cutting through the room. "You're either nodding off or hungover half the time, and when you're not, you're looking for your next fix. You think I haven't noticed?"

Dave's glare hardened, his voice dropping to a dangerous growl. "You don't know what the fuck you're talking about."

"Don't I?" Stephen challenged, stepping closer, his drumsticks clenched tightly in his hands. "We're all barely holding on here, man. You, Eric, Perry… hell, even me. And I'm just trying to find something, anything, that reminds me why I loved this shit in the first place."

The room fell into a heavy silence, the tension crackling between them like static. Finally, Dave leaned back, letting out a bitter laugh. "So, what? You're just gonna go play some funky side project while the rest of us figure out how to clean up this mess?"

Stephen sighed, his tone softening. "It's not about ditching the band, Dave. It's about keeping myself sane. I can't sit here and watch everything fall apart without doing something for myself."

Dave stared at him for a long moment, his expression unreadable. Then, with a slow shake of his head, he muttered, "Perry's gonna lose his shit when he hears about this."

"Yeah, well, "Stephen said, his voice weary, "Perry's been losing his shit for years. What's one more thing?"

Dave gave him a dark chuckle, his lips twisting into a bitter smirk. "You're not wrong." He looked down at his guitar, plucking a few dissonant notes as if trying to drown out the conversation. "Go do your side gig. Just don't act surprised when Perry burns this whole thing to the ground."

Stephen nodded, his expression tight but resolved. "I'll deal with Perry when the time comes. I just wanted to be straight with you before it all comes out."

Dave didn't look up, his focus fixed on his guitar. "Yeah, well, thanks for the heads-up, "he said flatly.

Stephen hesitated for a moment, as if waiting for Dave to say something more. When it became clear he wouldn't, Stephen turned and headed for the door. But just as he reached it, Dave's voice stopped him.

"Hey, "Dave said, still not looking up. "If this really is the end… make sure you leave it all out there. Don't hold back."

Stephen paused, glancing back at him. "Same to you, man, "he said quietly. "Same to you."

With that, he stepped out into the night, the glow of the Sunset Strip lighting up the horizon like a faded memory. Inside, Dave kept playing, the mournful melody filling the empty room, a sound that echoed with everything they were about to lose.

The television sat propped on a dusty crate in the corner of Perry's half-renovated living room, its glow the only light in the dim space. The house in Venice Beach was supposed to be his sanctuary, a place to recharge, but at the moment, it felt more like a construction site. Exposed beams crisscrossed the ceiling, drop cloths covered the furniture, and the faint smell of sawdust hung in the air.

Perry sat on the floor, a bottle of wine next to him and a half-burned joint balanced on the edge of an ashtray. His eyes were glued to the screen as the images of the L.A. Riots filled the room. Buildings burning, people running through the streets, broken glass and flames reflecting off camera lenses, it was chaos, raw and unfiltered, playing out in real time. Perry's bare feet tapped restlessly against the hardwood floor as he leaned forward, his fingers tangled in his dark hair.

The riots had started the night before, the moment the verdict came down. Four LAPD officers, caught on tape beating Rodney King, had been acquitted. Perry had been following the case, like everyone else in L.A., but the verdict still hit like a gut punch. He couldn't say he was surprised, not really. But there was something about seeing it play out, the brutality on tape and the utter lack of justice, that made his stomach churn.

The news was on every channel, the anchors' voices hushed and somber as they tried to narrate the chaos. Perry barely heard them, his focus on the images. A man stood in front of a liquor store engulfed in flames, shouting into the camera with tears streaming down his face. "They don't give a shit about us! This is what we've got to do to make them listen!" The camera cut to another street, where people smashed windows, grabbed whatever they could carry, and disappeared into the shadows. The National Guard was already moving in, soldiers in fatigues climbing out of trucks with rifles slung over their shoulders.

"Fucking hell, "Perry muttered under his breath, reaching for the wine bottle and taking a long swig. The world felt like it was ripping apart at the seams, and the TV was showing him every raw, unfiltered moment of it.

Casey's voice called out from another room, muffled by the sound of power tools. "Perry? You watching the riots again?"

"Yeah, "he replied, his voice distant. He didn't look away from the screen as she walked into the room, wiping paint off her hands with a rag. She stopped when she saw him, her expression softening. He looked like he hadn't moved in hours, his gaze locked on the screen as if he could absorb it all through sheer willpower.

She walked over and sat beside him on the floor, her shoulder brushing his. "It's everywhere, "she said quietly, her eyes flicking to the TV. A police car flipped onto its side as flames roared behind it, casting eerie shadows across the faces of the crowd. "Feels like the city's finally snapped."

"Feels like the world's finally snapped, "Perry replied, his voice low and sharp. He took another swig of wine, then set the bottle down with a thud. "This isn't just about Rodney King. This is everything. Years of getting pushed down, ignored, treated like shit. This was bound to happen."

Casey nodded, her eyes thoughtful. "I get it. But it's scary as hell to watch."

Perry's gaze stayed fixed on the screen. "Scary, yeah. But it's fucking honest." He gestured toward the TV with a sweep of his hand. "This? This is real. It's ugly and violent, but it's not fake. People are showing the truth, what happens when you push them too far."

The camera cut to a woman standing in front of a burning building, her voice hoarse from shouting. "They don't see us. They don't hear us. Well, they'll fucking see us now."

Casey sighed, leaning back on her hands. "It's like the whole city's on fire."

Perry turned to her, a strange gleam in his eyes, his mind already racing. "Yeah, "he said slowly, the words coming out like they carried weight. "It's like… like they're putting on a fucking show. Burning the city down for everyone to watch, like it's some sick form of entertainment."

Casey frowned, unsure where he was going with this. "I guess."

He leaned forward, resting his elbows on his knees, his fingers tapping against his temple. "Think about it. People are glued to their TVs right now, watching this like it's a movie. They're horrified, sure, but they can't look away. It's like… porno for pyros."

Casey blinked, caught off guard by the phrase. "What?"

"Porno for Pyros, "Perry repeated, his voice gaining momentum. He gestured at the TV again, where flames engulfed another building, the camera zooming in on the destruction. "That's what this is. People getting off on the destruction, on the violence, on the fucking anarchy of it all. They act like they're above it, but they're eating it up."

Casey stared at him, her expression a mix of concern and curiosity. "That's… dark, "she said, choosing her words carefully. "But you're not wrong."

Perry leaned back, his hands running through his hair as the idea began to take shape in his mind. "It's not just the riots, "he said, his voice picking up speed. "It's everything. The way people consume violence, stubbornness, destruction, it's all the same. They want the spectacle. They need it. And we give it to them."

Casey tilted her head, watching him closely. "What are you thinking?"

He paused, the wheels in his mind spinning too fast to catch up with. "I've been trying to put something together, "he said finally. "A new band. Something that's more… visceral.

Raw. Real. Jane's was one thing, but this? This is something else entirely. Something that captures this." He gestured again to the TV, his hand sweeping toward the flames.

"And you're calling it Porno for Pyros?" Casey asked, a faint smile tugging at the corner of her mouth.

Perry nodded, his eyes gleaming with excitement. "Yeah. 'Porno for Pyros.' That's the name. That's the vibe. The world's on fire, and everyone's getting off on it. Might as well play the fucking soundtrack."

Casey chuckled softly, shaking her head. "Leave it to you to find inspiration in the middle of an apocalypse."

Perry grinned, leaning back against the wall as the flames on the screen reflected in his eyes. "It's not the end of the world, Case. It's just the next chapter."

Meanwhile, Dave and Eric and a few friends had been experimenting with some new sounds. In late 1992, the studio was an almost monastic refuge for Dave Navarro and Eric Avery, a stark contrast to the chaos that had characterized the final years of Jane's Addiction. With Perry Farrell moving on to form Porno for Pyros and Stephen Perkins joining Mike Muir's Infectious Grooves, it was clear Jane's was over. After months of avoidance, Dave and Eric finally confronted the reality head-on, acknowledging what they had both silently known for a while.

"So this is it, "Dave had said one night, leaning against a graffiti-covered wall in the parking lot outside the rehearsal space. A cigarette dangled from his lips, unlit, as if he couldn't decide if it was worth the effort.

Eric, arms crossed, had nodded slowly, his gaze fixed on the cracked asphalt. "Yeah. It's done. He's got his new band. Stephen's doing his own thing. And us?" He looked up, meeting Dave's eyes with a flicker of frustration. "We're just standing here like idiots."

Dave chuckled, a dry sound. "Maybe. But I don't know how to quit playing, man. I need to make something. Something that's ours."

That conversation had planted the seed for what would become Deconstruction, a project as far removed from Jane's Addiction's bombastic energy as possible. While Jane's had been an explosion of chaos and color, Deconstruction was introspective, fragmented, and experimental, a quiet masterpiece in the making.

The studio was a cavernous, dimly lit space, the air heavy with the smell of old amplifiers and the faint metallic tang of coffee left too long in its pot. Eric stood in the middle of the room, bass in hand, plucking out a meandering riff that echoed hauntingly off the walls. It wasn't a song yet, but it had potential. Dave was perched on a stool, hunched over his guitar, cigarette dangling from his lips, his fingers running up and down the fret board in a flurry of arpeggios. The sound was angular, raw, but somehow beautiful, like something broken that still had sharp edges of brilliance.

"Wait, "Eric said, stopping mid-riff. "What the fuck was that you just did? Play that again."

Dave smirked but obliged, repeating the haunting, discordant pattern he'd just stumbled into. "This?" he asked, letting the last note linger in the air.

"Yeah, that, "Eric said, his eyes narrowing in concentration. He adjusted his bass strap and started playing a counter-melody, something dark but groovy, weaving around Dave's jagged riff like ivy climbing a broken wall.

"Shit, "Dave said after a moment, nodding in approval. "That's it. That's the vibe."

They played the loop over and over, the sound growing richer, more layered. It felt like they were carving something out of stone, chiseling away until the song revealed itself. Dave added flourishes, sliding harmonics, bursts of distortion, while Eric locked into a hypnotic rhythm, grounding the piece with his steady, deliberate playing.

After a while, they paused, the studio falling silent except for the faint hum of amplifiers. Eric grabbed a water bottle, taking a long drink, and leaned back against the wall. "You know, "he said, his voice quiet, thoughtful, "this feels… different."

Dave raised an eyebrow. "Different how?"

Eric shrugged, staring at the floor. "It's… ours. There's no bullshit. No drama. No Perry trying to hijack everything." He looked up, meeting Dave's gaze. "I love the guy, but I don't miss the circus, man."

Dave nodded slowly, understanding. "Yeah. This feels… honest. Stripped down."

"Stripped down?" Eric smirked. "Dude, you just played like eight million notes in the last five minutes."

Dave laughed, flipping him off playfully. "Hey, it's called texture, man. Look it up."

The next day, they brought in a session drummer, someone Eric knew from the local scene. He wasn't Stephen Perkins, but his playing was solid, restrained, giving the songs a minimalist foundation. In many ways, it was exactly what they needed, simple rhythms that left room for experimentation.

"Alright, "Eric said, nodding toward the drummer as they started a take. "Keep it tight. No flourishes. Just… pulse."

Dave adjusted his amp settings, dialing in a tone that was sharp but not overwhelming. As the drums began, a steady, almost mechanical beat, he launched into a riff that sounded like shards of glass falling in slow motion. Eric joined in, his bass-lines melodic but understated, creating a hypnotic interplay that felt both cold and emotional.

The producer, sitting in the control room, leaned into the talk-back mic. "What the hell is this one called?" he asked, his voice crackling through the studio speakers.

Dave shrugged. "I don't know. 'Iris,' maybe?"

Eric frowned. "Why 'Iris'?"

Dave grinned. "Because it sounds… delicate. Like it could fall apart at any second."

Eric rolled his eyes but didn't argue. The name stuck.

Between takes, the conversations were sparse but meaningful.

"Do you ever think about how weird this is?" Eric asked one afternoon, leaning against his bass amp. "We're making this… whatever this is, while Perry's out there doing his thing, and the world's still spinning."

Dave nodded, adjusting the strap on his guitar. "Yeah. But honestly? I don't care. I'm not trying to prove anything to anyone. I just want to make something real."

Eric studied him for a moment, then nodded. "Yeah. Me too."

By the time the album began to take shape, it was clear that Deconstruction wasn't just a side project; it was a statement. The songs were unconventional, sprawling, and deeply personal, rejecting the formulaic structures that dominated the 1990's alternative scene. Tracks like "L.A. Song" and "Single" felt like confessions, while instrumentals like "Iris" were hauntingly beautiful, their experimental nature pushing the boundaries of what people expected from two former members of Jane's Addiction.

And yet, as powerful as the music was, there was an unspoken understanding between Dave and Eric: this wasn't meant to last. They weren't trying to rebuild Jane's Addiction or even replace it. This was something entirely different, something fleeting, and maybe that was the point.

"It's weird, "Eric said one night as they packed up their gear. "This might be the best shit we've ever done, and no one's gonna hear it."

Dave smirked, slinging his guitar over his shoulder. "Then fuck 'em, "he said, his tone light but sincere. "We're not doing this for them."

Eric chuckled, shaking his head. "Yeah. I guess not."

They left the studio that night, the streets of L.A. quiet around them, their album nearly complete. Deconstruction would be a portrait of two artists at a crossroads, a quiet masterpiece born out of the ashes of something larger, something louder. And while the world might not have been ready for it, they were.

A Fresh Start?

By 1993, Perry Farrell wasn't just grappling with the next phase of his music career, he was busy pissing people off while doing it, exactly as he liked. In his Venice Beach house, a gutted, half-renovated mess of exposed beams, incense smoke, and tribal sculptures, he crouched on the floor, surrounded by half-drunk bottles of wine, ashtrays overflowing with joints, and an absurd number of crystals arranged in a pattern that only made sense to him.

"Perry, you know the label's losing their fucking minds about the name, right?" Martyn LeNoble leaned against the doorway, his Dutch accent cutting through the haze. He smirked, lighting a cigarette as he watched Perry drop another crystal into place like he was summoning some ancient force.

Without looking up, Perry grinned, twisting the crystal in his hand. "Good, "he said, voice sharp and biting. "Let 'em lose their minds. That's what they're paid to do. They freak out; I create. Circle of life."

"Yeah, well, they're saying it won't sell, "Peter DiStefano chimed in, slumping into a chair with his guitar strapped across his chest. He looked beat, his hair wild and his fingers twitching like he hadn't slept in days. "They're saying, 'Porno for Pyros is a deal breaker.' Their words, not mine."

Perry finally looked up, an amused spark in his eyes. "Deal breaker? They're lucky I didn't name it 'Fucking on Fire' instead." He leaned back on his hands, exhaling smoke. "The name's the least of their goddamn problems."

Peter ran a hand through his hair, glaring at Perry. "Yeah, well, it'll be our goddamn problem when they won't release the record. I'm not playing these songs to a fucking wall, Perry."

Martyn barked a laugh, flicking his cigarette ash onto the floor. "You're preaching to the wrong guy, man. Perry wants the suits to freak. You think he loses sleep over their bottom lines?"

"I don't lose sleep over shit, "Perry shot back, his voice growing sharp. He stood up, brushing ashes off his ripped jeans. "Listen, this isn't a fucking debate. The name stays. You don't like it, the label doesn't like it? I don't give a shit. They'll come crawling back when the first song hits, mark my words. They always do."

Peter leaned forward, frustration spilling into his voice. "Do you even want this band to make it? Or are you just trying to piss everyone off for sport?"

Perry's expression darkened. He stepped closer to Peter, jabbing a finger at him. "You think I'd put this much of myself into something I didn't care about? You think this is a game to me?" His voice dropped, low and lethal. "Porno for Pyros is gonna be bigger than Jane's. Bigger than any of us. And if you can't see that, maybe you're the one who's checked the fuck out."

The room went quiet, the tension heavy. Martyn raised an eyebrow but didn't say a word, clearly entertained by the back-and-forth. Peter, however, didn't back down.

"You better be right, man, "Peter said, his tone clipped. "Because if they pull the plug, you're gonna be out there explaining this shit, not me."

Perry leaned back, his grin returning, but there was a fire in his eyes now, an intensity that made it clear he wasn't backing down. "Trust me, "he said, his voice quieter but no less forceful. "They'll see. The name's perfect. It's everything this band is. It's fucking fire."

Martyn gestured toward the rough demo tape sitting on the table. "Well, they're gonna have a hard time ignoring that, "he said, smirking as he picked it up. "Say what you want about the suits, but even they can't argue with how good this shit sounds."

Perry's grin widened. "Exactly. They're scared because they know it's dangerous. The name, the sound, the vibe, it's gonna blow their neat little ideas about what a band should be to pieces."

Peter groaned, but a faint smirk tugged at the corner of his mouth. "Fine. Fuck it. Let's burn it all down, then."

"Now you're getting it, "Perry said, clapping Peter on the shoulder. "Let's scare the shit out of them."

Martyn shook his head, chuckling as he grabbed his bass. "You've got a way with people, man. A fucked-up way, but a way."

Perry tilted his head, his grin sharp as a blade. "That's the job, Martyn. That's the fucking job."

Martyn and Peter started plugging in their instruments as Perry turned toward the mic, his mind already racing ahead. In his gut, he knew they were onto something. The label could bitch and moan all they wanted, but he wasn't about to compromise, not on the name, not on the sound, not on the vision.

They ran through the demo tracks late into the night, the raw energy of the songs filling the empty space of Perry's half-finished house. By the time they wrapped, the tension had melted away, replaced by the kind of manic excitement that only came from creating something that felt alive.

Perry leaned against the mic stand, his shirt soaked through with sweat, his voice hoarse from hours of singing. "You hear that?" he asked, his voice low, almost reverent. "That's what they're afraid of."

Peter shook his head, slinging his guitar off his shoulder. "You're a stubborn bastard, Perry, but you might actually be onto something."

Perry smirked, lighting a joint as he surveyed the room. "Might? Come on, Peter. You know we're gonna fucking own this."

Martyn laughed as he packed up his bass. "Well, if nothing else, I'm here for the ride. Let's see how far we can take this circus."

Perry exhaled a cloud of smoke, his grin widening. "Far enough to leave a mark. Far enough that they'll never forget the name."

And in that moment, even Peter couldn't argue with him.

Perry stepped out of the booth, grabbing a towel to wipe the sweat off his face. His energy was still running hot, a mix of adrenaline and sheer determination that kept him bouncing on the balls of his feet. "Alright, let's hear it back, "he called out to the producer, his voice sharp with anticipation.

The playback started, filling the studio with the raw, magnetic pulse of "Pets." The guitars snarled, the drums rolled with a hypnotic groove, and Perry's voice soared over it all, equal parts haunting and sarcastic. Martyn closed his eyes, nodding along to the bass-line he'd laid down, a satisfied smirk pulling at his lips.

When the track ended, the room was momentarily silent, the echo of the last note hanging in the air like smoke. Perry turned to the band, his grin wide, teeth flashing. "That, "he said, pointing toward the speakers, "is why we don't play it safe."

Peter shrugged, his tone deliberately nonchalant. "Yeah, not bad. Could've used more guitar."

"Fuck you, "Perry shot back, laughing as he grabbed a bottle of water. "It's perfect, and you know it."

Stephen tapped his drumsticks against his knees, leaning forward with a satisfied nod. "It's got a groove, man. People are gonna feel that one in their bones."

The producer, seated at the soundboard, glanced over his shoulder. "You sure about the mix, Perry? Vocals are a little buried in the chorus."

Perry waved him off, pacing the room like a man possessed. "Leave it. The vocals don't need to be out front, they're part of the whole, like another instrument. People are gonna dig into it, let it wash over them. It's gotta feel alive, like it's breathing."

Martyn raised an eyebrow, leaning back in his chair. "Breathing? Man, you really are summoning spirits."

Perry shot him a mock-serious look. "Don't mock the process, Martyn. The spirits are listening."

Peter rolled his eyes but couldn't help the grin tugging at his lips. "You're so full of shit, Perry."

Perry grinned back, tossing his towel onto the couch and plopping down beside Peter. "And yet, here you are, following me into the fire."

The mood lightened as the band shifted into discussions about the next track on their list. Martyn scribbled notes in a battered notebook, while Stephen tapped out potential rhythms on a nearby snare drum. Perry leaned back, his gaze drifting toward the ceiling, his mind clearly already moving on to the next idea.

"Hey, Perry, "Stephen said suddenly, his voice breaking through the quiet. "What's the deal with the video? You keep talking about wanting it to be 'bigger than the music, ' but what does that even mean?"

Perry tilted his head, a sly grin creeping across his face. "It means exactly what it sounds like, Stevie. The video isn't just a promo, it's a fucking piece of art. Something people will remember long after the song's out of rotation. Something that gets under their skin."

Peter groaned, running a hand through his hair. "You're not gonna make us act again, are you? I'm still cringing from the last one."

"Relax, "Perry said, waving a hand dismissively. "This one's gonna be different. Surreal. Weird. People won't know whether to love it or hate it, but they'll be talking about it either way."

Martyn smirked, shaking his head. "Just make sure it doesn't get us banned everywhere before we even release the damn single."

Perry's grin widened, his eyes gleaming with mischief. "Oh, it'll probably get banned. That's half the fun."

The room erupted into laughter, the tension from earlier melting away. Even Peter, who had spent the better part of the session grumbling, couldn't suppress a chuckle.

As the evening wore on, they dove back into the music, their energy renewed. Tracks were fine-tuned, layers added, and through it all, Perry drove them forward, his vision sharp and unrelenting. By the time they called it a night, the studio felt alive with the echoes of what they'd created.

Standing in the doorway, Martyn looked back at Perry, who was still seated on the couch, flipping through his notebook, lost in thought. "You ever stop?" he asked, his tone half-teasing.

Perry glanced up, his expression unreadable for a moment before breaking into a sly smile. "When the world stops spinning, maybe."

Martyn shook his head, laughing softly as he headed out. Peter and Stephen followed, their footsteps echoing down the hall, leaving Perry alone in the quiet studio.

The demo tape sat on the table beside him, the raw tracks still hot from hours of recording. He picked it up, turning it over in his hands, his fingers brushing against the scrawled label: Porno for Pyros – Pets Sessions.

For a moment, he just stared at it, his mind racing with the possibilities. Then, with a small, almost imperceptible nod, he slipped the tape into his bag, grabbed his coat, and stepped out into the cool Venice night. The moon hung low over the horizon, casting a pale glow over the city, and as Perry walked toward his car, he couldn't help but smile. This was just the beginning.

A New Era is Born.

Porno for Pyros' self-titled debut album was released on April 27, 1993, and it wasted no time climbing the Alternative and Rock charts. The sound was raw, seductive, and completely unfiltered, a natural extension of Perry Farrell's wild creative vision. The first single, "Cursed Female, "had premiered a month earlier, its video a provocative blend of sensual imagery and surrealism that sent ripples through the industry. But it was the follow-up single, "Pets, "that catapulted the band to stardom, shooting the album to gold record status faster than any Jane's Addiction record had.

At the video shoot for "Pets, "Perry was everywhere at once, an untamed force of nature whose energy seemed to infect everyone on set. His movements were erratic yet purposeful, like a mad conductor orchestrating chaos. The director, trying desperately to maintain some semblance of order, waved his clipboard in frustration. "Perry, we need to stick to the storyboard!"

Perry laughed, a sharp, wild sound that silenced the crew. "Storyboard?" he barked, stepping closer, his eyes alight with challenge. "Fuck the storyboard! This isn't a movie. Its just us cats, sending a message. This needs to be subtle. It's the fucking words that matter, man, not the 'imagery'."

The director hesitated, glancing nervously at the producers watching from the sidelines, but Perry was already turning away, his focus elsewhere. "We're not here to look pretty, "Perry continued, his voice rising. "We're here to make them feel something. Even if it fucking hurts."

Martyn leaned against an amp, watching the scene unfold with a smirk. "You know, he's not wrong, "he said to Peter, who was tuning his guitar nearby.

Peter rolled his eyes but couldn't hide his grin. "Yeah, but do we have to make the director cry in the process?"

By the time filming wrapped, the atmosphere was charged. The footage was raw, electric, and undeniably powerful. As Perry watched the playback, his grin widened. "That's it, "he said, his voice low, almost reverent. "Classy but raw. Just….us."

The buzz was immediate. MTV News picked up on the energy like sharks catching the scent of blood in the water. Clips of the band dominated airtime, Kurt Loder reporting with a knowing grin, "Porno for Pyros, Perry Farrell's new project, is proving to be the successful new project no one saw coming."

The video for "Pets" became an instant sensation, its mix of surreal imagery and Perry's captivating performance striking a chord with a restless generation. Within weeks, it was on heavy rotation, and the band was everywhere, radio, television, magazine covers.

Rolling Stone put Perry's face front and center on their latest issue. Beneath the headline "Perry Farrell's New Revolution, "his eyes burned with intensity, his expression daring the world to keep up with him. The accompanying article described the band as "the next evolutionary step in alternative music, "a testament to Perry's ability to reinvent himself while staying true to his core.

The tour that followed was like stepping into another world. Night after night, they played to sold-out crowds, each venue packed to capacity with fans who moved as one, their fists raised high, their voices screaming every word. The energy was visceral, almost dangerous, and Perry fed off it like a predator.

Under the glare of the stage lights, he was magnetic, his every move calculated to provoke, to ignite something in the crowd. "You want truth?" he yelled one night, his voice cutting through the din like a blade. His eyes burned as he stared out at the sea of faces. "You think you'll find it sitting on your asses? You gotta' bleed for it!"

The audience roared back, their voices merging into a deafening wave of sound. Perry stood at the edge of the stage, his arms outstretched, as if ready to dive into the chaos. For those few hours, he was their prophet, their savior, and their destroyer all in one.

But outside the maelstrom of the shows, there were quieter moments. At dawn, while the world still slept, Perry would take his surfboard out into the Pacific, paddling beyond the breaking waves until he found a stillness that seemed to exist nowhere else in his life.

Out there, with the sun rising over the horizon, the ocean stretching endlessly before him, he found a strange, fleeting peace. He'd ride the waves in silence, his body moving instinctively, the rhythm of the sea grounding him in a way nothing else could.

As he sat on his board, the salt air filling his lungs, he whispered to himself, his voice barely audible over the sound of the waves. "This is it, "he said, staring out at the endless expanse of water. "This is the only place where I don't have to prove a damn thing."

For Perry, the balance between the intensity of the stage and the calm of the ocean was the only way to keep going. The revolution he'd sparked with Porno for Pyros was burning bright, but even he knew that fire couldn't burn forever. And yet, for now, he was content to ride the wave, to see how far it could carry him before it crashed.

Dave set the teacup down, his fingers lingering on the smooth ceramic as he mulled over the weight of Anthony's words. He wasn't sure if it was the incense, the calm of the room, or the sheer absurdity of sitting in this zen-like bubble with two of the most unpredictable musicians on the planet, but something inside him shifted.

"Alright, "Dave said finally, his voice steady but low. He looked up at Anthony and Flea, his dark eyes filled with something cautious but resolute. "Let's see where this goes. But no bullshit. If it's going to work, it's gotta feel... I don't know... honest."

Flea grinned wide, his energy breaking through the stillness of the room like sunlight through a cloud. "Honest? Man, we're all about honesty. Too fucking honest sometimes." He clapped Dave on the back, the sudden burst of motion jarring but somehow grounding. "You're gonna fit in just fine, brother."

Anthony nodded, a small, satisfied smile on his face. "We're not asking you to be anyone else, man. Just bring yourself. All the fucked-up, beautiful, dark, twisted shit. That's what we want. That's what we need."

Dave gave a small, almost imperceptible nod, his lips twitching into the faintest hint of a smile. He wasn't entirely convinced, of them, of himself, or of the future, but there was something about the energy in the room, the strange sense of purpose radiating off Anthony and Flea, that made him think this might be worth the risk.

Flea jumped up suddenly, unable to sit still any longer. "Holy shit, this is gonna be good!" he exclaimed, pacing the room like a kid who'd just been handed the keys to a candy store. "I can hear it already. Your guitar with my bass, Anthony's voice... fuck, it's gonna tear people's faces off...and be just-beautiful guys ."

Anthony chuckled, leaning back against the wall, his arms folded loosely across his chest. "One step at a time, Flea. Let the man breathe. He's not even officially in yet."

Flea stopped pacing and pointed dramatically at Dave. "You're in, "he declared, his grin widening. "You just don't know it yet."

Dave couldn't help but laugh, the sound low and almost reluctant. "Yeah, well, don't get ahead of yourselves. Let's just see if this works first."

Anthony's smile widened. "Fair enough. But trust me, man, when it does? It's gonna be some next-level shit."

Dave leaned back slightly, his hands resting on his knees as he took in the scene. The incense swirled lazily in the air, the faint hum of distant traffic filtering through the walls. It wasn't Jane's Addiction. It wasn't the chaos of Perry or the volatile push and pull of Eric and Stephen. It was different. Quieter, maybe. But no less intense. If anything, it felt sharper, more focused.

And in that moment, sitting in Anthony Kiedis' meditation room, surrounded by two musicians who had seen their own share of darkness and come out the other side, Dave thought maybe, just maybe, he could find something here. Something new. Something that might help him put the pieces back together.

The first jam session with The Red Hot Chili Peppers was held just a week later, in a rehearsal space that felt almost claustrophobic with the sheer amount of gear crammed into it. The air was thick, not with incense this time, but with the raw anticipation of something about to be born. Flea was already slapping out a furious bass-line when Dave walked in, his body moving in time with the rhythm, his face lit up with that manic, infectious energy he carried like a second skin.

Anthony stood off to the side, notebook in hand, scribbling lyrics or notes or god knows what, humming under his breath as he tried to keep pace with Flea's improvised groove. They both looked up when Dave entered, their expressions a mix of curiosity and expectation.

"Ready to fucking rip?" Flea shouted, his voice loud and wild, breaking through the stillness like a thunderclap.

Dave smirked, slinging his guitar strap over his shoulder. "Let's see if you can keep up."

The first few notes were hesitant, a feeling-out process as they each tried to find their footing. But it didn't take long for the room to catch fire. Flea's bass-lines roared and growled, a heartbeat that pushed everything forward. Anthony's voice slid in next, sharp and rhythmic, weaving in and out of the melody with that distinct, unmistakable cadence of his. And Dave, Dave's guitar soared above it all, his riffs slicing through the noise with an edge that was both precise and unpredictable.

By the time the first song ended, the atmosphere was raw with sweat and electricity. Flea was practically bouncing off the walls, his eyes wide and gleaming. "Fuck yes! That's what I'm talking about, my brothers!"

Anthony leaned against the mic stand, his breathing heavy, a grin stretched across his face. "I told you, "he said, pointing at Dave. "This is it."

Dave said nothing, just wiped the sweat from his brow and adjusted his guitar strap. But inside, he felt it too. A spark. A flicker of something that could grow into a blaze.

They played late into the night, the songs coming together in jagged pieces, raw and imperfect but alive with potential. And as Dave walked out into the cool Los Angeles night, his guitar case slung over one shoulder, he couldn't help but feel a cautious kind of hope. He didn't know if this was going to work, if it would last, or if it would burn out just as quickly as it had ignited. But for the first time in a long time, he felt like he was moving forward. And that, for now, was enough

Porno and Peppers.

Anthony Kiedis' home in Laurel Canyon was a sanctuary, an oasis of calm amid the chaos of Los Angeles. The walls were painted in soothing earth tones, and the air was thick with the scent of burning incense. In a dimly lit meditation room, Dave Navarro sat cross-legged on the floor, eyes half-closed, with Anthony and Flea. The silence in the room was deep, broken only by the soft clinking of ceramic cups as they sipped green tea, each of them lost in thought.

Anthony broke the silence, his voice steady and contemplative. "We gotta evolve.

Do something no one expects."

Dave ran a hand through his hair, a shadow of hesitation crossing his face. "Janes was… different, "he murmured, his voice distant. "More abstract. Darker…but man was it fucking 'fun'…in a sense."

Flea leaned forward; his usually animated face was unusually serious. "That's exactly what we need. Something real. Something fucked up."

Dave looked down at his tea, the liquid swirling in the dim light, his expression clouded with doubt. "You know about my history… with shit."

Anthony tapped his sobriety medallion, a knowing smile tugging at the corner of his mouth. "Who the fuck doesn't have history?" he chuckled; his tone laced with understanding.

They shared a look, a silent acknowledgment of shared battles, of scars that ran deep. In that moment, Dave felt a flicker of connection, of something solid to hold onto. Joining the Red Hot Chili Peppers was a step into uncharted territory, but maybe, just maybe, it was exactly what he needed.

In June, 1994, the Red Hot Chili Peppers entered The Sound Factory to begin the initial stages of writing and recording, of what would become *One Hot Minute*, with legendary producer Rick Rubin, who they'd worked with prior on the multi-platinum, *Blood, Sugar, Sex, Magik*.

The band completed a few basic tracks before Kiedis began having difficulty singing. He'd been through a dental procedure in which an addictive sedative, Valium, was used. The medication triggered a relapse, and he once again became dependent on drugs. Kiedis had slipped from five years of sobriety and began reusing heroin and cocaine - narcotics he'd sworn never to use again.

The band took a short break from recording as the summer of '94 brought a return to Woodstock, a festival reborn in a new age, one that would prove both a spectacle and a statement.

On August 12. The crowds gathered, stretching as far as the eye could see, a sea of faces, each one drawn by the promise of something electric, something unforgettable. It wasn't just about the music, it was a cultural reckoning, a passing of the torch from the rebellious spirit of the original Woodstock to a new generation finding its own voice in a chaotic world.

Porno for Pyros took the stage first, as the sun dipped low in the sky, casting golden hues across the massive crowd. Perry Farrell stood at the mic, his presence magnetic, his silhouette framed by the warm light. The opening notes of "Pets" rang out, and the crowd erupted, their energy rippling across the fields like a living thing. Perry moved with a frenetic grace, his voice raw and powerful, carrying every ounce of conviction that had made him a prophet of the alternative nation.

Martyn LeNoble's bass-lines rumbled like thunder beneath Perry's vocals, grounding the performance while Stephen Perkins' drumming hit like a heartbeat, primal and unrelenting. Peter DiStefano's guitar screamed and sang, weaving its own chaotic beauty through the mix. The band was tight, almost too tight for the loose, unpredictable spirit of the festival, but that tension only heightened their intensity.

Between songs, Perry spoke to the crowd, his words part sermon, part provocation. "You feel that?" he shouted, his voice rising above the din. "That's freedom, people. That's what they're scared of. You, all of you, being free. Don't let them fucking take it. Ever."

The crowd roared in response, fists raised, voices screaming back at him. Perry smiled, wild and electric, as if feeding off their energy. To those watching, it felt less like a concert and more like a ritual, a communion between the band and the thousands before them. By the time Porno for Pyros launched into "Tahitian Moon, "the sun had fully set, and the stage lights cast strange, shifting shadows over the band. The audience swayed and surged, lost in the music, their bodies moving as one.

Later that night, the Red Hot Chili Peppers took the stage, with Dave Navarro stepping into his new role with a mixture of nerves and exhilaration. The air had shifted; rain began to fall in a steady drizzle, turning the festival grounds into a mud-soaked playground for the thousands who didn't care. Dave stood with his guitar slung low, his black hair clinging to his face in the rain, his fingers dancing over the strings with a precision that belied the chaos around him.

They opened with "Give It Away, "and the crowd exploded. Each member was donning an enormous plastic, lit-up light bulb over their head. Flea bounced across the stage like a man possessed, his bass-lines surging through the mud and rain, while Anthony Kiedis prowled the mic, his vocals sharp and rhythmic. Dave's guitar added a new layer to the Chili Peppers' sound, darker, more intricate, with a tinge of the gothic surrealism he'd brought from Jane's Addiction.

By the third song, the light rain had let-up and Dave, caught a glimpse of Perry watching from the side of the stage, his face half-lit by the shifting colors of the lights. For a moment, it threw Dave off, a strange sense of being watched not with judgment, but with something else, approval, maybe.

The Chili Peppers closed their set with "Under the Bridge, "and as the song's melancholic chorus rang loud, the night felt suspended. The hundreds of thousands' voices singing along in perfect harmony, a shared moment of intimacy in the vastness of Woodstock.

Backstage, it was a mingling scents of rain, sweat, and cigarette smoke. Crew members hurried about, equipment dripping with water, while musicians and managers lingered in groups, buzzing with the residual high of the performances.

Dave spotted Perry leaning against a stack of amplifiers, a half-empty bottle of red wine in his hand. His painted face was streaked with rain, but his grin was intact, mischievous as ever. As Dave approached, Perry raised the bottle in a mock toast.

"Look at you, "Perry said, his voice warm and laced with pride. He clapped Dave on the shoulder, his grip firm. "You made it, man. From the mud of L.A. to the mud of this shit-show, right?"

Dave gave a sheepish laugh, his head dipping slightly. "It's not Jane's, but… it's good. Feels like something."

Perry nodded, his grin softening into something more genuine. "Nothing's ever like Jane's. That will never be replicated…for any of us fuckin' cats. But whatever you do now, make it yours. Don't let anyone tell you how it's supposed to be Dave. I tried that, for a long time. And I'm sorry um, well…I'm sorry Davey."

Dave studied Perry's face for a moment, searching for something unspoken. "You miss it?" he asked quietly.

Perry tilted his head, considering the question. "Every fucking day, "he admitted, his voice low, raw. "But sometimes, you've got to burn it all down to see what comes next brother."

They stood in silence for a moment, the sounds of the festival fading into the background. In that shared quiet, the weight of their history seemed to lift, if only slightly, replaced by something like understanding.

Perry drained the last of the wine and handed the empty bottle to a passing crew member. "Catch you in the waves, Navarro, "he said, turning to disappear into the crowd of artists and roadies, leaving Dave standing alone.

Dave watched him go, the rain starting to pick up again, drumming lightly against the tin roof of the backstage tent. He felt a strange mix of emotions, gratitude, nostalgia, and a faint flicker of hope. For now, the music was enough. It had to be.

Woodstock '94 would be remembered for its mud, its rain, and its music. But for Perry Farrell and Dave Navarro, it was also a reminder, of where they'd been, of where they were now, and of the undeniable pull of whatever was still to come.

One Tense Minute.

The studio was a cocktail of tension, sweat, and the faint metallic scent of overused cables. They were deep into the recording process for *One Hot Minute*, and every take felt heavier than the last. Flea's bass lines thundered with purpose, punching through the mix like a heartbeat, relentless and unyielding. Stephen Perkins wasn't there to lean on anymore, but Chad Smith, with his powerhouse precision, had locked into Flea's groove, creating a rhythm section that felt unshakable.

Dave sat hunched over his guitar, his fingers restless, teasing out notes like he was chasing ghosts. The weight of Rick Rubin's words hung in the air: Let it bleed. Dave knew what Rubin was asking, and it pissed him off in a way he couldn't fully explain. The kind of honesty the producer was pushing for felt like flaying himself alive. And yet, deep down, he knew Rubin was right.

Anthony paced near the mic stand; his bare feet silent on the studio's worn carpet. His eyes locked on Dave, their unspoken tension, a constant presence in the room. Anthony, dealing with his demons once again and the guilt that comes with it, recognized the same in Dave. But where Anthony's battles fueled his lyrics, Dave's seemed to drag him into a darker place, one he couldn't always find his way out of.

"You good, man?" Flea asked, breaking the silence as he adjusted the strap of his bass. His voice was light, but his eyes carried a genuine concern.

Dave gave a tight nod, not looking up. "Yeah, "he muttered, though the word carried no conviction. He twisted the tuning peg on his low E string, not because it needed adjusting, but because his hands needed something to do.

Rick Rubin leaned forward from his perch behind the mixing console, his calm, measured tone cutting through the simmering tension. "Take your time, Dave. But when you're ready, don't think. Just play. Feel it."

Dave exhaled sharply, shaking his head like he was trying to clear it. "Easier said than done, "he muttered, barely audible.

Anthony stepped closer, his tone softer than usual. "Look, man, "he said, gesturing toward the guitar in Dave's lap. "That thing in your hands? It's your voice. Say what you need to say with it. Don't hold the-fuck back."

Dave finally looked up, meeting Anthony's gaze. For a moment, the air between them shifted, the usual edge of their interactions replaced by something quieter. It wasn't friendship, at least not yet, but it was an understanding.

Chad broke the tension with a quick tap of his drumsticks, a steady beat that seemed to say, "Let's just fucking play already." Flea shot him a grateful look, then turned to Dave with a crooked grin. "Come on, Navarro. Stop being such a moody genius and show us what you got."

Dave smirked despite himself, the tension in his shoulders easing slightly. "Alright, assholes, "he said, adjusting his strap and plugging in. "Let's do this."

The red light above the booth blinked on, and Rick's voice crackled through the intercom. "Rolling."

Flea's bass hit first, a low, growling line that shook the room. Chad followed, his snare sharp and commanding, like the crack of a whip. Anthony swayed in place, eyes closed as he waited for his cue.

Dave hesitated for a fraction of a second, his fingers hovering over the strings. Then, as if a switch flipped inside him, he dove in. His guitar screamed to life, each note sharp and aching, a raw outpouring of everything he'd been holding back. It wasn't just music, it was pain, rage, and longing, a sound that seemed to cut straight through the air and into the marrow of everyone listening.

Anthony's voice entered, rough and soulful, wrapping around Dave's guitar like smoke. The song built, layer by layer, each instrument weaving together into something that felt both fragile and invincible.

When the take ended, the room was silent except for the soft hum of amps and the faint buzz of a snare drum. Rick leaned forward, his expression unreadable, before nodding once. "That's the one, "he said simply.

Dave set his guitar down, his hands trembling slightly. He didn't look at anyone, instead focusing on the floor as if trying to ground himself. Anthony clapped him on the shoulder as he passed, his grip firm but not overbearing.

"See? Told you, "Anthony said quietly, his voice carrying a rare note of warmth. "It's all in there."

Dave didn't respond, but his silence felt less like dismissal and more like acknowledgment.

Flea plopped down on the worn couch in the corner, grabbing a water bottle and taking a long swig. "Holy shit my brother, "he said, wiping his mouth with the back of his hand. "That sounded fucking amazing. You finally brought the fire, Navarro."

Chad grinned, spinning his sticks in one hand. "Yeah, man. That was some heavy shit. I think Rubin's got a hard-on for you now."

Dave finally looked up, a faint smirk tugging at the corner of his mouth. "Great. That's exactly what I need."

The stress of the room broke with a round of laughter, the kind that comes not just from relief but from the shared realization that they'd just created something special.

Rick leaned back in his chair, his hands steeples as he watched the band interact. He'd seen this dynamic before, the push and pull of personalities, the friction that made the music better, sharper. He didn't say anything, letting the moment settle naturally.

As the band began packing up for the night, Dave lingered by the window, staring out at the city lights. Anthony joined him, standing just close enough to speak without the others hearing.

"You alright?" Anthony asked, his tone careful.

Dave nodded, his eyes still on the view. "Yeah, "he said after a moment. "I think so….you?"

Anthony didn't answer, just gave him a pat on the back before heading out. Dave stayed a little longer, the weight of the night settling on his shoulders. Whatever this was, this band, this album, it was pushing him in ways he hadn't expected.

And for the first time in a long time, he wasn't sure if that was a good thing or a bad thing.

And the other three were already beginning to feel uncertain, and it was a feeling none of them knew how to shake.

But Dave always showed up ready to make something new and for now, that was enough.

The band pushed forward, their music carrying the weight of everything left unsaid, each note a fragile attempt to hold it all together.

But deep down, they all knew the truth: something had to give. And when it did, none of them would come out unscathed.

It was an awkward time, both within the band and in the way the world was reacting to *One Hot Minute*. Reviews were polarizing, some praised the record's depth and brooding intensity, while others accused the band of losing their soul. Headlines dissected every decision, every note, every lyric, and beneath it all, there was the unspoken truth: the 'Peppers' weren't sure themselves.

Dave sat in the green room after a press junket, flipping through a dog-eared copy of *Rolling Stone* with their faces plastered across the cover. Anthony was mid-pose, shirtless as always, exuding confidence. Flea was playful, his head cocked to the side. And there was Dave, the outsider, his face sharp and unsmiling, the image practically begging for readers to notice the tension between him and the rest of the band.

Anthony strode into the room, tossing his mic pack onto a table and grabbing a water bottle. He caught Dave staring at the magazine and rolled his eyes. "Let me guess, "Anthony said, twisting the cap open. "Another piece about how we're not fucking Blood, Sugar, Sex…whatever, anymore?"

Dave gave him a sideways glance, his lips twitching with a humorless smile. "You say that like you don't miss it."

Anthony paused mid-sip, his eyes narrowing. "What's that supposed to mean?"

Dave leaned back in his chair, crossing his arms. "You know exactly what it means. Every interview, every goddamn show, you're practically apologizing for me being here. Like you're afraid to own the fact that we're different now."

Anthony slammed the water bottle down, his voice low but edged with anger. "No one's apologizing for you. But don't kid yourself, you didn't make this shit easy, my man."

Before Dave could respond, Flea entered, his usual easygoing demeanor hardening as he sensed the tension. "You two assholes at it again?" he asked, his voice tight. He looked at Dave, then Anthony, shaking his head. "Can't you save this shit for after the tour?"

Dave scoffed, shoving the magazine aside. "Sure, Flea. Let's keep pretending everything's fine. That's working out great so far."

Flea stepped closer, his tone sharpening. "Look, man, we knew this was gonna be different with you, alright? But different doesn't mean bad. You're bringing something none of us can, so stop acting like you're the problem."

The room went quiet, Flea's lecture hitting home. Anthony looked away, tension etched into his face, while Dave stared at the floor, his jaw tight.

The next day, the band gathered for the "Warped" music video shoot, but the mood remained brittle. Perry Farrell might've thrived in tension, but for the Chili Peppers, it felt like a weight dragging them down. The set was dark and moody, the imagery far from the bright, frenetic energy of their earlier videos.

As the cameras rolled, Anthony leaned into Dave, the two of them locked in an uncomfortably intimate embrace that would later become one of the video's most infamous moments. It was supposed to be provocative, an image of unity in the face of their darker sound, but to Dave, it felt like just another performance, another mask to wear.

Between takes, Dave lit a cigarette and leaned against the edge of the set, staring out at the crew bustling around him. Flea approached, his bass still slung over his shoulder, and gave Dave a long look.

"You alright, brother?" Flea asked, his voice softer this time, the anger from before gone.

Dave shrugged, exhaling smoke into the heavy air. "Yeah, I'm great. Just living this fuckin' dream, man."

Flea didn't buy it. "This thing… it's bigger than all of us. You know that, right? You're part of it now, whether you feel like it or not."

Dave gave him a sidelong glance. "Sometimes I wonder if you guys even want me to be here."

Flea frowned, his voice firm. "We wouldn't be doing this without you, Dave. You're here because we fucking need you. Now, stop doubting that."

Dave didn't respond, just tapped ash off his cigarette and stared into the distance, the weight of what he'd just heard pressing against the weight of his own doubts.

By the time the video wrapped, the band was drained. Anthony disappeared as soon as they called cut, while Flea stayed behind to chat with the director. Dave lingered near the exit, watching the playback on one of the monitors.

The imagery was stark, sweaty, tangled bodies moving in rhythm with the music, flashes of raw intimacy against a backdrop of darkness. It was powerful, sure, but to Dave, it felt like it belonged to someone else, like he was a guest in a world he couldn't quite call his own.

"Hey."

He turned to see Chad standing behind him, his expression neutral but his tone softer than usual. "Don't let it eat you up, man, "Chad said, gesturing toward the monitor. "It's just a stupid video. Tomorrow's another day."

Dave nodded, but it didn't quite sink in. Tomorrow might be another day, but it felt like the same questions would still be waiting for him, unanswered and unrelenting.

As he walked out into the fading sunlight, Dave couldn't shake the feeling that *One Hot Minute* was a chapter being written in real-time, a story that was equal parts triumph and tragedy, its ending still out of reach.

The One Hot Minute Tour kicked off without a hitch, in Dublin, Ireland on October 1, 1995. But despite a first great show and an enthusiastic audience and crew, Dave's playing was slightly off and sporadic, and people noticed.

Backstage Anthony took a deep breath, forcing himself to keep calm.

"Hey Dave, whats um… are you doing okay?"

Dave, tired and full of of sweat, sat, lit a cigarette and looked at Anthony, confused, "I'm fine man. That was fucking awesome. What's wrong now?"

Anthony paces then stops and kneels down in front of him, attempting to remain cool, "You're not fine, man. We both know that. I've been there. Hell, I lived there. And now, for fuck's sake, I'm there again… and I'm telling you, it doesn't end well."

Dave's lips twisted into a faint, defiant smile, his voice edged with sarcasm. "Yeah? Its about time you admitted it." Shaking his head, "And stop pretending you're the poster boy for stability? We all know your relapsing, a lot!"

Anthony puts his hands on his hips and turns and starts to pace.

"At least I'm not trying to hide it, "Dave says, head down in his hands.

The jab hit harder than Anthony expected, but he didn't flinch. He turned back to Dave and leaned closer, lowering his voice. "You're right. You are, but don't think this is about me. This is about you. About us. About this fucking band. If you can't see that, then maybe you don't belong here."

Dave's smile faltered, his expression tightening. For a moment, it looked like he might fire back, but instead, he looked away, the tension in his jaw easing just enough to reveal the exhaustion etched into his face. "I can handle it, "he repeated, quieter this time, like he was trying to convince himself as much as Anthony.

Anthony stood there for a long moment, his frustration boiling beneath the surface. But he knew the truth, he couldn't force Dave to change. And, he knew he was being a typical junkie, primadonna, hypocrite. The decision had to come from him, and until then, all Anthony could do was watch the slow unraveling of someone he cared about…and himself.

A few nights later, backstage after a show, the tension reached a breaking point. The crowd outside was still roaring, their energy electric, but inside, the air was thick and heavy, weighed down by unspoken words. Flea stormed into the dressing room, slamming the door behind him.

"Alright, enough of this bullshit, "Flea snapped, his voice sharp and cutting through the stillness like a blade. He looked directly at Dave, his eyes blazing. "What the fuck are you doing to yourself?"

Dave, slouched on a couch, barely lifted his head. "I'm doing what I've always done, "he muttered, his voice flat.

"Bullshit, "Flea spat, stepping closer. "This isn't you, man. Not the you we wanted in this band. You're fucking phoning it in every night, and we're the ones picking up the slack. You think that's fair?"

Dave's eyes flicked toward him, a flicker of anger flashing across his face. "You don't know what the fuck you're talking about."

"Oh, I don't?" Flea shot back, his voice rising. "You think you're the only one who's been through shit? You know we all have! You think I don't know what it's like to want to disappear? Newsflash, Navarro, we've all been there. But this band doesn't work if we're not all in it, and right now, you're not." He begins to tear-up, "so either get your shit together brother, or get the fuck out."

The group fell silent, the weight of the situation creating a stand-still. Anthony sat in the corner, his expression unreadable, while Chad looked down at his hands, his fingers tapping nervously against his leg.

Dave sat up slowly, his movements deliberate, his expression unreadable. "You think it's that simple?" he said, his voice low, almost dangerous. "Just 'get my shit together'? Like it's some fucking switch I can flip?"

He points at Anthony, "Think its that easy for *him?* Oh but we don't dare fucking mention that elephant in the room…do we?"

Flea crossed his arms, his glare unwavering. "No, it's not simple. That's an entirely separate issue. But *your* issue? Well, it's a choice. And you're running out of time to make it."

Dave stood, his body tense, his eyes locking onto Flea's. For a moment, it looked like the two of them might come to blows, but then Dave shook his head, his shoulders slumping. "I don't need this right now, "he muttered, brushing past Flea and heading for the door.

Anthony stood, his voice cutting through the room before Dave could leave. "Dave, You walk out that door, and you better think real motherfucking hard about why you're here in the first place, my brother"

Dave froze, his hand on the doorknob. He didn't turn around, didn't say a word. After a moment, he opened the door and walked out, leaving the rest of the band in a silence that felt heavier than anything they'd ever played on stage.

"That went well, "Chad muttered, breaking the tension with a bitter laugh.

Anthony ran a hand through his hair, his frustration evident. "He's drowning, and he doesn't even see it."

"Shut up Anthony! We've been down this same fucking road with you! Numerous times. And apparently, we're on that road again." Flea sat down heavily, his anger fading into something closer to despair. "You even thinking you have any room to talk is…." He stops, stands back up. "I don't know how much longer we can keep this up, "he says in a tone of despair as he walks out the door.

The room fell silent again, Chad and Anthony lost in their own thoughts. The band had been through so much, had fought so hard to keep going, but now it felt like they were standing on the edge of something they couldn't control.

Dave didn't come back that night. The next show was in two days, and no one was sure if he'd show up. For the first time, the future of the Red Hot Chili Peppers felt uncertain, and it was a feeling none of them knew how to shake.

When Dave finally returned, it was with the same haunted look in his eyes, the same weight pulling him down. But he showed up. The band pushed forward, their music carrying the weight of everything left unsaid, each note a fragile attempt to hold it all together.

The live performances grew increasingly volatile, their intensity bordering on combustible. Each night felt like a razor's edge, with the crowd roaring louder, the music hitting harder, and the band's internal fractures becoming more and more visible. Anthony could feel it with every song, every lyric screamed into the mic. Dave played like a man with something to prove, his solos blistering, raw, but there were cracks, missed notes, moments of hesitation that hadn't been there before. And everyone could see it.

Flea, always trying to stay the optimist, despite the situation, tried to rally the group during soundchecks. "We're on fire out there, man! The crowds fucking love it!" he'd say, his voice charged with adrenaline, his enthusiasm almost desperate.

But Anthony could only nod, his mind clouded with worry every time he caught a glimpse of Dave slumped against an amp between songs, his face pale, his hands trembling. He knew the signs, because he's lived them, and is *living* them more and more.

One night, in a cramped dressing room before the show, Anthony finally broke the silence. "Alright, Navarro, "he said, throwing his towel onto a chair. His voice was casual, but his eyes were sharp. "You're playing like a fucking demon out there Dave, but offstage you look like death warmed over. I can't make you stop no more than anyone can make me, but you've got to fucking pull back, pace yourself. Stay in fuckin' check, man."

Dave, sitting on the floor with his back against the wall, looked up with tired eyes. He forced a smirk. "I'm fine, man. Just… burning the candle at both ends, you know how this shit goes."

Flea, sitting nearby tuning his bass, glanced up, the tension in the room palpable. "Maybe we all just need a break, "Flea offered, his voice careful, trying to diffuse the situation before it escalated. "especially you two."

Dave sighed, leaning his head back against the wall, his smirk fading. "I don't need a fucking intervention, alright? I'm doing what I need to do to keep this train moving."

Chad, leaning against the far wall, crossed his arms. "The train's moving, yeah, but it's running off the goddamn tracks, "he said bluntly.

Dave's jaw tightened, and for a moment, the room went silent. Anthony stood up, running a hand through his hair, frustration boiling just beneath the surface.

"You think you're holding it together, but you're not, "Anthony said, his voice sharp but not unkind. "And Dave, you and I can't keep pretending like everything's fine when it's not."

Dave met his gaze, defiance flickering in his eyes. "What do you want me to say, huh? That I'm fucked up? That I'm struggling? Fine. There. Yes, I am! Happy now?"

Anthony shook his head, his expression softening. "No, man. I'm not happy. None of us are. But we're in this together, and if one of us (gesturing to Dave and himself) is going fucking down, we all are."

The truth Anthony spoke was undeniable and for a moment, no one spoke.

Finally, Flea broke the silence, standing and slinging his bass over his shoulder. "Let's just get through tonight guys." he said, his voice weary but resolute. "One freak-fucking-'show' at a time."

Dave nodded slowly, pushing himself to his feet. "One show at a time, "he repeated, but his tone lacked conviction.

That night's performance was electric, a thunderous display of everything the band had to give. Dave poured himself into every note, his guitar screaming with an intensity that left the crowd in awe. But behind the blistering solos and the roaring applause, the fractures grew deeper.

Backstage after the set, the energy was subdued, the high of the performance already fading. Dave sat alone in a corner, his guitar still slung across his lap, his fingers absently plucking at the strings.

Anthony approached, a bottle of water in hand, and handed it to Dave without a word. Dave took it, nodding his thanks, his eyes downcast.

"You killed it out there, "Anthony said, his voice quiet.

Dave let out a hollow laugh. "Yeah, for how long though?"

Anthony sighed, sitting down beside him. "As long as we can, man. As long as we fucking can."

Dave didn't respond, but that truth, the truth of Anthony's words, lingered between them.

As the tour stretched on, the cracks became more and more impossible to ignore. Dave's absences grew more frequent, his energy more erratic. Some nights, he was the driving force of the show, his playing electrifying, his stage presence magnetic. Other nights, he was barely there, his movements sluggish, his focus slipping.

The band pressed on, each of them grappling with their own frustrations and fears. Flea tried to keep the mood light, cracking jokes and pulling pranks, but even his boundless energy couldn't mask the strain. Chad retreated into himself, his drumming becoming more aggressive, as if trying to pound out his frustrations with every beat.

And Anthony… Anthony fought to hold it all together. He decided he'd try to get sober once again, while still on tour the added stress of watching his band-mate, and friend, completely unravel.

One night, after a particularly grueling show, Anthony found himself alone on the hotel balcony, staring out at the city lights. The door behind him slid open, and Dave stepped out, a cigarette dangling from his lips.

"You should get some sleep, "Anthony said without looking at him.

Dave shrugged, leaning against the railing. "Sleep's overrated."

They stood in silence for a moment, the distant hum of the city filling the air.

"You ever think about what comes after this?" Dave asked suddenly, his voice quiet.

Anthony turned to him, his brow furrowed. "What do you mean?"

"This, "Dave said, gesturing vaguely. "The band. The shows. All of it. What happens when it's over?"

Anthony exhaled, his gaze returning to the city below. "You focus on what's next. You find something to fight for, man. Shit, who knows?"

Dave nodded, his expression thoughtful. "Yeah. Maybe."

But even as he said it, Anthony could see the doubt in his eyes, the weight of uncertainty pressing down on him. And he knew, deep down, that this situation wasn't sustainable.

The Urge to Change.

The release of *Good God's Urge* in the spring of 1996 should have been a moment of triumph for Porno for Pyros. Their sophomore album had been crafted with the same unconventional vision Perry Farrell had always championed, blending dreamy soundscapes with Perry's signature lyrical musings about spirituality, nature, and human connection. But the reception was lukewarm, the matchstick that set their debut on fire now seemed dimmer in the eyes of critics and fans alike.

The reviews were polite but uninspired, phrases like "solid effort" and "lacking the bite of their debut" peppered the write-ups in major publications. Sales lagged behind expectations, and the album failed to make the same cultural impact as its predecessor. Even the devoted fans who packed their shows seemed restless, unsure of where the band was heading.

Perry tried to shrug it off, putting on his usual defiant front during interviews. "Look, man, we're not here to spoon-feed people what they think they want, "he said to Spin with a flick of his wrist. "We're here to take them somewhere else entirely. If they don't get it, that's on them, not us."

But behind closed doors, things were unraveling in a way that even Perry couldn't ignore. The biggest blow came when guitarist Peter DiStefano was diagnosed with testicular cancer. The news hit the band like a gut punch, stopping them in their tracks as Peter began treatment. Recording sessions were rescheduled, live dates were canceled, and for a time, it felt like everything was on hold.

Peter, ever stoic, tried to downplay the severity of his diagnosis. "It's just another fight, you know?" he told the band, his voice calm despite the weight of his words. But Perry could see the exhaustion in Peter's face, the quiet fear that lingered beneath the surface.

"We'll figure this out, "Perry told him one night after a stripped-down rehearsal, his voice firm, his hand resting on Peter's shoulder. "You focus on getting better. That's all that matters right now."

The band's future felt uncertain, but then came a call from the producers of Howard Stern's biopic, *PRIVATE PARTS*. They wanted Porno for Pyros to record a song for the soundtrack, and they had an idea that would both fill the gap left by Peter's absence and create a moment of musical alchemy: bring in Flea and Dave Navarro.

Flea was already a fixture in Perry's orbit, his kinetic energy and adventurous spirit making him a natural fit. Dave, on the other hand, was a more complicated piece of the puzzle. He had drifted in and out of Perry's world since his exit from the Red Hot Chili Peppers earlier that year, and while their friendship remained intact, the idea of working together again carried an unspoken weight.

"Flea and Dave?" Stephen Perkins said when Perry pitched the idea during a quiet meeting at the studio. "That's... a lot of energy in one room. Could be good. Could be a fucking disaster."

Martyn LeNoble raised an eyebrow, leaning back in his chair. "You're sure about this? Bringing in two guys with their own shit going on?"

Perry shrugged, a wry grin tugging at his lips. "It's one song. It's not like we're making an album. Besides, those two together? It'll be magic."

Peter, sitting off to the side, managed a faint smile despite the fatigue etched into his face. "Hell, If they can keep up with Perry, more power to them."

The studio session was set, and when the day came, the energy in the room was incredible. Flea arrived first, his ever-present kinetic energy filling the space as he bounced from one conversation to the next. "Alright, let's get weird, "he said, slapping Stephen on the back before launching into a riff on his bass that immediately turned heads.

Dave showed up shortly after, quieter but no less intense. He exchanged polite greetings with the Porno for Pyros crew, his demeanor guarded but professional. Perry watched him closely, noting the tension in Dave's movements, the slight hesitation in his voice.

The song, "Hard Charger, "was a raw, punk-infused anthem, the kind of track that demanded chaos and precision in equal measure. With Flea's unpredictable bass-lines and Dave's sharp, biting guitar, the sound came alive, a fiery fusion of energy that crackled through the studio.

Perry stood at the mic, his voice cutting through the mix with a snarling intensity that felt like both a celebration and a challenge. "Louder!" he barked at the engineer, his eyes blazing. "I want it to feel like a goddamn riot!"

As they worked through take after take, the room seemed to hum with a wild, unrelenting energy. Flea and Dave locked into an unspoken rhythm, their playing weaving together in a way that felt natural despite their different styles. Stephen's drumming anchored it all, his steady pulse driving the song forward even as the rest of the band pushed and pulled at its edges.

During a break, Flea leaned over to Dave, his grin wide. "Man, this is some crazy shit, "he said, shaking his head in disbelief.

Dave smirked, his fingers idly strumming his guitar. "Yeah. It's kinda' got that old feel, doesn't it?"

Perry watched them from across the room, a satisfied smile tugging at his lips. He could feel it too, that spark, that intangible magic that had always defined the best of his music.

By the time they wrapped, the room was electric with the kind of energy that left everyone buzzing long after the final note had been played.

"That..that definitely works for me, my friends , "Flea said, wiping sweat from his brow.

Dave nodded, a faint smile on his lips. "Yeah. It felt…fucking" good. "Almost like old times."

Perry clapped Dave on the shoulder, his eyes gleaming. "Told you, man. We still got it."

For Peter, who had stopped by briefly to watch from the control room, the session was a bittersweet reminder of what he was missing. But as he listened to the playback, he couldn't help but feel a sense of pride in what they had created, a testament to the resilience of the band and the spirit that kept them moving forward, no matter the obstacles.

The song went on to feature prominently in PRIVATE PARTS, its raw energy resonating with fans and critics alike. For a brief moment, it felt like the band had recaptured the fire that had made them so compelling in the first place. But even as the world celebrated the track, the members of Porno for Pyros knew that their journey was far from over, and that the challenges ahead would test them in ways they had yet to imagine.

The Big Idea.

Perry Farrell sat in a corner of his Venice Beach loft, his eyes scanning over ancient texts spread before him. It was a clash of worlds, ancient wisdom crammed into a modern shell, tribal masks hanging alongside abstract art, incense smoke curling upward like a silent witness to his thoughts. Lost in words that seemed to whisper from another realm, he was digging into mysteries, seeking meaning in esoteric writings of the past. Symbols and phrases floated in his mind, and he felt himself sinking into a place of deep reflection. This was how he prepared his days lately: grounding himself in the cosmos, trusting the invisible web that connected everything.

But today, something stirred differently. As he poured over a passage about transformation, an idea crept into his mind, sudden and electric. He sat back, letting it sink in, his fingers brushing across the yellowed paper.

From the television in the background, a music critic's voice filtered through, sharp and dripping with analysis. "As grunge fades and metal resurges, the architects of alternative seem torn between rebirth… and extinction."

The words felt like a challenge. Perry's eyes flicked toward the screen, narrowing slightly, his fingers drumming against the notebook sitting in his lap. Rebirth. Extinction. The critic had no idea how close to the bone those words cut, how much they mirrored the thoughts already swirling in his mind.

The smell of organic food and freshly ground coffee was nearly suffocating as Perry, Dave, and Stephen sat around the table in the small cafe. Plates of untouched food cluttered the space between them, but no one seemed hungry. Perry's gaze drifted toward a pile of sugar packets on the table, which he began arranging into jagged, almost ritualistic patterns, his mind clearly somewhere else. Across the table, their manager, Ted Gardner, leaned forward, trying to cut through the tension that was enough to choke on.

"Are you even fucking listening, Perry?" Ted snapped, his patience visibly fraying.

Perry didn't look up, his hands still fiddling with the sugar packets. "I'm always listening, Teddy, "he replied, his voice light and dismissive. "That's my problem. Too much goddamn listening."

Ted let out a sharp breath, leaning back in his chair. "Jesus Christ, Perry. I'm not here to play games. We need to talk about what the hell is next. Jane's is dead. Eric's out, for good this time, he's not even taking your calls anymore. So what's the fucking plan?"

Stephen, sitting with his arms crossed, broke his silence. "He's right, Perry. Eric's gone, and we don't have a bass player. That's not a small fucking detail to skip over."

Perry finally looked up, his eyes gleaming with that untouchable mix of mischief and conviction. "Details, details, "he said with a smirk, waving a hand like the question was irrelevant.

Stephen narrowed his eyes, leaning forward. "You can't just keep pretending like shit will magically work itself out, man. We don't even have a fucking lineup right now. Or a plan. What the hell are we doing?"

Dave, who had been uncharacteristically quiet, finally leaned back in his chair, lighting a cigarette. He took a drag, exhaling slowly before muttering, "He's winging it. Same as always."

Perry grinned, his smirk widening as he gestured toward Dave. "And look where winging it's gotten us so far, huh? Lollapalooza? Jane's? Porno? You think any of that came from sitting down and making fucking spreadsheets?"

Ted slammed a hand on the table, silencing the growing tension. "Enough with the riddles, Perry. Seriously. You're not gonna charm your way through this one. What's next?"

Perry leaned back, crossing his arms, his grin softening into something more thoughtful. "What's next..." he repeated, his voice trailing off like he was savoring the words. "We start fresh. Not bigger but smarter. We take everything we've learned, all the bullshit, all the pain, and we turn it into something new."

Stephen frowned. "With who? Because unless Eric's been replaced by some cosmic bass player you're about to pull out of your ass, I don't see how this works."

Perry pointed at Stephen, his grin returning. "That's the spirit, Perkins. Doubt me just enough to keep me sharp."

Stephen rolled his eyes. "Not doubting you, man. I'm doubting reality. It takes more than fucking vibes to make a band."

Dave tapped ash from his cigarette, his tone cutting through the room. "Yeah, and it takes more than a half-baked idea to get anyone to give a shit. You got anything real, Perry? Or are we just sitting here waiting for one of your epiphanies to turn into a paycheck?"

Perry's grin faded slightly, but the fire in his eyes didn't dim. He leaned forward, locking eyes with Dave. "You want real? I've been diving into something bigger than us, man. Bigger than this room, bigger than the fucking industry. I'm talking about a re-born movement, even if for just a moment. Music's just part of it. The energy, the memories, shit that sticks in people's souls long after whatever fuck-stick band ends. That's what I want to build on."

Stephen shook his head, clearly unconvinced. "Okay, great. Sounds cool and all, but how the hell are we supposed to pull that off when half of us are barely holding it together?"

Perry's expression softened, though his voice carried a sharp edge of defiance. "We've always been half-broken. That's the point, man. People don't want perfect. They want real. And this", he gestured between them, "is as real as it fucking gets, boys."

Ted rubbed his temples, muttering something under his breath before finally speaking. "You're gonna need more than philosophy to sell this, Perry. No bass player, no clear plan, no goddamn budget… It's a hard sell."

Perry laughed, the sound sharp and full of conviction. "Ted, baby, you're thinking too small. This isn't a 'sell.' This is just an idea - and a damn good one. And boys, people don't need to buy in, they just need to feel it. I mean come on, that's one thing us cats got going for us - we understand what it takes to pull that off. "

The cafe was silent, Perry's idea settling over them. Dave took another drag from his cigarette, his gaze unreadable, while Stephen sat back, his arms still crossed, his expression a mix of doubt and begrudging respect.

Ted finally stood, his chair scraping against the floor. "Alright, Perry. But if this all falls apart, don't come crying to me."

Perry smirked, leaning back in his chair. "If it falls apart, it just means we were too big for them to handle…or I'm just plain, stupid."

The manager's voice cut through the quiet. "Eric's not budging. He's… done."

Perry barely looked up from his creation, muttering more to himself than anyone else. "The universe always provides what we need, Teddy. Okay?"

Dave shot him a frustrated look, his face tight with impatience. "Jesus Christ, here we go again. What we need is a bassist, Perry. Not fucking fate."

At that moment, Perry's attention shifted. Through the cafe window, he spotted Flea walking by, laughing with a group of friends, his energy so vibrant it seemed to radiate from him.

Perry's demeanor changed instantly, his eyes brightening with a sudden spark of realization. Without another word, he stood, motioning toward the door. "Here's our answer, "he announced, already heading outside.

Dave threw his hands in the air, muttering, "What the fuck now?" as Perry disappeared through the door.

Outside, Perry burst onto the sidewalk, his movements quick, almost frantic as he waved Flea down. "Flea!" he called, his voice cutting through the noise of the street.

Flea turned, eyebrows lifting in surprise as he spotted Perry. His face broke into a wide grin, his voice booming with genuine excitement. "Perry fucking Farrell!"

They embraced, a moment that held the weight of years of friendship, of surfing together, of wars fought and survived, of a bond that ran deeper than the music.

Perry pulled back, his eyes gleaming. "I got a proposition that'll blow your mind."

Flea laughed, his grin widening. "Those usually cost me money… or my sanity."

Perry leaned in, lowering his voice, his tone brimming with excitement. "Both, probably. And immortality."

Ten minutes later, Flea was seated at the table with the rest of the band, his vibrant energy seeming to clash with the tension in the air. He grabbed a glass of water and glanced around the table, finally breaking the silence. "Alright, Farrell. Spill. What's this genius idea of yours?"

Perry grinned, leaning forward as if he were about to reveal a great cosmic secret. "It's simple - Jane's Addiction."

Flea raised an eyebrow, sitting back in his chair as he processed the words. "Jane's, huh? What about it? Thought that ship had sailed. Didn't you guys torch the whole thing?"

Dave groaned, rubbing his temples. "Exactly. That's what I've been saying. Eric's out. He's not budging, and Perry thinks fate's just gonna toss us a new bassist like a fucking gift from the heavens."

Stephen cleared his throat, glancing at Flea. "No bassist, no band. That's the reality. Perry's been dodging that part of the equation like it's not important."

Perry's grin widened as he pointed at Flea. "That's because we've already got one sitting right here."

Flea blinked, then let out a sharp laugh, shaking his head. "Oh, come on, man. You're not serious."

Perry's expression didn't waver. "Dead serious. Look, you already know the deal. You're the only one who can pull this off. You've got the chops, the vision, the energy. You're the only bassist who can fill Eric's shoes and still bring something completely new to the table."

Flea leaned forward, resting his elbows on the table, his face serious now. "Dude….you realize I've got my hands full with the Peppers, right? We've got our own shit going on."

Dave folded his arms, his patience clearly running out. "Look, Perry, I love the optimism, but Flea's got his own thing, and you're asking him to commit to something that's not even fucking together yet. We don't even have any new songs, let alone a plan."

Perry nodded, unfazed. "Of course I know that. But this isn't just another band." He turns to Flea, "look, this is Jane's Addiction, brother. This is the band that rewrote the stupid rules when none of those other L.A bands, except *yours,* would dare take chances. I mean, kind of but you know? Shit, why not keep it going?:

Flea, reluctant, "I don't know Per…:"

Perry cuts him off, excitedly, "Look, the whole fucking grunge bullshit is dead, and the bands that are still around? They all sound the goddamn same. But nobody sounds like Jane's…nobody. Flea, look man, we're not talking some grand, fucking huge, year-long outing here. Smaller tour with small, quaint production, for a few months and…"

Dave rolls his eyes.

Flea smirks, cutting in, "Small and quaint?" Laughs, "Yea right Perry."

Perry continues, "…but it will be refreshing for the old cats that stood by us, and something completely new for a new generation of kids who buy our records now, but were too young, or never got the chance to see us live."

There was a pause as Flea buttered a piece of toast while the other three gave each other a glance.

Then finally, he let out a long breath, a crooked smile tugging at his lips. "Alright, Perry. I'll jam with you guys. See if there's still any magic left. But I'm not promising anything beyond that."

Perry slapped the table, his grin triumphant. "That's all I need, brother. One jam. After that, the music will speak for itself."

Flea continues to his toast, "Dave, you know I love you, and you absolutely know I love playing with you but…"

Dave, knowing what he's concerned about, cuts him off, "I'm off the needle. Over a year now , buddy."

Flea looks up and grins, reaches over to Dave to give his shoulder a squeeze.

"Ok, I guess uh, let me know what the next step is."

Dave muttered under his breath, his tone dripping with sarcasm. "And, here we fucking go."

Stephen smirked, raising his coffee cup in a mock toast. "To the beautiful disaster ahead."

Flea grinned, shaking his head as he grabbed a piece of toast from his plate and rustling Dave's hair with his other hand. "You guys are out of your damn minds, you know that?"

Perry leaned back, his eyes gleaming with excitement. "And that, Sir, is why it's gonna work."

A Relapsing Reunion.

Flea set his bass down, sweat glistening on his brow as he grinned. "Man, you could feel that shit, right? Like… the earth moved."

The newly-reformed Jane's Addiction was in a non-disclosed studio recording, "So What, "a song they initially wrote in 1986, however never finished recording it. It would be released as a new single for the forthcoming compilation album, *Kettle Whistle,* which would be released to coincide with the reunion tour, which was to be called, appropriately, "The Relapse Tour."

Perry nodded, wiping his face with the back of his hand, his expression a mix of exhaustion and satisfaction. "It's alive. This isn't just us playing, it's a fucking entity."

Stephen leaned on his drumsticks, shaking his head with a wide grin. "If we can do that here, in an empty fucking warehouse, imagine what it's gonna sound like in front of a crowd."

Dave lit a cigarette, his hands still trembling slightly from the intensity of the session. "Yeah, if we can make it through without tearing each other apart, "he said, half-joking, though his tone carried a hint of tension.

Perry ignored the jab, pacing the room, his mind already racing ahead. "We need to run it again. It's there, but it's not perfect yet. Not raw enough. Not dangerous enough."

Flea raised an eyebrow, sitting on an amp. "Perry, man, it was fucking dangerous. I could feel my ribs vibrating."

"That's good, "Perry shot back, his eyes blazing. "But I want it to feel like your soul's gonna crack open. That's the level we're hitting."

Stephen groaned, tossing a towel over his shoulder. "Jesus, Perry, give us a second to breathe before you make us bleed all over again."

Perry smirked, pacing back toward his mic stand. "Bleed. That's the whole point, Stevie. No one remembers safe. No one gives a fuck about clean. They remember what cuts them open."

Dave exhaled a cloud of smoke, watching Perry with a wary amusement. "You ever think maybe you're the one who needs to bleed less?"

Perry spun around, pointing a finger at Dave, his grin feral. "Oh, I bleed plenty, Navarro. That's why this works."

The room fell silent for a moment, the intensity of Perry's words hanging in the air. Then Flea stood, slinging his bass back over his shoulder. "Alright, then. Let's bleed. One more run, but if this doesn't kill me, I'm taking a fucking lunch break."

Stephen laughed, already settling back behind his kit. "Deal. Let's rip it."

They launched into "Mountain Song" again, the sound even sharper, more visceral, each of them pouring every ounce of themselves into the music. The warehouse shook with the force of it, the echoes carrying far beyond the walls, a sound so alive it seemed to pulse with its own heartbeat.

When they finished, the silence was almost deafening, the air thick with sweat, smoke, and the buzz of adrenaline.

Dave leaned back against the wall, catching his breath, his cigarette still dangling from his lips. "Alright, I'll give you this one, Perry. That… that was fucking dangerous."

Perry leaned into his mic stand, his face lit with a victorious grin. "Told you. Now, imagine what it'll do when we take it live."

Stephen pulled off his headphones, tossing them onto the drum riser. "If we don't destroy the venue first, it's gonna blow people's minds."

Flea cracked open a bottle of water, chugging half of it before grinning at the group. "Alright, Farrell. I'm in. Let's burn this shit down."

The energy in the room shifted, the exhaustion fading under the realization of what they'd just created. It was more than music, it was a declaration, a reminder of what they were capable of when they pushed themselves to the edge.

Perry grabbed his notebook from a folding chair, flipping through pages filled with scribbles and diagrams that only made sense in his head. "This isn't just a reunion guys, "he said, his tone serious now, the grin fading as his eyes swept over the group. "This is a resurrection. We're bringing Jane's back, but it's not gonna be like before. It's gonna be better, louder, harder. We're gonna remind people why we burned so fucking bright in the first place."

Dave looked up from where he was sitting on the floor, his expression skeptical but intrigued. "And if it doesn't work?"

Perry stared at him for a long moment, his eyes unblinking. "Then we go down in flames, as usual. But we go down as four degenerates who at least fucking tried to leave a mark."

Stephen shook his head with a laugh, picking up his sticks again. "You're a lunatic, Perry."

"Damn right I am, "Perry replied, a desperate expression creeping across his face. "But the fact is, I love you guys, so very much. And quite frankly, you are all I have. It fucking hurts, but I wouldn't have it any other fucking way."

Dead silence and solace spread from one member to the next. Flea's eyes became red, swollen and watering. Dave simply stared at Perry, knowing that despite all the animosity, Perry wasn't putting on a show. He was being real. And it stung. This was not 'Perry Farrell.' No, this was Perry Bernstein, the kid from Queens, desperate to be someone, and longing for compassion, and more importantly, companionship.

Perry stood and continued, "Now let's make history."

The band sat back for a moment to let what they'd just heard, sink in. The air was electric, not with chaos this time but with clarity, an understanding that they weren't just playing music. They were carving something eternal out of the fleeting madness of their lives. And this time, they were ready to take it as far as it could go.

Lines stretched down blocks as fans waited at ticket booths, buzzing with anticipation, while MTV News blared updates about the band's comeback. Behind the scenes, the pressure was building, and as the days counted down to the first show, the band fought through the fatigue, each of them driven by something more than the music, a need to prove themselves, to reclaim what they had lost.

The night of the opening show at Hammerstein Ballroom in New York was charged with an electric excitement that seemed to vibrate through the walls. Backstage, Perry meticulously arranged crystals on a small altar, his face a mask of concentration. Stephen tapped out a rhythm on a practice pad, hands steady and methodical, while Flea stretched his arms behind his head, his gaze focused and intent. Dave Navarro sat apart from them, staring at his own reflection in the mirror, his hands trembling slightly.

Perry noticed the slight tremor in Dave's hands. He stood, brushing off his knees, and moved toward him quietly. "Hey, "Perry said, his voice low, reaching out.

Dave didn't look up at first, his eyes locked on his reflection. "Hey, "he finally replied, his voice flat and distant.

Perry crouched down beside him, slipping a hand into his pocket. When he pulled it back out, he was holding a small bag, its contents unmistakable. He held it up between two fingers, his expression unreadable. "Need something to take the edge off?" Perry asked, his voice carrying the weight of their shared history.

Dave stared at the bag, a storm brewing in his eyes. He exhaled slowly, the memories rushing back all at once, moments of brilliance, collapse, escape, and destruction. After a long, tense pause, he nodded. "Yeah, "he muttered, his voice barely audible. "Yeah, I do."

The stage lights dimmed, and the roar of the crowd swelled, shaking the entire building. When the band stepped onto the stage, the noise was deafening, a wall of sound that seemed to pulse through the venue like a living thing. The opening riffs of "Stop!" tore through the air, and the band attacked their set with a raw, feral intensity. Perry stalked the stage like a wild prophet, his movements unpredictable, his voice slicing through the noise. Flea's bass-lines throbbed like a heartbeat, while Stephen's drums hammered the audience with a primal rhythm. Dave's guitar shrieked and wailed, sharp and jagged, each note carrying a scream that seemed to resonate deep in the audience's bones.

Three-quarters into the set, the band disappeared briefly, leaving the crowd restless and murmuring, until the spotlight shifted to the center of the venue. There, a second, high-rise stage had been erected, a smaller platform that loomed over the crowd like a pulpit. The lights came up, and Perry's voice cut through the air as the band launched into "Classic Girl." The audience roared, their voices rising to meet Perry's as he prowled the narrow stage, the intimacy of the performance drawing them in.

The set rolled seamlessly into "Chip Away, "Stephen and Flea's, aggressively - sounding drumbeat pounding like a ceremonial rhythm, haunting and hypnotic, anchoring the performance with a sound so heavy it seemed to echo long after each note. Perry moved to the edge of the platform, leaning dangerously close to the crowd as he let the last, primal screams of the song reverberate through the venue.

Finally, the opening chords of "Jane Says" rang out, and the crowd erupted in a roar that drowned out the band for a moment. The high-rise stage seemed to transform, the song's bittersweet nostalgia settling over the audience like a wave. Fans swayed together, arms raised, voices mingling with Perry's in a moment that felt both cathartic and communal. The lights softened, bathing the band in a golden glow that seemed to freeze the moment in time, leaving the crowd hanging on every word.

As the last notes faded, Perry leaned into the mic, his voice carrying a weight of both exhaustion and exhilaration. "We're not done yet, "he growled, his grin almost predatory as he pointed back toward the main stage.

The band descended from the high-rise stage, weaving their way through the ecstatic crowd as fans reached out, desperate to touch even the briefest piece of the band's energy. By the time they returned to the main stage, the audience was at a fever pitch, the anticipation crackling through the room like electricity.

They closed the night with "Ted, Just Admit It…, "Perry's voice rising like a scream from the depths, his body twisting and contorting with every line. The band threw themselves into the song, their energy frantic and unrelenting, as if they were exorcising something dark and unspoken. Flea's bass-lines throbbed with menace, Stephen's drumming hit like thunder, and Dave's guitar screeched with an almost painful beauty. Perry tore into the final chorus, his voice raw, his eyes blazing, his entire body trembling with the weight of the moment.

When the final notes echoed into silence, the band stood together at the edge of the stage, bathed in a cascade of applause and screams. Perry bowed his head, his arms spread wide, while Dave leaned on his guitar, sweat dripping from his face, his chest heaving with each breath. Stephen tossed his sticks into the crowd, grinning as the fans scrambled for them, and Flea raised his bass high in the air, his smile bright and feral.

For a moment, the four of them stood together in the lights, the fractures and tensions forgotten as they soaked in the adoration of the crowd. Whatever darkness lingered backstage, whatever struggles they carried, it didn't matter right then. In that moment, they were whole. In that moment, they were Jane's Addiction.

The tour was a series of highs and lows, each show bringing moments of euphoria that were almost immediately followed by darkness. The stage was their sanctuary, a place where they could lose themselves, where the music consumed everything else. But as the days wore on, the inevitable cracks in the comraderary began to show. Crowds grew, the applause thundered, but the music loosened, the edges fraying as Perry started missing cues, his focus slipping.

Dave's hands shook more often, his movements becoming erratic, and Stephen and Flea exchanged glances, their eyes filled with a quiet, unspoken worry. They could feel the storm building, each show bringing them closer to something they couldn't control. Flea, who usually carried an air of calm, began pacing more between shows, his frustration brewing beneath the surface. Stephen, ever steady, tried to keep the rhythm locked, but even he felt the weight pressing down.

One night, as rain pelted the windows of their tour bus, the tension finally broke. Flea stormed into the back lounge, his face flushed with frustration, his movements sharp and deliberate. Perry and Dave sat slouched in the shadows, their eyes hollow, the weight of the tour pressing down on them like a physical burden.

Flea didn't hold back. His voice was sharp, cutting through the dull hum of the bus's engine. "This shit has to stop, "he said, his gaze fixed on both of them, his tone carrying a weight that couldn't be ignored.

Perry looked up slowly, his face distant, like he wasn't entirely present. "What has to stop?" he asked, his voice flat, as if the words cost him energy he didn't have to give.

"Both of you, "Flea snapped, his frustration barely contained, the words boiling over before he could stop them. "This bullshit. You're killing the music."

Dave shifted in his seat, leaning back defensively, his tone dismissive. "We're fine."

Flea's eyes flashed with anger as he pointed an accusatory finger at them both. "Fine? Are you fucking kidding me? The music's suffering. It's all suffering."

Perry's face tightened, his voice edged with defiance as he leaned forward, staring down Flea. "The shows are sold out. What the fuck else do you want?" he barked, his tone sharp, an edge of anger bleeding through his words.

Flea shook his head, his voice carrying a raw intensity that silenced the room. "It's not about that, Perry. It's about not destroying everything you've built. Brother, you... both of you... you're two of my best fucking friends, and you're forcing me to watch you die."

The silence that followed was deafening. The rain hammered against the bus windows, the sound sharp and relentless. Flea let out a heavy sigh, running a hand through his hair as he stepped back, his voice softening but no less serious. "I can't fucking do this. Not like this."

He stormed out, leaving Perry and Dave in the suffocating quiet of the lounge. The hum of the bus engine filled the void, and for a long moment, neither of them spoke. Perry stared at the floor, his mind somewhere far away, while Dave rubbed his temples, the tension building in the pit of his chest.

Finally, Dave broke the silence, his voice quiet and strained. "Maybe he's right."

Perry didn't respond immediately. His gaze stayed locked on the stained carpet beneath his boots. When he finally spoke, his voice was low, barely a whisper, carrying the weight of too many sleepless nights and too much unspoken guilt. "Maybe. But not tonight."

Dave leaned back, closing his eyes, the exhaustion overtaking him, as the bus rattled down the dark, rain-slicked highway. Whatever storm they were heading into, it felt inevitable now. None of them had the strength to stop it. Not yet.

The final show of the tour was in Los Angeles, at the Palladium, a venue that had once been their proving ground. Now it felt like a confessional, a place where the music could bleed out every regret, every mistake, every broken piece of what they had become. The sold-out crowd roared as the band took the stage, the lights cutting through the dark like searchlights, scanning for something they couldn't name.

Perry stood at the mic, his hands gripping it tightly, as if it were the only thing anchoring him to the moment. He looked out at the crowd, a sea of faces screaming his name, and for a moment, he felt the weight of it all pressing down on him. The lights were blinding, the heat suffocating, but it wasn't the physicality of the moment that overwhelmed him. It was the knowledge that this might be the last time.

Flea counted them into "Ocean Size, "his baseline booming through the speakers like a tidal wave. Perry grabbed the mic stand, his voice cracking as he sang the opening lines, his words carried on a tide of desperation. Dave's guitar screamed, distorted and raw, each note a testament to his state of mind, unsteady but trying, trying so fucking hard. Stephen was solid as always, his drumming the heartbeat of the band, the one thing that could still keep them tethered to the stage.

They burned through the set with an intensity that was as much a release as it was a cry for help. Perry prowled the stage, spinning in circles, his movements erratic, his energy unpredictable. He pointed into the crowd, shouting at faces he couldn't see, his voice ragged. Dave leaned heavily into his guitar, his head bowed, sweat dripping onto the strings. Flea, shirtless and glowing under the stage lights, danced with his bass, trying to keep the energy alive, while Stephen's steady rhythm filled the room like a heartbeat, pushing them forward even as the edges began to fray.

When they reached "Jane Says, "the air in the Palladium shifted. The room softened, the crowd's collective voice rising with Perry's as they sang along to every word. Perry stepped back from the mic, letting the audience take over, their voices carrying the song in a way that was both beautiful and heartbreaking. Dave's acoustic strumming was loose but familiar, the chords washing over the room in waves of nostalgia and grief.

Perry stood at the edge of the stage, watching the crowd sway and sing, their voices blending into one. He could feel the emotion surging through the room, but it didn't feel like victory. It felt like a goodbye. He glanced over at Dave, who avoided his gaze, focused entirely on his guitar, his fingers trembling slightly. Flea caught Perry's eye, his expression unreadable, but there was a flicker of something there, disappointment, maybe, or concern. Stephen kept his head down, his focus locked on the drums, like he couldn't afford to look up and see what was falling apart around him.

And as the final chords of "Jane Says" hung in the air, Perry turned to the band. He felt the ache in his chest, the kind of ache that comes with knowing something is over. The crowd erupted into cheers, their energy undiminished, but on stage, it felt like the air had been sucked out of the room.

They walked off stage in silence, their faces drawn, their bodies heavy with exhaustion. Backstage, the tension was palpable. Perry sat in a corner, wiping the sweat from his face with a towel, while Dave slumped onto a couch, his head in his hands. Flea paced the room, his bass still slung over his shoulder, his movements sharp and agitated. Stephen methodically packed up his drumsticks, his expression blank, his silence louder than anything he could have said.

Perry finally broke the silence, his voice quiet, almost hoarse. "That's it, isn't it?"

No one responded. Dave didn't even lift his head, and Flea stopped pacing but didn't turn around. Stephen glanced at Perry but said nothing, his hands still busy with his drum kit. The weight of the unspoken agreement settled over them like a shroud.

Flea finally spoke, his voice low but steady. "If this shit keeps up, there's not gonna be anything left of us."

Dave let out a bitter laugh, leaning back into the couch, his eyes bloodshot. "Pretty sure there isn't much left now."

Perry looked down at the floor, his hand tightening around the towel in his lap. He knew they were right, but admitting it felt like tearing out a piece of himself. The tour had been named "The Relapse Tour" as a joke, but now the words felt prophetic. They had come full circle, back to the same darkness they had once escaped, only now it felt deeper, harder to climb out of.

"We'll take a break, "Perry said finally, his voice lacking its usual conviction. "Figure shit out. We always do."

Stephen stood, his movements slow, deliberate. He looked at Perry, his expression soft but firm. "This isn't like before, Perry."

Perry's jaw tightened; his gaze fixed on the floor. "It's never like before."

The room fell into silence again, the sound of the crowd still cheering faintly in the distance, like an echo of something they couldn't quite reach anymore. Perry leaned back against the wall, closing his eyes, the cheers fading into the background as the weight of everything finally settled on him a ton of bricks.

Love and kicking.

The Relapse Tour had come with a whirlwind of late nights, surreal sets, and a backdrop of endless faces, but among the flashing lights and relentless energy, Perry found himself captivated by someone unexpected.

Etty Lau, one of the tour's background dancers, had an undeniable presence on stage. She moved with the kind of grace and intensity that made her impossible to ignore, and for Perry, who had seen it all, she became a rare point of fascination. Born to Chinese immigrants, Etty was more than just a dancer; she was a singer with her dreams, grounded yet fierce, and carried herself with a quiet confidence that set her apart.

Perry first noticed her during a rehearsal. While the band ran through a chaotic sound check, Etty stood to the side, practicing her movements in perfect focus, unaffected by the noise around her. As he watched her, Perry felt something stir: curiosity, admiration, and maybe even envy of her calm.

Over the weeks, the two began to talk. It started casually, exchanging quick words backstage or during long bus rides, but it quickly grew into something deeper. Perry found himself drawn to her steadiness, the way she seemed to see through the haze of the tour and into something more meaningful.

One night, during a stop in New Orleans, Perry invited her to sit with him on the hotel balcony. The air was thick with humidity, the sound of distant jazz drifting through the streets. Etty sipped tea, her legs tucked beneath her, while Perry leaned against the railing, his eyes on the city below.

"You don't seem fazed by all of this, "Perry said suddenly, breaking the comfortable silence.

Etty looked up at him, her expression curious. "By what?"

"The madness, "he said, gesturing vaguely toward the world beyond the balcony. "The noise, the chaos, the endless fucking grind."

She smiled, a small, knowing smile. "I grew up in it, Perry. My family moved to the States with nothing. We had to fight for everything. Noise doesn't scare me, it's just background."

Her words lingered with Perry, long after the conversation ended. There was something about her that felt solid, unshakable, and for someone like Perry, who had spent his life teetering on the edge, it was intoxicating.

By the time the tour reached its final leg, Perry and Etty were inseparable. Their connection was electric but grounding, a strange paradox that Perry couldn't quite understand but didn't want to question. It wasn't lost on the rest of the band.

During a rehearsal in Los Angeles, Flea caught Perry watching Etty as she rehearsed with the other dancers. He smirked, nudging Stephen with his elbow. "Looks like Perry's finally got a muse, "he said, his voice low but teasing.

Stephen followed Flea's gaze, a grin tugging at his lips. "About time, "he muttered.

But being with Etty didn't magically fix everything. Perry was still Perry, impulsive, volatile, and prone to self-destruction. There were nights when the weight of the tour and his own demons pressed too hard, when he'd retreat into the darker corners of himself, unreachable even to her.

One such night, after a particularly grueling show in Atlanta, Etty found Perry sitting on the hotel bathroom floor, his back against the wall, his head in his hands.

"You okay?" she asked, kneeling beside him.

He didn't look up. "Um, yea I'm just so damn tired, "he said simply, his voice heavy.

Etty reached out, brushing her fingers against his arm. "Then stop, "she said softly.

He let out a bitter laugh. "You think it's that goddamn easy?"

"No, "she admitted. "But I think you're strong enough to try."

Her words struck something deep within him, and for the first time in a long time, Perry felt a flicker of hope.

Etty's presence became a quiet but powerful influence. She didn't try to change Perry, she understood that he was who he was, but she offered him something he hadn't felt in years: stability. And slowly, Perry began to lean on her, finding in her a balance that had always eluded him.

The rest of the band noticed the shift. Perry was still wild, still unpredictable, but there were moments when he seemed… calmer, more focused. Stephen, ever the observer, pulled Etty aside one day after soundcheck.

"Whatever you're doing, "he said, his voice earnest, "please don't stop."

After the tour ended, their relationship grew even stronger, blossoming in the stillness away from the stage.

They sat together on the back patio of Perry's home, a soft glow from the lights casting shadows around them. Sitting, wrapped up in each other, a bottle of wine between them, the night air cool and quiet.

Perry took her hand, his voice soft but filled with conviction. 'Etty… I love you.'

Etty looked at him, her eyes filled with warmth but tinged with hesitation. She let out a small sigh, her voice hesitant. 'I love you too, Perry. I do. But…'

Perry's expression shifted, sensing the weight in her words. 'But what? Tell me.'

She glanced down, her fingers tracing the rim of her glass. 'It's… it's the heroin, Perry. I can't ignore it. I want a life with you, but I need stability. I want a family, and I can't build that on… uncertainty.'

The words hung between them, heavy and unspoken until now. Perry nodded slowly, feeling a mix of guilt and frustration.

'I can do it, ' he said, his voice filled with a determination he wasn't entirely sure he believed himself. 'For you. I'll quit.'

Etty squeezed his hand, her gaze steady. 'I'll be here with you. But Perry… it has to be real.'

The detox was brutal, an unforgiving war that stripped Perry down to his rawest self. What was once an escape mechanism for the sake of art, something he raved about openly and swore by to the public, without shame had grown to something more. Heroin had become a 'physical addiction.' He had to use it, just to feel physically normal. They 'high' and romance of the drug was long gone. It was now medicine. A medicine his body, not Perry, craved. He locked himself away in his room for hours, sometimes days, his body wracked with tremors, sweat dripping off him in waves as he wrestled with the gnawing hunger that never seemed to subside. He screamed into the pillow until his voice gave out, clutched the sheets as though they were the only thing keeping him from being swept away. The air in the room felt suffocating, dense with pain and desperation.

Etty was always there, unshaken, a quiet, resolute presence in the middle of the storm. She didn't hover, she knew Perry needed to fight his own battles, but she never let him feel alone. she'd sit with him on the edge of the bed, her hand resting on his, her voice soft but steady.

"You're stronger than this, "she would say, her words calm but firm, willing him to believe them. "I know you are. You've got too much left to do to let this fucking garbage win."

But not every battle ended in victory. There were nights when Perry lost, when the pull of heroin overpowered even the strongest of his intentions. Those nights, Etty would find him slumped in a chair or sprawled on the floor, his eyes hollow, the needle discarded nearby.

Her face would twist with heartbreak, her voice trembling with frustration as she confronted him. "Perry, what the fuck are you doing?" she'd demand, her voice a mixture of anger and pleading. "You told me you were done with this. You promised me."

"I'm trying!" he'd snap back, his voice hoarse, defensive. "I'm really, really trying, Etty. I'm doing my fucking best!"

One night, she came back from the store, arms full of groceries, to find him in the middle of shooting up. The room reeked of sweat and sickness, and the wall next to him was dotted with stains, old, dried blood from months of use. The spoon in his hand clattered to the floor as he looked up, startled. A thin stream of blood sprayed from his arm, spattering the wall, its red stark against the faded paint.

For a moment, they just stared at each other, Perry frozen mid-act, Etty standing there, the grocery bags slipping from her fingers to the floor.

"I'm sorry baby, "he said, his voice cracking under the weight of guilt. His eyes were red-rimmed, and his face was a mask of shame. "I'm really fucking sorry."

Etty's face softened, but her voice stayed firm. She wasn't going to let him drown himself in excuses. "Then try harder, Perry, "she said, stepping closer. "You don't get to do this to yourself. You don't get to do this to us. You're my best friend, and you're a goddamn genius. You think I'm just gonna stand here and let you waste that?"

Before he could say anything, she reached forward and knocked his kit, needle, spoon, everything, off the table with one quick, decisive motion. It hit the floor with a dull clatter, the liquid in the syringe spilling out onto the hardwood.

"You don't need this shit, "she said, her voice low but fierce, her eyes locked on his. "You think you do, but you don't. It's lying to you, Perry. And you're better than this."

Her words hit him harder than he wanted to admit. He sat there, staring at the mess on the floor, his head in his hands. For a long time, neither of them spoke.

Finally, Etty knelt in front of him, her hand reaching out to lift his chin. "I love you, "she said, her voice breaking slightly, but her eyes were unwavering. "But I can't save you. You've got to save yourself. And if you don't, Perry... you're gonna lose me too."

The statement was raw. And it was final. Perry stared at her, the ultimatum pressing down on him like a stone. Somewhere deep inside, he felt something shift, a flicker of clarity, a faint reminder of the man he wanted to be.

For the first time in what felt like months, Perry nodded, his voice barely audible. "Okay, "he said, his hands shaking. "Okay. I'll do it. I'll try."

Etty reached out and took his hand in hers, squeezing it tightly. "Not for me, "she said. "For you. Do it for you."

That night, as Perry lay in bed, his body trembling and his mind screaming for relief, Etty stayed by his side. She didn't leave, even when he begged her to, even when he lashed out in frustration. She held his hand, whispered encouragement, and reminded him that he wasn't alone.

The road to sobriety was long and uneven, marked by relapses and regrets, but in that moment, something had changed. Perry had found a reason to fight, a reason to push through the darkness. And even as the shadows loomed, he clung to that reason, knowing that it might just be enough to save him.

As the worst of the withdraw finally began to subside, Perry sat on the couch, staring at the ocean through their window. Etty joined him, handing him a cup of tea, her movements quiet and deliberate. She sat beside him, tucking her legs underneath her, and they sat in silence for a long time, the waves outside their only soundtrack.

"Why?" Perry asked suddenly, his voice barely above a whisper. "Why didn't you leave?"

Etty turned to him, her eyes shining with a mix of exhaustion and love. "Because I knew you'd find your way back. And because I couldn't stand the thought of you doing it alone."

Perry looked at her, his throat tightening with emotion. "I don't deserve you."

Etty shook her head, a faint smile on her lips. "Maybe not. But you have me anyway."

Months later, when Perry finally emerged from the shadow of addiction, his body was leaner, his face sharper, but his eyes carried a clarity they hadn't held in years. He walked into the kitchen where Etty was making tea, and for the first time, he allowed himself to feel proud.

"I'm…I'm fuckin' clean, E." he said simply, his voice steady but thick with emotion.

Etty turned, her face breaking into a radiant smile as she crossed the room and threw her arms around him. "You did it, "she whispered, her voice filled with awe.

Perry pulled back just enough to look at her, his smile breaking through. "No. We did it."

They stayed like that for a long time, holding each other in the quiet of their home. For the first time in years, Perry felt like he had a future, a life that was real and steady and worth fighting for. And as he looked into Etty's eyes, he realized he hadn't just found sobriety, he'd found a reason to keep it.

Don't Try This at Home.

For some reason, Dave Navarro decided to open the doors of his house in the Hollywood Hills, to the mayhem of the valley below. It wasn't an announcement or a plan, more of a mood that crept in, like the way a party starts without anyone ever officially declaring it. His only rule: "Come into the house, you get in the photo booth." Simple, non-negotiable, and absolutely binding.

At first, it seemed like a quirky idea. The booth had been a whim, something Dave had installed during a lull in touring. It sat inconspicuously in the corner of the room, a relic from an old arcade he'd found downtown. But once people started coming through the door, it transformed. The photo booth became a confessional, a stage, and a kind of filterless truth-teller.

The first week was tame by Dave's standards, strippers, a few band mates, the occasional Hollywood hanger-on who wandered up the hill in search of something to do. They'd step into the booth reluctantly at first, unsure what Dave was aiming for. But soon, word spread, and the energy of the house shifted.

By the second month, the photo booth wasn't just a feature of the house; it was *the* house. Every guest, from pizza delivery drivers to A-list celebrities, found themselves in its frame. The strips it spit out didn't just capture faces; they told stories. Some were blurry and chaotic, others composed and strangely serene. The booth didn't care if you were drunk, high, famous, or nobody. Its lens treated everyone equally.

On this particular evening, the house was packed, the air electric with conversation and the sharp tang of cigarette smoke. Rose McGowan stood by the pool in a vintage dress, chain-smoking and laughing loudly with Keanu Reeves, who held a whiskey in one hand and a lit joint in the other. Billy Corgan, visibly tipsy, was arguing with a record executive over the merits of releasing singles versus full albums.

In the middle of it all, the door burst open, and Twiggy Ramirez stumbled in like a man who'd just escaped from a mental asylum.

"Dave! Holy shit, you gotta help me!" Twiggy shouted, his voice cracking with a mix of panic and exhaustion. His hair was sticking out in every direction, his shirt half-untucked, and his boots scuffed from what looked like miles of walking.

Dave, perched on the edge of the counter, a cigarette dangling between his fingers, didn't even flinch. "Jesus Christ, Twiggy, "he said, taking a drag. "What the fuck happened to you?"

Twiggy gestured wildly at the floor, his hands trembling. "The floor's fucking breathing, man. Your house, it's alive! I was driving here, and my steering wheel turned into a goddamn snake. A fucking snake, Dave! So I got out of the car and walked. But, I think my legs might not even be real anymore!"

Dave exhaled slowly, studying Twiggy like he was deciding whether to be concerned or entertained. "Sounds like you've been hitting the ketamine again? Hmm? Or is this some new crazy shit you've discovered?"

"K and… maybe a little of something else, "Twiggy admitted, his voice dropping into a sheepish mumble. "But that's not the point. The point is, I might be trapped in another dimension."

Dave smirked, flicking ash into a nearby tray. "Here's an idea dude, get in the photo booth. Maybe it'll confirm if you're still in this reality."

Twiggy froze, his gaze darting toward the booth like it was the gates of hell. "No fucking way, man. What if it steals my soul? Or worse, what if it proves I don't have one?"

Before Dave could respond, the door swung open again. This time, it was , grinning like a lunatic and holding a goat on a leash.

"Yo, Dave!" Flea shouted, dragging the goat into the middle of the room. "Check this out! Found him wandering around on Sunset. Isn't he fucking cool?"

Dave blinked, momentarily thrown off. "Flea, why the fuck do you have a goat?"

"Why not?" Flea replied, crouching down to scratch the goat's chin. "His name's Gary. He's chill as hell."

Twiggy backed up, pointing a shaking finger at the animal. "That's not a goat. That's the fucking devil."

Flea looks up at Twiggy grinning, but confused, "Wait, what?"

Dave shook his head, chuckling as he stubbed out his cigarette. "Twiggy, you're tweaking so hard, Gary could start reciting the Bible backwards, and it wouldn't make this night any weirder."

Flea laughed and led Gary toward the photo booth. The goat, remarkably calm, stepped inside without resistance. A minute later, the strip emerged, showing Gary's stoic expression in four identical frames.

"That goat's got more composure than most of the people here, "Dave muttered, tossing the strip onto the counter.

Twiggy, now sitting cross-legged on the floor, stared at the photos like they were a sacred text. "Gary's fucking deep, "he whispered. "I think he gets me."

As the months went on, the photo booth captured everything: Marilyn Manson dragging in a mannequin and posing with it like it was his girlfriend; Billy Zane trying to convince Leonardo DiCaprio to reenact a scene from Titanic; Natalie Imbruglia giggling uncontrollably as she crammed into the booth with three record executives.

Some nights were pleasant, fun and "normal, "the atmosphere filled with laughter, music, and the clinking of glasses. Other nights though, had a darker edge, the photo strips revealing raw vulnerability or exhaustion in the faces of their subjects. The booth didn't just document the house, it documented the people who passed through it, their highs and lows, their beauty and flaws.

long after the party had ended, Dave sat alone in the kitchen, flipping through the pile of photo strips scattered on the counter. A strip of Twiggy, wide-eyed and sweaty, caught his attention. In the final frame, Twiggy was smiling faintly, his panic giving way to something that almost looked like peace.

Dave smirked and lit another cigarette. The booth didn't lie.

Detox and a New Millennium.

The detox hospital was sterile, its walls painted in dull shades of beige that seemed designed to sap any sense of individuality or rebellion. The sound of beeping monitors and shuffling footsteps filled the halls, a monotonous backdrop to the internal battles being fought in every room. For Dave Navarro, this was the beginning of a war he wasn't entirely sure he wanted to win. The first week had been hell, body-rattling seizures, vivid hallucinations, and pain so deep it felt like it lived in his bones.

The staff had seen it all before: rock stars dragged in by desperation or their handlers, swearing this time would be different, before sneaking out for one last hit. But Dave stayed. He clenched his teeth through the worst of it, his pride keeping him from asking for more than the bare minimum of medication to dull the withdrawals. He told himself, If this is what it takes, then fuck it. I'll take it.

He spent long, sleepless nights staring at the ceiling, feeling every nerve in his body scream for relief. It wasn't just the physical pain; it was the memories that crept in, sharp and unrelenting. The faces of band mates he'd let down, the shows he could barely remember, the moments he'd thrown away chasing a high. They all haunted him now, refusing to be drowned out.

The staff said the worst was over by day seven. By then, he could eat without gagging and hold a conversation without his mind splintering into a thousand pieces. But he still felt raw, like his skin had been peeled away and the world was pressing directly against his nerves. He hated every second of it, but he also clung to it, knowing that the discomfort was a sign he was alive, that he was still fighting.

When he was well enough to walk unassisted, Dave moved on to the rehab facility overlooking the ocean. It was less a hospital and more a halfway house for broken people trying to stitch themselves back together. The sound of waves crashing against the shore was constant, a strange mixture of soothing and taunting. The ocean didn't give a fuck about his struggle, but it was there, steady, unchanging, a reminder that life kept moving no matter how much pain you were in.

The therapy sessions were brutal at first. Dave sat in the circle with his arms crossed, his face a mask of indifference, his answers clipped and sarcastic. But the other people in the room weren't fooled. They saw right through it because they'd all worn that same mask at some point.

"Dave, why do you think you're here?" the therapist asked one afternoon, her voice calm but firm.

He smirked, leaning back in his chair. "Because I partied too hard, doc. Isn't that why we're all here?"

The therapist didn't flinch. "You're here because you're killing yourself. And if you don't start being honest about why, this is just another pit stop before your next overdose."

That simple fact disturbed Dave more than he wanted to admit. For the first time, Dave didn't have a clever comeback. He stared down at his hands, his fingers tracing the faint scars on his arm, reminders of every time he'd told himself, Just one more hit.

The turning point came in the middle of the night, during one of his usual bouts of insomnia. He stood by the window, watching the moonlight shimmer on the water, when the reality of everything he'd lost came crashing down. He thought about Perry, about Stephen, about Eric, how they'd all burned so bright together, only to fall apart under the weight of their own demons. He thought about the fans who had screamed his name, the friends who had tried to pull him back, the opportunities he'd thrown away.

He didn't cry, Dave Navarro didn't cry, but he felt something break loose inside him, a dam he didn't even know he'd built. For the first time, he let himself feel the full weight of his grief, his guilt, his shame. And in that moment, he made a decision: he was done. Not for his career, not for the band, not even for the people who loved him. He was done for himself.

By day 30, the tension in his body had eased, his hands had stopped shaking, and his mind was clearer than it had been in years. He sat in the therapy circle, the ocean a constant presence in the background, as he shared his story.

"Yeah, so I've heard it a fucking million times, "he said, his voice steady but raw. "But ignored it, or figured it was 'big book' bullshit. But yeah… sometimes you gotta hit rock bottom all over again to remember why you climbed out the first time."

The room was silent, the weight of his words settling over the group. They nodded, some murmuring quiet affirmations, but no one interrupted. They all knew that place he was talking about, the rock bottom that felt endless until you clawed your way out.

As the session ended, Dave lingered by the window, watching the waves roll in and out. He didn't feel triumphant, but he felt steady. And that was enough for now.

The next week, Dave packed up his few belongings and stepped out into the sunlight, ready to leave the rehab facility behind. The city stretched out before him, daunting but full of possibility. He wasn't naïve, he knew the temptations would always be there, whispering to him when the nights got long or the pressure built up. But for the first time in a long time, he felt like he had a fighting chance.

He called Perry from a payphone outside the facility, the receiver cold in his hand. Perry answered on the third ring, his voice as sharp and irreverent as ever.

"Well, if it isn't the prodigal son, "Perry drawled. "How's the monastic life treating you?"

Dave laughed, a sound that felt foreign but good. "I'm clean, Perry, "he said, his voice firm. "Really clean. No more bullshit."

There was a pause on the other end of the line, and when Perry spoke again, his tone was softer, almost vulnerable. "Good, "he said. "That's good, man. We need you. And by 'we' I'm talking about the world. You're too fucking talented to leave." There was a silence, then, "and I'm sorry kiddo…for any part I had in all the fucking mess. Truly I am. Please know that."

Dave, tearing up but confident, exhaled and said, "I am too to my brother. I'll see you around sometime." And with that, he hung up.

Dave leaned against the phone booth with Perry's words settling over him. They weren't just about the music, they were about the brotherhood they'd built, the bond that had somehow survived all the shit they'd put it through.

"Okay. Shit, 'm back, "Dave said simply. And for the first time in years, he actually believed it.

Dave spent the next several months locked in his home studio, writing and recording. He was sober and focused.

Perry Farrell found himself sitting alone at the bar of the Sunset Marquis Hotel. It was one of those nights where the atmosphere buzzed with a strange energy, high-end crowds drifting through, laughter mingling with the clinking of glasses and the hum of conversations. Perry sipped on mineral water, watching the crowd with an expression that was half amusement, half contemplation.

A fan approached Perry and nervously, "Um, hey Perry. Big fan of Jane's... and Porno."

Perry extended his hand. As they shake hands, he asks nervously, stuttering, "So uh, um, any chance of another album? Um, from either, um band?"

Perry briefly looks away, then says, "you never know what the fucking universe brings, right, kid?" He smiles.

The fan smiles, "a, right on. Cool." He turns and slowly walks back to his table.

Perry turns back, his voice a quiet murmur to the bartender. "Some moments change everything. You just don't know it yet."

The Hollywood Hills mansion was alive, pulsing with bass, smoke, and shadows. Partiers drifted in clusters, glasses in hand, some leaning in to murmur over lines of powder dusted across glass tables. Dave Navarro leaned against the wall, almost blending in, yet standing apart in his detachment. Now in his early thirties, with heavily lined eyes and a perpetual smirk, he looked like he belonged and didn't care at the same time.

Through the crowd wove Tommy, an old friend, wiry rocker with unending energy and hair to match. He was pulling Carmen Electra by the wrist, her leather jacket and smudged mascara giving her an air of gritty allure that drew gazes wherever she went.

"Dave!" Tommy's shout barely cut through the music. "I got someone you gotta meet, man!"

Dave's eyes narrowed as he looked Carmen up and down, amusement glinting through his aloofness. "Oh yeah? What the hell are you dragging this poor girl into?"

Carmen scoffed, sizing him up. "Poor girl? You think I don't know what I'm doing, sweetie?"

Tommy grinned, thrilled by the crackling tension. "See? You two are gonna get along just fine. Dave, this is Carmen. Carmen, Dave. Now, play nice, alright?" And with a smirk, he slipped back into the crowd, leaving them alone.

"So… you're Carmen, "Dave said with a smirk, taking a drag from his cigarette. "Thought you'd be taller."

Carmen grinned, cool and unfazed. "And I thought you'd a tad fucking cooler. Guess we're both a little disappointed."

Dave chuckled, a low sound that mingled with the noise around them. "Shit. Alright, okay Mouse. You got a mouth on you."

"Oh, I'm a 'Mouse' now?" she shot back. "What's that make you? Some kind of sad little bird? Tweet- fuckin - tweet, Dude"

Dave took another slow drag, his eyes gleaming. "Maybe I am. I've *certainly* Got been called worse. Got any crumbs for me?"

Their laughter softened the tension, just slightly. Carmen reached over, snatched his cigarette, and took a long drag, blowing the smoke back in his face with a smirk.

"Bad habit, "she said, challenging.

Dave leaned in, his grin widening. "You got any better ideas?"

They locked eyes, the noise around them fading as a charge sparked in the silent exchange.

PART THREE

The Coachella Call.

It was early 2001 and Perry Farrell's life had taken on a quieter rhythm. The beautiful disaster of Jane's Addiction had given way to smaller projects, personal growth, and the occasional whispers of a reunion that never quite materialized. He was content, for the most part, watching the industry morph and change, staying connected enough to feel relevant but distant enough to keep his sanity. And yet, when his phone rang late one evening, he had no idea it was about to pull him back into the world he thought he'd left behind.

Perry was lounging in his home studio, headphones slung around his neck, a faint hum of experimental tracks filling the air. The caller ID flashed Paul Tollett, an old friend and co-founder of the Coachella Valley Music and Arts Festival. Perry picked up, his voice casual.

"Paul, what's up, man? How's my brother from 'Wilton days?"

Paul laughed, then his tone was quick, urgent. "Perry, we need your help. Coachella's in trouble."

Perry straightened in his chair, his fingers brushing over the knobs of his mixer. "Trouble how? You just brought it back, didn't you?"

"Yeah, and it's fucking drowning, "Paul admitted, the exhaustion clear in his voice. "We're barely scraping by. Ticket sales are low, and we can't lock down a headliner. If we can't pull this off, Coachella's dead. Goldenvoice is dead. And Rick…" Paul hesitated. "Rick's broke. He sold his house, his car, everything, to get this festival going again."

"Jesus, "Perry muttered, leaning back and staring at the ceiling. "Why the fuck would you guys put everything on the line like that?"

"Duh, because we fucking believe in it?" Paul shot back, a touch of defensiveness creeping into his voice. "And so did you once. We're trying to create something different, man, something that's not just about top-40 bullshit. But we're running out of time, and we need something big to save it."

Perry was silent for a moment, his mind already racing. He could hear the desperation in Paul's voice, the weight of everything they were carrying. Finally, he sighed, rubbing a hand over his face. "What do you want me to do?"

"We need Jane's Addiction, "Paul said bluntly. "As the headliner. You're the only act that can pull this off. People would lose their fucking minds, Perry."

Perry let out a sharp laugh, though there wasn't much humor in it. "You know what you're asking, right? Jane's hasn't played together in years. We didn't exactly part ways singing kumbaya."

Paul didn't miss a beat. "You're Perry Farrell. If anyone can pull this shit together, it's you. Look, we don't just want you. We need you."

Perry's jaw tightened, his fingers drumming against the desk. "What about Rick?" he asked, his voice softer now.

Paul hesitated again before speaking. "He's in deep, Perry. He's not gonna ask, but I will. He needs help. He needs ten grand just to keep this thing afloat until ticket sales come through."

"Jesus Christ, "Perry muttered under his breath. He stood up, pacing the room, the weight of everything sinking in. Jane's Addiction, back together. Could it even work? Could he even handle it?

"You're killing me, Tollett, "Perry finally said, though there was a flicker of amusement in his voice. "Ten grand and the band? You sure you're not asking for my firstborn, too?"

Paul chuckled nervously. "No kids, Perry. Just the band. And, uh, the money."

Perry let out a long breath, running a hand through his hair. "Fine. I'll wire Rick the money. But getting Jane's back together… that's a whole other shit-show. Don't hold your breath."

Paul's voice lit up with relief. "You're a fucking legend, Perry. Thank you."

"Yeah, yeah, "Perry said, shaking his head. "You better pray this thing doesn't blow up in your face."

The morning had started slow, the sky with the kind of overcast gloom that made Venice Beach feel intimate, as if the world had folded in on itself. Perry Farrell's balcony overlooked the expanse of sand and rolling waves, the usual chaotic energy of Los Angeles muffled by the soft, steady crash of the ocean.

Perry and Etty moved in sync, their bodies flowing through yoga poses with practiced ease. The morning ritual had become their shared grounding point, a way to reconnect with themselves and each other in the quiet hours before the day's noise took over. Perry's movements were fluid but restrained, his mind split between the present and the thoughts that had been swirling in his head for weeks.

Etty, glowing in the early stages of her pregnancy, shifted into a graceful pose, her breath steady. She glanced at Perry, watching the subtle tension in his jaw, the way his mind seemed elsewhere. Her curiosity finally broke through the calm.

"Do you miss it?" she asked, her tone light but probing, her words hanging in the air like the lingering scent of the incense burning nearby.

Perry paused mid-pose, holding himself steady, his eyes fixed on the horizon. The question caught him off guard, though he'd been asking himself the same thing for months. He took a deep breath, letting it fill the silence before responding.

"I miss... the energy, "he admitted, his voice low but unguarded. "The magic. The danger. All of it."

Etty shifted into a seated position, her gaze steady on him, calm but unwavering. "So bring it back, "she said simply, her words sinking into the space between them.

Perry glanced at her, intrigued but hesitant. "Bring it back?" he echoed, arching an eyebrow. "And do what, babe? Blow it all up again?"

Etty tilted her head, her expression soft but firm. "No, "she replied. "Make it different this time."

That simple statement settled into him like a seed planted in fertile ground, sparking something that had been lying dormant. Perry lowered himself out of the pose, sitting cross-legged on the yoga mat, his fingers tracing the edge of his knee.

"Different how?" he asked, his voice tinged with curiosity, the edge of skepticism in his tone softened by the way he looked at her.

Etty smiled, her hand instinctively resting on the small curve of her belly. "Sober, "she said, her voice steady. "Present. Connected. Not for them, Perry. For you. For us."

Perry chuckled softly, shaking his head as a faint grin pulled at the corner of his mouth. "You're something' else, you know that?" he said, glancing sideways at her. "Here I was thinking I'd be the one giving the pep talks when this little one shows up."

Etty laughed, the sound warm and grounding, before meeting his gaze again. "Well, someone's gotta keep you fucking honest, "she teased, her smile widening.

Perry exhaled deeply, leaning back on his hands as he let her words settle into him. The idea wasn't new, he'd been circling it for weeks, if not months, but hearing her say it out loud made it feel real. He looked at her, at the strength in her gaze, the quiet fire in her voice, and for the first time in a long while, he felt grounded in something bigger than himself.

"Well, "he said, his grin turning into something sharper, more determined. "I might just be ahead of you on this."

Etty raised an eyebrow, intrigued.

"I didn't wanna say anything until, you know, "he gestured toward her belly with a sly smile. "Our future band mate shows up. But yeah. I think it's about fucking time to make something magical again."

Etty tilted her head, her smile softening as she watched him, a flicker of something unspoken passing between them. She reached out, her hand resting on his knee, a quiet reassurance in her touch.

"I think it's time too, "she said.

Perry sat forward, crossing his arms over his knees as he stared out at the waves, his mind already racing with possibilities. But this time, it wasn't the frantic, negative energy of the past, it was something steadier, more focused. This wasn't about proving anything to anyone. It was about building something real, something lasting, something that wouldn't tear itself apart the way everything else had.

He glanced back at Etty, her presence a grounding force in the storm of his thoughts. "You're gonna keep me honest, huh?"

"Always, "she replied with a grin, her voice playful but resolute.

Perry exhaled again, his shoulders relaxing as he allowed himself to lean into the idea. For the first time in years, the future didn't feel like a weight pressing down on him. It felt like a door cracking open, a sliver of light spilling through, waiting for him to step through.

As they returned to their poses, the sun finally broke through the clouds, casting a warm, golden light over the balcony. Perry moved with a renewed energy, his focus sharper, his movements more deliberate. Something had shifted, and he could feel it in every breath, every stretch, every beat of his heart.

The next morning, Perry sat at his kitchen table, a cup of coffee steaming in front of him. His phone sat on the table, glaring at him like an unwelcome guest. He knew what he had to do, but that didn't mean he was looking forward to it.

He scrolled through his contacts, landing on Dave's number. Taking a deep breath, he pressed call.

Dave picked up after a few rings, his voice casual. "Perry. This is unexpected."

"Yeah, well, I'm full of surprises, brother. You know that." Perry replied, trying to keep his tone light. "First of all, I listened to the new recordings you sent me."

"You did? Already? Dave says, slightly surprised. "So, what did you think? And dude, be fucking honest."

"Fucking loved it, man!" Perry says, genuinely. "Quite the departure sonically, from your usual style but beautiful songs brother, seriously."

Dave gives a smile, "Well thanks Perry. Coming from your crazy ass, it means a lot"

"When you putting it out, "Perry asked.

"Um, I think the record company is thinking sometime this summer. Not sure of exact date yet."

Perry responds, slightly excitedly, "Oh yea? Might be perfect timing, publicity-wise, I mean."

Dave, confused look on his face asks, "Uh, what do you mean by that?"

Perry leans back in his chair, "Listen, I'm just gonna cut to the chase. Coachella wants Jane's Addiction to headline. Paul and Rick are in deep shit, and they're asking for a miracle. I told them I'd make the calls, but… I don't know, man. What do you think?"

Dave was silent for a moment before letting out a low whistle. "Jane's Addiction headlining Coachella. Damn…that's um, fucking massive."

"Yeah, "Perry said, nodding even though Dave couldn't see him. "But it's not gonna be easy. Eric's probably gonna tell me to 'fuck off, ' and Stephen…" He trailed off, not needing to finish the thought.

Dave chuckled. "You're really selling this, man." He pauses, thinking.

Perry gives him a moment and stays silent.

Then Dave puts the phone back to his mouth, "But fuck it. If Stephen will agree…I'm in."

"Seriously?" Perry asked, his eyebrows shooting up.

"Seriously, "Dave replied. "But you're making the call to Eric. No way I'm stepping in that fucking minefield."

Perry laughed, shaking his head. "Yeah, thanks for the vote of confidence."

And just as they both predicted, the call to Eric Avery didn't go as smoothly.

"Why now, Perry?" Eric asked, his tone more weary than angry. "Why the fuck would I want to go through all that again?"

"Because it's Coachella, "Perry replied, trying to keep the frustration out of his voice. "Because this is a chance to do something that fucking matters."

Eric sighed heavily. "I don't know, man. I've got a good thing going. A great woman, a new band, completely sober...no drama and zero-bullshit." He pauses, sighs, "Why? Why the hell would I potentially mess that up?"

"Because you're a fucking major part of this thing that we made?" Perry said, his voice steady. "Jane's isn't Jane's without you. And because deep down, well, I think you know... you want to."

There was a long pause before Eric finally spoke. "Christ Perry Farrell, always the 'master of manipulation.'" He shakes his head, exhales, "I'll think about it." Eric promptly hung up the phone.

But Perry knew. Sadly, he knew Eric wouldn't be getting back to him.

Perry wandered through the crowded venue, the low hum of conversation and the pulse of music filling the air. He wasn't just there to mingle, his mind was already spinning with the puzzle pieces of what a reformed Jane's Addiction might look like.

By the bar, he spotted Chris Chaney, nursing a drink and chatting with a small group of people. Chris had earned a reputation as one of the most skilled and adaptable bass players on the scene. His work with Alanis Morissette had shown both range and restraint, and Perry respected the hell out of that. More importantly, Chris had the kind of steady energy that Perry knew the band desperately needed.

Perry smiled, weaving through the crowd as he approached. "Chris Chaney, "he asked, extending his hand, his tone casual but brimming with intent.

Chris turned, looking slightly surprised but immediately breaking into a grin. "That's me. Perry Farrell, how are you, man?" he replied, shaking Perry's hand warmly.

"Got a minute?" Perry nodded toward an empty table in the corner. "I've got a proposition that might interest you."

Chris raised an eyebrow, curiosity gleaming in his eyes. "Alright, "he said, grabbing his drink and following Perry.

As they sat, Perry leaned forward, his voice dropping to a serious tone that cut through the noise of the party. "I'm bringing Jane's Addiction back, "he began, watching Chris's reaction closely. "We've been asked to headline Coachella. Those crazy cats are going to give it another go."

Chris's eyes widened, and for a moment, he looked like he wasn't sure if Perry was joking. "You're fucking with me, right?" he asked, laughing nervously. But when Perry didn't crack a smile, Chris's expression shifted. "Wait... you're serious? Holy shit. You're actually serious."

"Dead serious, "Perry said, his tone steady. "I'm also pondering doing a new tour. But it's going to be different this time, ya know? Something we can all be proud of."

Chris leaned back in his chair, his fingers tapping lightly on the edge of the table as he processed the idea. "Aaaand, you want me... to fill in for Avery?" he asked, a grin tugging at the corners of his mouth.

"You've got the goods we need, "Perry replied without hesitation. "And the skill to bring something new to the band. I've seen what you can do, brother. You've got that thing, whatever the fuck you call it, that makes people pay attention."

Chris studied him for a moment, his expression thoughtful but intrigued. "Well, damn, "he finally said, breaking into a full grin. "I mean, I'm in. But, just out of curiosity…" He chuckled, raising an eyebrow, with a smirk, "Do the other guys know their band's getting back together?"

Perry laughed, leaning back in his chair. "Well, they're in as far as Coachella goes. We'll see how everyone re-connects. You know, get a sense of the vibe. If it goes off without a hitch and feels fucking great…as it should, yea, I'm gonna fucking push for more of it."

Chris shook his head, laughing along. "Yeah, that's what I fucking thought. You're a piece of work, Farrell."

They clinked their glasses together, sealing the beginning of what would be a pivotal chapter in the band's history.

As the night went on, Perry found himself buzzing with a renewed sense of purpose. He knew bringing the band back together would be far from easy, but something about Chris's energy reassured him. It felt like the universe was beginning to align, piece by piece.

By the time the party wound down and the streets of New York glowed under the soft haze of streetlights, Perry felt a flicker of hope he hadn't felt in years. The fire was still there, smoldering, waiting, and now, with Chris on board, he felt like they had the first ember to reignite it.

For Chris, the handshake wasn't just an agreement, it was a leap into the unknown. Jane's Addiction wasn't just any band; it was a cultural force, a legend with as much volatility as brilliance. And as he walked away that night, he couldn't help but feel the weight of what he'd just agreed to.

"Here we fucking go, "Chris muttered to himself, a smile creeping onto his face as he stepped out into the cool night air.

Back in his hotel room, Perry poured himself a glass of wine and stared out over the city, his mind alive with possibilities. The idea was no longer just a flicker, it was a roaring fire, and for the first time in years, he felt ready to step back into the flames.

But this time, it had to be different. He wouldn't...no, he *couldn't,* let the band fall apart again, not like before. This time, they'd rise, stronger and sharper, built on a foundation that wouldn't crumble. And as he sat in the quiet glow of the New York skyline, he let himself believe it was possible.

A few days later, the band stood together in a rehearsal studio, the tension was nearly non-existent, for a change. The years hadn't erased their history, but they'd grown personally and there was a sense of hope, rather than despair.

As Perry stepped up to the mic and Stephen counted them in, the first notes of "Stop!" filled the room. For a moment, it was like nothing had changed.

Perry glanced around, a small smile tugging at his lips. Maybe, just maybe, they could pull this off.

A Renewed Jubilee.

The heat of the Coachella Valley was stifling that April night in 2001, but the energy in the air was electric. Thousands of fans packed into the Empire Polo Club, the festival grounds alive with neon lights, pulsing beats, and an almost tangible sense of anticipation. For many in the crowd, this wasn't just another festival. This was Jane's Addiction, back together, headlining one of the most hyped events in recent memory.

Perry stood backstage, adjusting his mic and pacing as the muffled roar of the crowd seeped through the walls. Beside him, Dave tuned his guitar, his face a mix of focus and nervous energy. Chris Chaney, recruited for the Coachella show, was in the corner plucking at his bass, warming up with a quiet intensity that matched the weight of the moment. Stephen sat at his drum kit, twirling his sticks, a small grin on his face as he tapped out a rhythm against his thigh.

Perry exhaled, pulling at the hem of his shirt as he turned to the band. "Alright, boys, "he said, his voice carrying that familiar mix of mischief and intensity. "Let's give these fuckers a show they'll never forget."

The band walked onto the stage to an eruption of cheers that felt like a physical force, shaking the ground beneath them. Perry stepped up to the mic, his silhouette illuminated against the desert sky, his voice booming as he yelled, "Coachella! Are you ready to lose your fucking minds?"

The opening notes of "Stop!" tore through the speakers, and the crowd surged forward, a sea of bodies moving as one. Perry prowled the stage like an untamed force, his voice cutting through the night as he leaned into every lyric, feeding off the raw energy of the fans. Dave's guitar ripped through the air, sharp and haunting, while Chris's bass-lines rumbled like an earthquake, grounding the chaos with a steady rhythm. Stephen's drumming was relentless, his beats hitting like thunder, driving the band forward with an intensity that felt unstoppable.

Mid-set, Perry took a moment to address the crowd, his voice echoing across the desert. "You know, "he said, grinning, "they said this wasn't gonna work. Said we were done, over. Well, fuck that. Jane's Addiction isn't going anywhere."

The crowd roared in response, their voices rising in unison, a testament to the impact this band had made, even after years of silence.

When they launched into "Three Days, "the atmosphere shifted. The song's sprawling, epic structure enveloped the crowd, pulling them into its hypnotic rhythm. Perry's voice was raw and emotional, his delivery full of vulnerability and power. Dave's guitar solo cut through the night, a moment of pure catharsis that left the crowd in awe.

As the final notes of "Jane Says" rang out, Perry sat on the edge of the stage, leaning out toward the crowd as they sang along, their voices blending with his. For a moment, it felt like the band and the audience were one, connected by something intangible but undeniably real.

Backstage after the set, the energy was electric. Perry leaned against the wall, drenched in sweat, a wide grin on his face. "Fucking incredible, "he muttered, reaching for a bottle of water.

Dave nodded, wiping his face with a towel. "They still want it, man. They fucking want it."

Stephen leaned back in a chair, his drumsticks tapping against his knee. "So, what's next?"

Perry's eyes gleamed as he straightened up, a familiar spark of mischief flickering to life. "What's next? We take this show on the road."

Sitting in a cramped conference room at Live Nation's headquarters, Perry outlined his vision to the team. "This isn't just about Jane's, "he said, his voice steady but commanding. "This is an attempt to reignite something lost. Not just Jane's but the 'scene.' It's a revival, man. A jubilee."

Dave smirked from his seat across the table. "So, it's a party, but with guitars?"

"Exactly, "Perry shot back, grinning. "A big, loud, sweaty, beautiful fucking party."

The plan took shape quickly: a summer-long tour hitting amphitheaters and festival grounds across North America, with Jane's Addiction as the headliner and a rotating lineup of a couple of supporting acts. Perry pulled together a mix of bands that spanned generations, emerging artists looking for their big break alongside veterans who'd been part of the scene since the beginning. It was ambitious, risky even, but Perry thrived on risk.

Martyn LeNoble, from Porno for Pyros would join for several dates on bass, providing a bridge between the past and the present. His style brought a familiar yet refreshed energy to the band's sound.

As the tour dates were announced, tickets sold out almost instantly. Fans, both old and new, flooded the venues, eager to witness the return of a band that had defined an era.

The Jubilee tour kicked off in June, with the band stepping onto the stage in front of tens of thousands of screaming fans. The set-lists were a mix of classics and deeper cuts, each show a journey through the band's history.

Another special element of this tour was the release of *Trust no One,* on June 19, Dave Navarro's long-awaited solo album. The band took a short break from the tour, planned a release party and Dave did some press promotions. The album was mostly praised by critics and during some of the band's the following touring dates, Dave would perform a song or two from the album. It was a proud moment for a man who had finally put the pieces of his life back together, for the first time, in a long time. And his band-mates were just as proud.

In rehearsal, they'd spent weeks revisiting songs they hadn't played in decades, dusting off tracks like "Obvious" and "No One's Leaving, "which felt as fresh and urgent as they had when they were first written. There were moments of tension, arguments over arrangements, Perry pushing for perfection, Dave pushing back, but it all came together when the lights went up and the music began.

During a show in Detroit, MI., Perry paused mid-set to address the crowd. "You know, when we started this band, we didn't give a fuck about fitting in. And looking at all of you out there tonight, I can see we did something right."

The crowd erupted, their cheers filling the night as the band launched into "Mountain Song, "the bass-line rumbling like an earthquake as Dave's guitar soared above it.

As the tour progressed, it became clear that this wasn't just a reunion, it was a reaffirmation of Jane's Addiction's place in music history. Critics hailed the tour as a triumph, praising the band's ability to evolve while still staying true to their roots.

For Perry, it was a reminder of why he'd started all of this in the first place. Watching the crowds night after night, seeing the faces of fans who had grown up with their music alongside a new generation discovering it for the first time, he felt something he hadn't in years, a sense of purpose, a sense of connection.

And as the final show of the tour approached, Perry found himself thinking about the future. Jane's Addiction was back, but where would they go next? For now, though, he was content to live in the moment, to soak in the applause and the energy and the sheer joy of it all.

Because if there was one thing he'd learned, it was that moments like this didn't come around often, and when they did, you had to hold on with everything you had.

Some "Stray" Cats.

Sunlight glinted off the infinity pool as Etty reclined on a lounge chair, cradling baby Hezron. The sound of flip-flops slapping against concrete grew closer, a lazy rhythm breaking the calm.

Perry appeared, his sun-bleached hair dripping and wet-suit pulled down to his waist. Sand dusted his tanned skin as he casually propped his surfboard against the wall. His movements were unhurried, a man who had learned to embrace the flow of life instead of fighting against it.

Etty stood up, stretching with a smirk. "Hope you had fun. Your turn."

She passed Hezron to Perry, then handed him a baby bottle. Perry cradled his son with the same practiced ease he showed handling his board, his face softening as he looked down at the baby.

"Hey little man, "he said softly, gently adjusting Hezron's tiny fingers around the bottle. The baby gurgled, a sound that seemed to bring a rare, genuine calm to Perry.

Etty was already moving toward the surf gear. "Water looks perfect, "she said, grabbing a board and flashing him a quick grin. With that, she disappeared toward the beach, leaving Perry and Hezron to their own world.

Inside the house, still in his wet-suit, Perry sat cross-legged on his meditation cushion, Hezron resting contentedly in the crook of his arm. The baby's eyes fluttered closed as he drank from the bottle, his small body snug against Perry's chest. Perry reached over to his phone, pressing the speaker button.

The sound of a guitar amp buzzing filtered through the line, followed by a familiar voice.

"Yo, Perry, "Dave answered, his tone relaxed but carrying the faint rasp of too many cigarettes. In the background, faint metallic notes rang out as he adjusted the strings on a guitar.

"Hey brother, not too much. Finishing up a three-month, pain-in-the-ass restore on a '59 Les Paul, "Dave continued, the grin in his voice unmistakable. "She's singing like an angel now."

Perry chuckled. "Nice, man. You're still sweet-talking your guitars more than people, huh?"

"Gotta treat the real ladies in my life with respect, "Dave quipped, a quiet laugh following his words.

A soft clicking sound came over the speaker, steady and rhythmic. "Stephen, you there?" Perry asked.

"Yeah, yeah, I'm here, "Stephen replied, his voice warm and calm. The faint sound of drumsticks tapping echoed faintly in the background. "Working on some beats. Nothing serious, just messing around."

Perry's lips curved into a sly smile. "Yeah, because, uh… I've got an idea."

On the other end of the line, Dave let out a soft groan. "Here we fucking go. Dude, we just got off tour a few months ago!"

"Relax, "Perry said, adjusting the bottle in Hezron's mouth as the baby gave a soft sigh. "I've been thinking. The three of us… We made something nobody else could touch. And was evident by the tour, those cats want fucking more, boys. And maybe it's time to make something again."

Stephen chimed in before Dave could reply. "You're talking about a new Jane's record?"

"Sort of, "Perry said, his tone careful, like he was testing the waters. "Not the same Jane's. Something new but built on what we had. Cleaner. Perhaps? I don't, man…more connected?"

Dave's voice came through, a mix of sarcasm and genuine curiosity. "Cleaner? You're not exactly selling me on that."

Perry laughed lightly. "I'm serious, man. Think about it. No drama. No shit. Just the music. Stephen's been killing it with Banyan for years now, people love it, right, Stevie?"

Stephen hummed in agreement. "Yeah, Banyan's been good to me. I've been able to stretch out, try new things, but…" He trailed off for a second, tapping his sticks on something metallic, "but I miss what we had. That energy. That edge…I don't know, maybe?."

"That's what I'm talking about, "Perry said, his voice growing more animated. "We do this, but we do it right this time. No baggage. No ego."

Dave's laugh crackled through the phone. "No ego? Laughing, "Have you met yourself, Perry?"

Perry smirked, stroking Hezron's soft hair. "Hey give an old Jew a chance, Davey. I've evolved, man. I've got fucking crystals and a baby now. I mean, I'm zen as shit!"

Stephen broke in with a laugh. "He's not wrong, Dave. I've seen him in full-on, yoga-dad mode."

Dave sighed, the sound of a chord ringing out as he strummed lightly. "Alright, Farrell. Say more. What's this new idea of yours?"

Perry's smile widened, the spark of inspiration lighting up his face. "Let's start slow. Jam a little. See where it goes. No pressure, no label breathing down our necks. Just the three of us, making noise like we used to."

There was a long pause on the other end of the line before Dave finally spoke. "Alright. I'm in. But if this goes sideways, I'm blaming you."

"Deal, "Perry said, his voice light with relief.

Stephen's voice came through, steady and warm. "Alright, let's see what we've got left in us."

Perry looked down at Hezron, the baby now fast asleep, his tiny fist curled against Perry's chest. For the first time in years, Perry felt like he was standing on the edge of something extraordinary, something worth fighting for.

Outside, the waves crashed against the shore, their rhythm steady, unbroken. Etty's silhouette moved across the sand, her board tucked under one arm as she disappeared into the surf. Perry closed his eyes for a moment, breathing in the possibility of what was to come.

· When the band found themselves in the recording studio, in November of 2002, it had a different kind of energy now, refined, focused, but no less intense. It wasn't the reckless abandon that had driven *Nothing's Shocking* or *Ritual de lo Habitual.* This was something deliberate, a quiet storm they were learning to harness. As they worked through each track, Perry felt it in his bones: they were forging something entirely new, a sound that honored the past but wasn't chained to it.

Perry leaned back in the booth, wiping sweat from his brow. The take had gone better than he expected, the music flowing like it used to but with a precision they'd never quite mastered before. Across the room, Dave twirled a pick between his fingers, his face betraying a rare look of satisfaction. Stephen twirled a drumstick idly, his usual calm confidence radiating through the glass as he waited for feedback.

Bob Ezrin's voice came through the intercom again. "Alright, let's take five. You've earned it, "he said with an approving nod.

The band shuffled into the control room, grabbing water bottles and towels. Perry leaned against the soundboard, his energy still buzzing from the take. "What'd you think, Bob? Did we bleed enough for you this time?" he asked with a smirk.

Bob chuckled softly, his sharp eyes scanning the board as he adjusted a few levels. "You bled. But what I heard? That was something more. That was control, "he replied.

Dave plopped into a chair, his guitar still slung over his shoulder. "Control. That's a new one for us, "he muttered, his sarcasm softened by a faint smile.

Stephen nodded in agreement, sipping from a water bottle. "Yeah, but it's working. You feel that pocket we hit? That's the sweet spot."

Chris leaned casually against the wall, tuning his bass. "Sweet spot or not, you guys are a pain in the ass to keep up with, "he teased, drawing a round of laughter from the others.

Perry shot him a playful look. "Hey, Chaney, if you're gonna hang with us, you better toughen up. This isn't Alanis' world anymore."

Chris grinned. "Oh, I'm plenty tough, Farrell. Just making sure you guys can keep up with me."

The banter flowed easily, a stark contrast to the tension that had once defined their time in the studio. Perry couldn't help but feel a flicker of pride. They weren't just surviving, they were thriving, building something fresh without losing the heart of what made Jane's Addiction, well, Jane's Addiction.

Bob interrupted their chatter, gesturing to the soundboard. "Come here for a second, "he said, his tone more serious now. The band crowded around as he hit play, the speakers filling the room with the playback of their last take. It was raw yet polished, the layers of Chris's intricate bass lines weaving effortlessly with Stephen's driving rhythm and Dave's haunting guitar melodies. Perry's vocals floated above it all, powerful and restrained, a reflection of the balance he was finally beginning to find within himself.

"This, "Bob said, pausing the track, "is what you've been chasing. This isn't just nostalgia or trying to relive the past. This is something new. And it's damn good."

For a moment, no one spoke. Dave leaned forward, elbows on his knees, studying the floor. Stephen's usual calm demeanor broke slightly, a hint of a proud smile creeping onto his face. Chris gave a small nod, his confidence quiet but evident. Perry, arms crossed, glanced around the room. He could see it in their faces, the realization that this wasn't just a reunion. It was a rebirth.

"Well, shit, "Perry said, breaking the silence with a grin. "Guess we've still got it."

Dave smirked, finally looking up. "Don't get cocky, man. We've still got three more tracks to nail."

"Yeah, but admit it, Navarro. That felt good, "Stephen said, his voice steady but warm.

"Better than good, "Chris added. "That was fucking tight."

Bob leaned back in his chair, his expression softening. "It's tight because you're all listening to each other. You're playing like a band again. Don't lose that."

Perry nodded, his expression serious now. "We won't." He looked around at his band-mates, his voice steady as he added, "Not this time."

Perry's stern declaration was an unspoken agreement, however it was understood by everyone in the room. They'd been through too much, individually and together, to let it slip away again. The past couldn't be erased, but the future was theirs to shape. And for the first time in a long time, it felt like they were ready to face it.

The day of the "Just Because" video shoot crackled with a kind of intensity that only Jane's Addiction could bring. The rented warehouse, decked out with towering lights and sleek rigs, hummed with the buzz of a high-budget production, but there was an edge to it, something a little reckless just beneath the surface. Perry Farrell moved through the set like a predator sizing up its prey, his sharp suit catching the glare of the lights as he prowled between takes. His hair was slicked back, his eyes gleaming with that unpredictable mix of charm and mischief that had always made him magnetic. Crew members darted around, adjusting angles and shouting commands, but Perry barely noticed. He was locked in, radiating the confidence of a man who knew the stakes and planned to own every second of the spotlight.

"Alright, let's go from the top!" the director yelled, his voice booming over the din of activity.

Stephen Perkins tapped his sticks against the edge of his snare, warming up as he shot a grin at Chris Chaney, who was tuning his bass with methodical precision. "Tight but loud, "Stephen muttered, mostly to himself, before flashing a quick thumbs-up to Chris.

Across the room, Dave Navarro leaned against his amp, absently plucking at his guitar strings, as a makeup artist touched up his face. "You think we've played this track enough yet?" he asked, his tone dry but with a faint edge of amusement.

Perry, pacing nearby, caught the question and smirked. "Come on Dave, this isn't your first music video-rodeo. They play it and we fake it, until the footage is perfect, "he shot back, his voice light but carrying a conviction that left no room for argument.

"If its not burned into our skulls first, never wanting to hear it, much-less play again." Dave muttered under his breath, shaking his head with a small grin as he positioned himself on his mark.

The song's opening riff roared to life, filling the cavernous space with its sharp, punchy groove. The cameras rolled as the band launched into the performance, each of them locked into their roles like they'd been doing it forever, and in some ways, they had. Stephen's drumming was airtight, his rhythm commanding the room, while Chris's bass-line thumped steadily, grounding the track with a groove that was smooth but powerful. Dave's guitar cut through the mix like a blade, his fingers moving effortlessly over the frets, each note sharp and precise.

And then there was Perry. Prowling the stage with a swagger that only he could pull off, he leaned into the mic stand, his body moving in time with the music as if it was part of him. His voice filled the space, smooth yet dangerous, carrying the song's biting hooks with the kind of charisma that couldn't be faked. When he snarled out the chorus, "Just because!", his expression was fierce, almost triumphant, and the camera lingered on him, capturing every bit of that raw magnetism.

Between takes, the director shouted adjustments. "Perry, more intensity on the next one! Dave, angle toward the camera a bit more! Chris, just keep doing whatever the hell you're doing, it's perfect."

Perry wiped the sweat from his brow, laughing as he grabbed a water bottle. "More intensity?" he echoed, raising an eyebrow. "What does this guy think I'm holding back?"

Stephen tossed him a towel, chuckling. "Probably doesn't know you've only got one setting, over the top."

"You know it, "Perry shot back, flashing a grin.

Chris, leaning on his bass, smirked. "He's just trying to keep up with the spectacle that is Perry Farrell."

"That's right, Sir" Perry said, winking as he took another swig of water before heading back to the mic stand.

When the cameras rolled again, the band played with a precision that felt both practiced and spontaneous, the kind of tightness that only came from years of chemistry, even with Chris as the new guy. Dave shredded through his solo, his guitar screaming in perfect harmony with the track's unrelenting energy. Stephen's drumming was a masterclass in controlled chaos, every hit sharp and intentional, while Chris's bass-lines added a layer of finesse that gave the song its polished edge. Perry, as always, was the focal point, his every move commanding attention as he prowled the stage, his eyes darting between the cameras and the imaginary audience he seemed to conjure in his mind.

Finally, "Cut, "The director called out after the last take, and the room exhaled as one. The tension broke into scattered applause from the crew, some clapping while others wiped sweat from their brows.

"That's a wrap, "the director announced, sounding satisfied but exhausted.

Perry turned to the band, his grin wide. "Fucking nailed it, "he said, his voice carrying that unmistakable mix of pride and relief. He caught Dave's eye, and they exchanged a nod, a rare, silent moment of mutual recognition.

"Yeah, that felt good, "Dave admitted, running a hand through his hair as he set his guitar down. "Clean, tight… almost too tight for us."

Stephen laughed, throwing an arm around Dave's shoulder. "You saying we're growing up, man? Because I'm not ready for that conversation."

Chris shook his head, smirking. "If this is grown-up Jane's, I think I can live with it."

MTV wasted no time jumping on the band's return. Within days of the shoot, teaser clips flooded the airwaves, with Kurt Loder hyping the band's evolution as a "triumphant reinvention." "Jane's Addiction is back, "Loder declared, "and they've never sounded sharper." The buzz spread quickly, fueled by glowing headlines: JANE'S ADDICTION RETURNS TO CLAIM THE ALT-ROCK THRONE.

"Just Because, "hit the airwaves like machine gun rounds. It climbed *Billboard's* Top 200, Alternative, College Radio and Rock charts, almost overnight. With its polished, sleek production and addictive hook, the single was finding an audience *far* beyond the band's original fan-base. For Perry, it was both exhilarating and surreal. He couldn't deny the satisfaction of hearing their track on mainstream radio, of knowing they'd created something that resonated across the spectrum.

During a late-night celebratory drink, sparkling water for Perry, he leaned over to Dave with a mischievous grin. "So, "Perry said, tapping his glass against Dave's, "still think this shit's too polished?"

Dave rolled his eyes but couldn't help smiling. "Don't let it go to your head, man."

"Oh, it's already there, "Perry shot back, his grin widening.

As the night wound down, they all knew something had shifted. This wasn't the old Jane's Addiction, and it didn't need to be. It was something new, something sharp, something ready to carve its place into a new era of music. And for the first time in years, they felt like they were standing on solid ground.

Large venues were alive again with the sound of Jane's Addiction. The excitement was undeniable, a force that seemed to vibrate through the air as fans old and new filled arenas, theaters and festivals across the country. The stage setups were bigger, the lights brighter, but the raw energy that had always defined the band remained. Fans wore vintage *Nothing's Shocking* and *Ritual de lo Habitual* T-shirts, mingling with younger crowds wearing freshly printed merch bearing the sharp, modern logo of Jane's latest era. It was a meeting of generations, all bound by a shared love for a band that refused to fade.

As they walked out to play for yet another sold-out crowd, Dave took a moment to glance at the sea of faces. There was something different about his expression these days. His sharp wit and natural sarcasm were still intact, but there was a weightlessness in his demeanor, a sense that he was fully present in a way he hadn't been before. The noise of the crowd swelled as they took their places, and he leaned toward Perry, smirking.

"Man, they really missed us, huh?" Dave said, his tone light but tinged with emotion, his fingers already settling on his guitar strings.

Perry, exuding his trademark mix of swagger and intensity, clapped Dave on the shoulder, a broad grin spreading across his face. "Damn right they did, "he said, his voice carrying the energy of the moment. "Yup! Now, once again, let's give 'em them the show boys."

The crowd erupted as the opening chords of "Ocean Size" rang out, the sound washing over them like a wave. Perry prowled the stage with his signature theatricality, his movements fluid and commanding, his voice cutting through the roar of the audience with a precision that sent chills down spines. Stephen's drumming thundered, grounding the chaos with a steady, driving rhythm, while Chris's bass lines added a new layer of depth and finesse to the familiar songs. Dave, his guitar slung low, tore through his solos with a confidence that brought the crowd to a frenzy.

The chemistry between them felt undeniable. This wasn't a band phoning it in or coasting on nostalgia. There was a fire, a sharpness to the music that made it clear they were here to prove something, to themselves, to their fans, to the critics who had written them off over the years.

Backstage after a show, the energy lingered like static electricity in the air. Perry threw a towel over his shoulder, his face still flushed with adrenaline. Etty was waiting for him, cradling baby Hezron, who wore oversized noise-canceling headphones that made him look like a miniature rock star in training. She smiled as Perry approached, handing the baby over to him.

"You killed it out there, Babe, "she said, brushing a strand of hair from his face.

Perry grinned, holding Hezron close. "We all did, "he replied, his voice soft but filled with pride.

The media had taken notice of the band's resurgence. Magazine covers plastered with their faces appeared on newsstands across the country. Rolling Stone declared, "The Kings of Alt-Rock Return, "while *SPIN* ran a photo of Perry and Etty on the red carpet with the headline, "Jane's Addiction: Back with a Vengeance." The articles detailed the band's journey, how they had nearly self-destructed, how they had clawed their way back from the brink, and how their music had evolved into something sharper, more focused, but still unmistakably theirs.

Interviews showcased a more candid, introspective side of the band. Dave, often the most guarded of the group, opened up about his struggles with addiction and his journey to sobriety.

"It wasn't easy, "he admitted in one interview, his voice steady but tinged with vulnerability. "But hitting rock bottom was the best thing that ever happened to me. I had to remember why the music mattered, why I mattered." His words struck a chord with fans, many of whom had followed his tumultuous journey and found hope in his comeback.

Stephen, ever the anchor, spoke with a quiet humility that belied his importance to the band. "For me, it's always been about the music, "he said in an interview. "No matter what we've been through, this… this right here, playing together, that's what keeps me grounded. That's what keeps me going."

For Perry, the comeback felt like both a triumph and a vindication. The moments on stage, looking out at the thousands of fans who sang along to every word, felt like proof that everything they'd endured, the fights, the chaos, the breakups, had been worth it. But there was also a new sense of peace in him, a calm that hadn't been there before. His relationship with Etty and the grounding presence of Hezron had shifted something in him, giving him a perspective that made the highs and lows of the music world feel more manageable.

On the nights they weren't performing, Perry and Etty became fixtures on the red carpet, their appearances exuding an effortless glamour that the media couldn't get enough of. They were rock royalty, but there was a warmth to them, a genuine connection that shone through in every photo. Perry, who had once thrived on chaos, now seemed to thrive on balance. He still had that spark of rebellion, that edge that made him who he was, but it was tempered by something softer, something real.

The band's resurgence wasn't just about the music, it was about the story they were telling, a story of survival, reinvention, and the unbreakable bond between them. And as they stood together on stage, playing for crowds that roared their approval, it was clear that this wasn't just a comeback. It was a new chapter, one they were writing together, and one that promised to be as unforgettable as the ones that had come before.

Reality Bites.

By November 2003, Carmen Electra and Dave Navarro were walking down the aisle, their relationship officially stamped into the tabloids, their lives an open book for public consumption.

MTV's reality show *Til Death Do Us Part: Carmen and Dave* offered a raw, often unfiltered look at their lives together, exposing the world to the whirlwind of their marriage, the highs and lows, the passion and the volatility. It was mindless-fodder dressed up for prime-time, their love story turned into a spectacle. Millions of viewers tuned in every week to watch the laughter, the screaming matches, the makeup sex hinted at but never shown. It was messy, complicated, and very, very real, or at least, it seemed that way.

"You know, this show is going to ruin us, "Dave said one night after the cameras had packed up for the day. He was sprawled on the couch, guitar in hand, strumming absentmindedly as Carmen lounged nearby, flipping through a magazine. The glow of the TV lit the room, but the silence between them was heavier than the airwaves.

Carmen didn't look up, her tone sharp but still playful. "Or maybe it'll make us stronger, "she shot back, her voice laced with defiance. "We're showing people what real love looks like, ups, downs, all of it."

Dave stopped strumming, his fingers hovering over the strings as he turned to look at her. "Yeah, but this isn't real, Carmen. It's… edited. Packaged for people to consume. They don't want to see us happy. They're waiting for us to fuck up, to crash and burn so they can feel better about their shitty lives."

She sighed, setting the magazine down and tossing a pillow at him. "Maybe that's just you being paranoid."

He caught the pillow, his smirk fading, replaced by a hint of something darker, heavier. "Maybe, "he muttered, the word trailing off. "Or maybe this whole thing is a ticking time bomb, and we're too wrapped up in it to hear it ticking."

Carmen sat up, her eyes narrowing. "So what, you're just waiting for us to fail? That's what you think?"

Dave shook his head, but his expression gave him away. "No, "he said softly, almost too softly. "I just… I've seen this before. When people start looking at you like a product instead of a person. It doesn't end well."

"You think you're some tortured artist, "Carmen had told him once, her voice filled with frustration. "But you're just torturing yourself."

That line echoed in his head now as he stared at the guitar in his lap. She wasn't wrong. A part of him had always lived on the edge, looking for the cracks in things, finding the flaws in moments that should've been perfect. It was his nature, his curse. And maybe that's why the cameras made him so uncomfortable. They weren't just capturing their lives; they were magnifying every imperfection, every argument, every insecurity.

Carmen moved closer, sitting on the arm of the couch, her expression softening. "You think I don't get it?" she asked, her voice quieter now. "The pressure? The feeling like you're being watched all the time? But we signed up for this, Dave. We knew what we were getting into. And we're not doing it for them, we're doing it for us. For the life we want to build."

Dave looked up at her, his dark eyes searching hers for something, reassurance, maybe, or understanding. "And what if the life we're trying to build gets swallowed up by this shit?" he asked, his voice barely above a whisper.

Carmen reached out, brushing a strand of hair from his face. "Then we fight for it, "she said simply. "We don't let them win. We don't let this show, or the press, or anyone else take what's ours."

There was a fierceness in her tone that made Dave pause. He wanted to believe her, wanted to believe that they were strong enough to withstand the scrutiny, the manufactured drama, the endless noise of the cameras and the tabloids. But a part of him couldn't shake the nagging doubt, the sense that they were playing a game with no clear rules and no guarantee of winning.

"You've got more faith than I do, "he admitted, his voice tinged with both admiration and resignation.

Carmen smiled, leaning in to kiss him lightly on the forehead. "That's why we balance each other out, "she said. "You keep me grounded, and I remind you to stop being such a cynical bastard."

Dave chuckled, a genuine laugh that broke through the tension hanging between them. "Fair enough, "he said, setting the guitar aside and pulling her into his lap.

They sat like that for a while, the quiet settling over them like a fragile truce. The cameras would be back tomorrow, the world would continue watching, dissecting, and judging their every move. But for now, it was just them, a man and a woman trying to hold on to each other in a world that seemed determined to pull them apart.

The reality show would continue, the episodes playing out like chapters of a messy, unpredictable story. And as they navigated the ups and downs, the love and the arguments,

Dave couldn't help but wonder if Carmen was right, if showing the world their flaws could somehow make them stronger.

But deep down, a part of him knew that love, like music, wasn't about perfection. It was about passion, about finding harmony in the discord, about showing up even when the notes didn't quite hit the mark.

By fall of the next year, Dave had more of a reason to drop the attitude and continue his positive progression and was riding high with a profound sense of accomplishment... and closure.

On October 4, 2004, Dave Navarro's Book, *Don't Try This at Home*, was released. A raw and unflinching memoir chronicling the wild, drug-fueled year of 1998 when his Hollywood Hills home became ground zero for a vortex of drug-fueled mayhem, fame, and personal reckoning. The book, co-written with Neil Strauss, fresh off the success of co-authoring Motley Crue's *The Dirt*, a *New York Times,* Number-One Bestseller, was part diary, part confession, and part sociological experiment, exploring Navarro's spiral into addiction and self-destruction.

The idea for the book had been brewing for years, though Navarro had kept it largely under wraps. While the photo booth in his home captured raw, unscripted moments during the height of his indulgence, it was Strauss who helped Dave translate those images and anecdotes into a cohesive narrative. Together, they crafted a story that didn't just shock, it illuminated the layers of pain, humor, and humanity beneath the surface of excess.

"People thought I was hosting these parties because I was living my best life, "Navarro wrote. "The truth is, I was barely surviving. The booth didn't lie, but I was lying to myself every single day."

Behind the scenes, Neil Strauss had been instrumental in helping Navarro shape the narrative. Strauss, already renowned for his ability to capture the raw, unvarnished truth of rock star lives, pushed Navarro to dig deeper than just recounting the wild anecdotes.

"Neil didn't let me off easy, "Navarro later said in an interview. "He kept asking, 'Why? Why did you let it get this bad? Why did you keep going?' I didn't have answers at first. Writing this book wasn't just telling stories; it was like ripping myself open and letting all the shit spill out."

The collaboration wasn't without its challenges. Navarro was still wrestling with the ghosts of his past while writing, revisiting painful memories and confronting truths he'd buried for years. But the process became cathartic. By the time the manuscript was complete, Navarro felt like he'd finally found a way to take ownership of his story.

Upon its release, *Don't Try This at Home* was met with a mix of fascination and praise. Readers devoured the behind-the-scenes stories of Hollywood debauchery, but many were struck by the vulnerability Navarro revealed.

Critics called it "unflinchingly honest" and "a must-read for anyone who's ever wondered what lies beneath the surface of rock star glamour." Fans of *The Dirt* embraced it as a grittier, more personal counterpart, while others praised Navarro's ability to balance dark humor with raw emotion.

"Navarro doesn't ask for sympathy, "one reviewer wrote. "He doesn't glorify his lifestyle or try to justify his choices. He simply lays it all out, beautiful, ugly, and everything in between."

In the months following the book's release, *Don't Try This at Home* became a cult favorite among readers fascinated by rock-and-roll memoirs. The photo booth parties, which had once been the stuff of urban legend, were now immortalized in print, their absurdity and tragedy laid bare.

Tough Decisions and a Memoir.

The peace and excitement of the road felt a world away from where he found himself now, back at home, staring at financial documents he could barely process, his face drawn tight with frustration and worry. Perry sat at the dining table, the stack of papers in front of him threatening to topple over. Bills, overdue notices, contracts, each one a reminder that the world he had built was shifting under his feet.

The music industry was taking a nosedive, and every time Perry turned on the news or checked his emails, it felt like another punch to the gut. He saw images of empty record stores, once bustling with energy, now barren and deserted, their shelves gathering dust. The places where he'd once browsed albums for hours, soaking in the atmosphere, were disappearing, replaced by the cold, digital void of online downloads and piracy. Sales reports were grim, numbers plummeting with no end in sight. The world he'd once thrived in was shrinking, collapsing, and he could feel it pressing in on him, suffocating.

The shift to digital had gutted everything. People didn't buy albums anymore, they didn't even buy songs, not really. Most people could just download whatever track they wanted for free. If bands were lucky, someone might shell out a dollar to download a single, but even then, most musicians would see only a fraction of a cent from the sale. Perry had always been in love with the tactile nature of music, the feel of the vinyl, the art on the covers, the physical act of holding a piece of someone's soul in your hands. Now, it felt like all of that was evaporating, and along with it, the livelihood of thousands of artists.

"It's not just the music, "Perry muttered to himself one night, staring at his laptop screen in the dim glow of his home office. He leaned back in his chair, rubbing his temples, the weight of it all pressing down on him. "It's the whole fucking ecosystem."

Touring, once a part of the cycle, had now become the cycle. With record sales practically nonexistent, all the money was coming from live performances from the road. But even that wasn't simple anymore. Record companies, desperate to recoup their own losses, were now pushing for what they called "360 deals." Perry had sat through enough meetings with suits in expensive ties, hearing the pitch. It always sounded like a sales gimmick: "We'll support you, help you tour, help you get back out there. All we ask for is a cut of everything, touring, merchandise, publishing."

Etty appeared in the doorway of Perry's study, cradling their newborn son, Izzadore. She leaned against the frame, watching him for a moment before speaking. "How bad is it?" she asked, her voice gentle but firm.

Perry sighed, running a hand through his disheveled hair. He closed the laptop with a bit more force than necessary, forcing a strained smile that didn't quite reach his eyes. "Nothing we can't handle, "he muttered, though the tremor in his voice betrayed him.

Etty stepped closer, adjusting Izzadore in her arms. Her expression was cautious but unyielding. "Perry, "she said, her tone steady, "don't bullshit me. Whats wrong?"

Perry let out a long exhale and stood up from his chair. "Everything, Babe." Perry muttered bitterly, pacing the room while she fed Izzadore. "They already fucking take like, ninety percent off the albums we sell, and now they want more. They want to own us, Every damn t-shirt we sell, every fucking ticket stub, ours. They want a cut of it."

Etty looked up from the baby, her expression calm but attentive. "And if you don't sign one of these deals?" she asked.

"They don't support the tour for the record. And, they most certainly support and tour you want to do. when there is no record to support." Perry said, throwing up his hands. "No tour money, no contract renewal, nothing. You're left out there on your own."

Etty tilted her head, her voice thoughtful but firm. "But isn't touring what you do best? You've built your whole life on being able to get out there and bring people to you."

Perry stopped pacing, looking at her. She was right, of course. Touring was his element, the stage his sanctuary. But this wasn't the same world anymore. The cost of touring, travel, crew, gear, had skyrocketed, and without the backing of a label or a contract with a large-scale promoter, it could bankrupt even the biggest bands. And now, if they signed these deals, the labels would own not just the records but everything attached to them. Perry hated it, hated how small and calculated it all felt.

Some nights, he'd sit in the dark, just him and the numbers, wondering how it had all gone to hell so fast. The DIY spirit that had fueled Jane's Addiction in its early days felt impossible now, swallowed by an industry more desperate and ruthless than ever.

Etty would find him there sometimes, her expression soft, supportive. She'd sit beside him, silent but steady, grounding him even when he felt like he was coming undone.

The sky over the shore was open, gray and blue with hints of rain in the air, as Perry sat, hopeless with a feeling of defeat, holding a glass of wine. He'd just suggested to Etty that perhaps it would be best, that she leave him, that he'd failed her as a husband…and the boys.

Etty's expression hardened, anger flashing across her face. "Are you fucking kidding me, Perry?" Her voice rose, firm and unrelenting. "You think I'd leave you just because things are rough? What kind of woman do you think I am?"

Perry looked away, his shame evident. His voice came out low and cracked. "I just... I wanted to give you more than this. I wanted to be better. Better for you, for Hezron, for Izzy."

Etty stepped closer, placing Izzadore gently into his bassinet before reaching out to Perry. She cupped his face in her hands, forcing him to meet her gaze. Her eyes softened, though her tone remained resolute. "Listen to me, "she said, her voice steady but fierce. "You are not a failure. You are the man I chose. The father of my kids. The man I love. And I don't give a damn about the money or the career. We've been through worse. We'll get through this, Perry. Together."

He searched her face, the weight of her words pressing against the wall he'd built around himself. "But what if I can't fix it?" he whispered, his voice barely audible and eyes that were beginning to water, "I mean...What if, if it turns out I'm no longer capable? To ya know...give you guys what you fucking deserve?"

Etty smiled then, a small but genuine smile that seemed to cut through his despair. "What we deserve, you idiot" she said, her voice softening, "is you. That's all we've ever needed. And you're enough, Perry. You've always been enough."

The room fell into a quiet calm, the only sound the soft breathing of their newborn son. Perry reached out, taking Etty's hand in his, holding it tightly as if it were the only thing keeping him afloat. For the first time in days, he felt a flicker of hope.

He nodded, his voice steady but quiet. "Together, "he repeated, the word carrying a weight that felt both heavy and freeing.

Etty leaned down, pressing her forehead to his. "Damn right, "she said, her smile widening.

As she pulled away, Perry glanced back at the stack of papers, the laptop, the reminders of the struggle they were facing. It wasn't over, not by a long shot. But as he looked at Etty, standing strong and unyielding beside him, and then at Izzadore, sleeping peacefully in his bassinet, he felt a sense of resolve building within him.

They had weathered storms before, and they would weather this one too. Together. Plus, he a something new in mind. Something refreshing.

Perry's latest project, Satellite Party, was a leap in a new direction. It was meant to be a fresh start, a way to reinvent himself and bring something different to the stage. The band was raw, experimental, and Perry had poured his heart into every track, crafting each song with a vision that was both bold and daring. But finding an audience proved to be more difficult than he'd anticipated.

Small venues replaced the massive arenas he'd once commanded, and where tens of thousands used to chant his name, now there were only hundreds , some of them curious, others simply unaware of the legacy he carried. Perry played each show with the same fire, but the energy was different. It was intimate, almost vulnerable, a far cry from the untamed chaos of his Jane's Addiction days.

'This isn't what I fucking signed up for, ' he muttered one night, slumping into a worn-out chair backstage after another small club performance. The walls were bare, the room cramped, a stark contrast to the opulent green rooms he was used to.

Etty sat beside him, placing a gentle hand on his shoulder. 'Babe, every great artist reinvents. Sometimes it's slow at first.'

Perry looked at her, his eyes dark and tired. 'I feel like I'm starting from scratch. Like they don't give a damn who I was or what I did.'

Etty leaned closer, her voice soft but firm. 'Maybe that's a good thing. Maybe this is a chance to find out who you really are, without the madness. Besides, ' she added with a smirk, 'you always loved a good fight.'

Rebirth?

The idea consumed Perry over the following days, his mind racing with possibilities as he jotted notes on scrap paper, napkins, and whatever else was within reach. His home office transformed into a war room, maps pinned to the walls, lists of bands scribbled in marker, his old notebooks from the original Lollapalooza tour pulled out and spread across the desk. He barely slept, his thoughts spinning with the logistics of it all.

Etty found him one night, hunched over his desk, eyes bloodshot but alight with purpose. She stepped into the room, cradling Izzadore, who had finally fallen asleep. "You're going all in on this, aren't you?" she asked, her voice quiet but tinged with amusement.

Perry looked up, his expression softening as he met her gaze. "It's all I can think about, "he admitted, running a hand through his hair. "I can't let it die, Etty. Not like this. It needs to evolve. It needs to mean something again."

She smiled, stepping closer and kissing the top of his head. "Then make it mean something, Babe. You've always been good at that."As she walked off, "Now cheer the fuck up, Sir."

A week later, Perry sat in a sleek conference room at C3 Presents, the company that had been working with him to conceptualize the new Lollapalooza. The polished table was strewn with blueprints of Grant Park, spreadsheets detailing potential costs, and lists of dream lineups. Jane's Addiction's agent , Marc, who was now Global Head of William Morris Endeavor's Music Division, sat across from him, tapping his pen against the table as he walked them through the pitch.

"All right, "Marc began, leaning forward, "we're looking at a three-day event. Friday through Sunday. Four main stages, smaller tents for electronic acts, and a dedicated area for local and emerging artists. We want it to feel like everything Lolla used to be, boundary-pushing, eclectic, but also grounded in what people expect now. We need to think big. Kanye, Radiohead, Foo Fighters - big."

Perry nodded slowly, his fingers drumming against the edge of his chair. "And we're locking it to Chicago?" he asked, his voice thoughtful.

Marc nodded. "Chicago's perfect. It's central, it's iconic, and Grant Park can handle the crowds. Plus, the city's backing us on this. They want it as much as we do."

Another voice chimed in, Charlie Jones, one of the co-founders of C3. "The challenge, "Charlie said, his Texas drawl slow and deliberate, "is convincing people this isn't just a nostalgia act. We've gotta prove it's not some throwback to the '90s. It's gotta feel new, relevant. That's the hook."

Perry leaned back in his chair, his eyes narrowing as he thought. "New, but with heart, "he said finally, his voice low but steady. "The heart of what it was back then. It was always about more than the music, guys. It was the art, the activism, the culture. We're not just selling tickets. We're creating a fucking experience."

Marc grinned, nodding. "Exactly. And we start with the bands. Big names to draw the crowds, but we make room for the weird shit too. The experimental, the underground. That's what'll set it apart."

Perry's face lit up, a mischievous glint in his eye. "We'll need installations, "he said, his voice gaining momentum. "Art pieces all over the park. Giant, interactive stuff. Make people feel like they're stepping into another world."

"And the activism, "Charlie added. "We bring in Greenpeace, Amnesty International, all the big ones. Give them space, let them speak. That's a big part of the old Lolla spirit."

"Fuck yes. Exactly, "Perry said, slamming his hand on the table. "That's what I'm talking about. I've always tried to get that notion across gentlemen…It's not just a festival, it's a goddamn, fucking movement"

As the weeks turned into months, the pieces began falling into place. Bands started signing on, the lineup shaping up to include a mix of icons and fresh faces: The Killers, Wilco, and Arcade Fire alongside rising stars and niche acts that Perry personally scouted. Each booking brought a new wave of energy, the dream beginning to solidify into something real.

One afternoon, Perry stood in Grant Park with a small group of planners, his boots sinking into the soft earth as he surveyed the sprawling space. The Chicago skyline loomed behind him, the buildings casting long shadows over the park. He pointed toward a wide-open section near the south end. "Main stage there, "he said decisively. "Facing north, with the skyline as the backdrop. That's the shot people will remember."

The group nodded, taking notes as they followed Perry's lead. He could see it already: the lights, the crowds, the music reverberating through the city. It was a vision that felt both ambitious and attainable, a rebirth of something that had once been untamed and wild, now refined and focused.

Later, as he walked back toward his car, Marc fell into step beside him. "You're really seeing this, huh?" Marc asked, his tone more curious than skeptical.

Perry glanced over, a small smile tugging at the corners of his mouth. "It's gonna be beautiful, Marc. You'll see."

Marc chuckled. "I don't doubt it, buddy. But you know this is just the beginning, right? Pulling it off is one thing. Keeping it alive? That's the real work."

Perry stopped, turning to face him fully. "We'll keep it alive, "he said, his voice firm. "We'll make it something they can't ignore."

And as they left Grant Park that day, the vision for the new Lollapalooza burned brighter than ever, a beacon of what was possible when ambition met determination. Perry could feel it in his bones, this was his next chapter, and he was ready to write it.

A Marriage Faces the Music

The restaurant was dimly lit, the kind of place where people whispered secrets over expensive wine and forgot the outside world for a while. Carmen and Dave sat across from each other, the candles between them flickering like the last sparks of a fire that once burned bright.

Dave stabbed his fork into his salad, a little too forcefully. "You know, I've been thinking…" he started, his voice rough, eyes fixed on his plate.

Carmen leaned back, her fingers toying with the stem of her wine glass. "That sounds dangerous…and rare" she teased, though her smile didn't quite reach her eyes.

He smirked, but it faded fast. "Nah, seriously. Shit's been, well, crazy, hasn't it?"

"Yea, I'd say 'crazy' one word for it, "she said with a small laugh. "I can't even remember the last time we spent more than a couple of hours in the same damn room without one of us rushing off to do something. You've got your gigs, I've got my shoots… it's like we're living separate lives under the same roof."

Dave nodded, his jaw tightening. "Yeah, and hell, I've been trying, you know that, right, Mouse? Trying to make it work. But maybe… maybe this just isn't something we can fix." He takes a drink of water. Then, "We've.."

She cuts him off, "I know what you're thinking, you're thinking that we're both putting more effort into our stupid selves, than into 'us.' "

There's a pause, Dave looks down at his plate, cutting his steak.

She looks at him with melancholy eyes, then continues, "Am I right, Bird? Its okay, say it."

Dave hesitantly looks up, leans back in his chair. "Yea sweetie, that's um pretty much whats been tinkering around in my dumb-ass head lately."

The words hit, not like a dropped bomb, but more of a small rock hitting water. Carmen's chest tightened, slightly but she nodded slowly. "Yea buddy, I've been thinking the same thing, "she admitted. "I love you, Dave, I fucking love you. But sometimes it feels like we're forcing this. And the more we force it, the more it feels like we're breaking something."

Dave leaned forward, rubbing his hand over his face. "Yeah, it's not about love though, is it? I mean, I fucking adore you. Always will. But this…" He gestured between them. "This whole marriage thing? Maybe we're just not built for it?" He looks to the side, sighs, "Shit, I don't know."

Carmen let out a shaky breath, her fingers tightening around the glass. "We're great at being best friends though, right?" she said softly. She then sits back, lightly pounds the table with both hands, in a slightly frustrating manner "But…fucking all to hell, maybe that's all we were supposed to be, huh."

Dave's lips twitched into a small, sad smile. "Yeah. Sucks to admit it, though."

"Big-time, dude" she agreed, her laugh half-choked by emotion. "But you're still my favorite pain in the ass, Navarro."

"And you're still my favorite weirdo, Electra, "he shot back, his grin widening. He reached across the table, his tattooed hand covering hers. "We're not losing each other. I mean, not really. Right?"

"Hell no, "Carmen said firmly, her eyes shining with unshed tears. "You're not getting rid of me that easy. I'll still check in, make sure you're not turning into some washed-up rock star."

"And I'll make sure you don't take yourself too seriously with all your Hollywood, modeling 'E True Hollywood' nonsense. Deal?" he replied with a wink.

They both laughed, loud and real this time, drawing a few curious glances from other diners. For a moment, it felt like nothing had changed, like they were still the playful, silly duo who always had each other's backs.

Outside the restaurant, the chill night air hit them as they stood together, unsure of what came next.

"Well, "Carmen said, pulling her coat tighter around her. "If this is it, I'd say we fucking nailed the breakup dinner. Five stars."

Dave snorted. "Damn straight. And for the record, I'm keeping the dog."

"Like hell you are!" Carmen shot back, shoving him playfully.

He laughed, throwing an arm around her shoulders as they started walking down the street. "You're lucky I like you, Electra."

"Yeah, yeah. Don't push it, Navarro, "she quipped, leaning into him.

They walked away into the night, their banter echoing down the empty street. For all the heartbreak, they knew they'd always have each other, maybe not as husband and wife, but as something even rarer.

NINJA.

Perry Farrell was slouched back in his Venice Beach office chair, legs up on the desk, his hand loosely holding a bottle of kombucha he hadn't touched in twenty minutes. His eyes were glued to his laptop screen, scanning through the next year's Lollapalooza lineup notes. The sound of the waves outside barely registered, it wasn't the ocean that held his attention these days.

His phone buzzed, interrupting the steady rhythm of his scattered thoughts. He reached for it lazily, but when he saw the name glowing on the screen, his hand froze mid-air. Trent Fucking Reznor.

He snatched it up immediately, putting it on speaker with a smirk already forming on his lips.

"Trent, "Perry said, his tone dripping with curiosity. "What's going on, man? Didn't think I'd be hearing from you today."

Trent's voice came through, calm but unmistakably deliberate. "Hey, Perry. Got something I've been chewing on for a while, and you're the guy to talk to about it."

"Well, you've got me on the line, "Perry said, leaning forward now, fully engaged. "Spit it out."

"Alright, "Trent started, his voice carrying just a trace of hesitation before firming up. "I'm putting Nine Inch Nails back on the road for one last fucking tour. And I want Jane's Addiction to co-headline it with us."

For half a second, Perry didn't say anything. He just let the idea drop into his brain like a grenade, the words reverberating. When he spoke again, his voice was somewhere between astonishment and sheer excitement.

"Hold the fuck up, "Perry said, laughing like he'd just heard the punchline to the dirtiest joke imaginable. "You're telling me NIN and Jane's, co-headlining? You're serious right now?"

"Dead serious, "Trent replied. His calm tone was a counterpoint to the energy that was already sparking in Perry's voice. "Think about it, man. Two of the biggest names from when the whole alt-rock thing blew up. Two bands that haven't shared a stage in decades. It's a goddamn slam dunk, man."

Perry let out a whistle, sitting back in his chair as the possibilities began to unfold in his mind. "Shit, Trent. That's not just a slam dunk, it's fucking next-level. What the hell do we even call a tour like this?"

"NINJA, "Trent said simply, as if it was the most natural thing in the world. "Nine Inch Nails. Jane's Addiction. You know fans…*and* the press, will eat that shit up."

Perry barked out a laugh, the kind that came straight from his gut. "Goddamn, that's good. NINJA. You're not fucking around with this, are you?" I assume is Marc packaging this?

"Of course. He's all in and loves it and, Nope, we aren't messing around, "Trent said. "This isn't some half-ass nostalgia trip. This is gonna be loud, stupid and fucking massive, my friend." We're going out swinging. I just need to know… are you in?"

Perry leaned forward, his voice dropping to something quieter but no less intense. "Like you even have to ask, brother. Fuck yeah, I'm in."

As soon as the call ended, Perry didn't waste a second. He punched in the number for Marc, and waited impatiently as it rang.

"Geiger, "Marc answered, his tone all business until he heard the excitement in Perry's voice. "What's going on, Perry? Was waiting for this call, "he says giggling with a half-smirk.

"So you think we've got something here, Marc?" Perry said, almost breathless. "Trent just called me. A co-headline tour with Nine Inch Nails? Love the name, by the way, "he said, giggling like a school boy, "NINJA! This shit's gonna blow up, Marc…"

Marc finally breaks in, "Yes! Okay, okay. Christ, Perry, take a goddamn breath, will ya?" Marc exhales and rubs his temples, then continues, "Yes, definitely a huge deal. But what about the band? Do you think everyone is ready to get back in your shit-storm of a saddle?"

"They'll be ready, "Perry said with confidence, though there was a flicker of doubt deep down. "This is too big to pass up, man. I mean, those cats gotta be on board for this…right?"

"Well, lets not count our horses before…never mind. Alright, "Marc said, already jotting down notes. "I've already started pulling the strings. But you better get your boys in line fast. I need confidence from all sides if this idea is going to move quick."

"You worry about the logistics, "Perry shot back. "I'll handle the guys."

The first call was to Stephen Perkins. Perry knew he'd be the easiest sell, Stephen had always been the band's backbone, the guy who showed up ready to play, no matter what.

"Perkins!" Perry said as soon as Stephen picked up. "Got a big one for you."

"Let me guess, "Stephen replied, already laughing. "Lollapalooza in space?

"Bigger, "Perry said, the grin clear in his voice. "Nine Inch Nails and Jane's. Co-headlining. What do ya think, man?!"

Stephen let out a whistle. "Holy shit. You're not fucking around, are you?"

"Never do, "Perry said. "But this is all Trent's idea. He just hit me with it, literally thirty minutes ago. So you in or what?"

"Do you even have to ask?" Stephen replied. "You me Perry. Just tell me when and where."

The next call, to Dave, wasn't as smooth. Dave had always been cautious about jumping back into the whirlwind that followed Jane's Addiction everywhere they went.

"Perry, "Dave said when he answered, his tone guarded. "What's going on?"

"NINJA, "Perry said, letting the word hang in the air for a moment. "Nine Inch Nails and Jane's. Co-headlining a fucking massive tour."

Dave paused. "Shit, "he said finally. "That's… big. But what's the catch, dude? What kind of mess are you dragging me into this time?"

"No mess, "Perry insisted. "It's clean, Dave. Tight. We're not going out there to fuck around, we're going out to remind people who the hell we are."

Another pause. Then, finally, Dave said, "Alright. I'm in. But if this goes sideways, Perry, I'm out. No bullshit, got it?"

"No bullshit, "Perry promised. "Just music."

Finally, there was Eric Avery. Perry hesitated before dialing, knowing this was the call that could make or break the tour. Eric had been out of the fold for years, unwilling to get pulled back into the drama that had defined Jane's Addiction's past.

"Perry, "Eric said when he picked up, his voice calm but distant. "How's it going? What do you want? And don't say, 'nothing.'"

"Eric, "Perry began, trying to keep his tone light. "This isn't a sales pitch. Okay, uh…it *might* be a slight sales pitch, but its more of a fucking invitation. Nine Inch Nails and Jane's. Co-headlining. It's gonna be massive, man."

Eric sighed. "I told you, Perry. I'm done with Jane's."

"I know, "Perry said quickly. "But this isn't just Jane's. This is fucking Nails. This is a chance to show the world something huge, something they'll never forget. Just… think about it, okay?"

Another sigh. Then Eric said, "I'll think about it. But no promises."

As Perry hung up the phone, he felt the familiar mix of excitement and anxiety that came with every big idea. The pieces were falling into place, but there was still work to do. Still, he couldn't help but smile. The NINJA tour was going to be something extraordinary, he could feel it. And for the first time in a long while, Perry Farrell felt like the best was still ahead of him.

The 'NINJA' tour was everything Perry had hoped it would be, big, loud, and unapologetically raw. Night after night, Nine Inch Nails and Jane's Addiction delivered a spectacle that felt like a celebration of the alternative rock explosion they'd both helped ignite decades earlier. The crowds were electric, and the energy onstage was undeniable, but underneath it all, there was the weight of everything it had taken to get there.

Perry paced backstage, the buzz of the crowd outside seeping through the walls. He adjusted his mic, the usual pre-show nerves hitting him harder than usual. As much as he thrived on the chaos of live performance, tonight felt different. It was the final stretch of the tour, and the outcome of what they'd accomplished was finally starting to sink in.

Dave sat on a chair behind his rig, quietly tuning his guitars. His focus was sharp, but there was a calmness about him now, a clarity that Perry hadn't seen in years. It was strange, in a way, reassuring but also a reminder of how much had changed.

"You ready to tear it up, brother?" Perry asked, his tone light, though his eyes carried a hint of something deeper.

Dave smirked, plucking a string. "Always, man. You're the one who's been pacing like a fucking lunatic."

Perry laughed, running a hand through his hair. "Just… soaking it all in, I guess. This whole thing, us being here, it's surreal, don't you think?"

Dave nodded, his expression thoughtful. "Yeah. Its all good, buddy."

Stephen Perkins walked in, drumsticks in-hand, beer in the other. He had been the glue holding everything together, his steady rhythm both onstage and off, a crucial anchor for the band. "Crowd's getting ready out there, guys." he said, grinning. "Let's go spread some love, shall we?"

Perry grinned back, his earlier nerves fading into excitement. He grabbed the signature bottle of red wine to take on stage and adjusted his wireless mic receiver on his hip, "Yup, as always. Love you all and let's go."

The stage lights dimmed, and the crowd erupted, their screams filling the arena like a tidal wave. As Jane's Addiction launched into the opening riff of "Mountain Song, "the energy from the applause was raw and intense, in the enclosed venue, that sent a warm, sudden breeze to the forward stage, a "wind, "that hit them within a millisecond.

Perry prowled the stage, his movements fluid and commanding, his voice cutting through the roar with a power that hadn't diminished in the slightest. Dave's guitar wailed, sharp and relentless, weaving through Stephen's thunderous beats and Chris Chaney's driving bass-lines. He had once again stepped into the role of bassist with a quiet confidence, his technical skill continued to add a new layer to the band's sound. He wasn't Eric, no one could be, but his precision and versatility always brought something fresh to the sets.

Halfway through the set, Perry grabbed the mic, his voice echoing through the venue. "We've been through a lot of shit to get here, "he said, his tone serious but tinged with a wild edge. "But you motherfuckers remind us why we keep coming back. This… this is what it's all about."

The crowd roared in response, their energy feeding into the band's performance. Perry turned to Dave, their eyes meeting for a brief moment, a shared understanding passing between them. They'd been through hell and back, but somehow, here again, they were still standing, still playing, still defying the odds.

After the show, the band gathered in the green room, their faces flushed with adrenaline, the smell of sweat and the lingering hum of amplifiers in their ears. Perry collapsed onto a worn-out couch, a bottle of water in his hand, his chest still heaving from the performance.

"That was fucking incredible, "Stephen said, his voice filled with genuine excitement as he tossed his drumsticks onto a nearby table. "They were hanging on every damn note."

Dave nodded, a rare smile breaking across his face. "Yeah. That might've been one of our best."

Chris, leaning against the wall, wiped his face with a towel, his expression calm but satisfied. "As always, you guys sure know how to bring the heat, "he said with a grin. "Makes my job easy."

Perry looked around the room, a sense of pride washing over him. "We did it, "he said, his voice quiet but firm. "We fucking did it."

There was a moment of silence, as the words hit-home. For all the struggles, all the fights, all the years of uncertainty, they'd managed to pull off something extraordinary, again, for more times now than any of them could recall. The 'NINJA' tour wasn't just a reunion, it was a statement, a reminder of who they were and what they could do.

Moments later, Trent Reznor walked in, his usual calm intensity radiating off him. He held a glass of water, his expression unreadable as he looked at Perry. "Hell of a set, "he said simply, his voice low but genuine.

Perry grinned, his earlier exhaustion momentarily forgotten. "Coming from you, that means a lot, "he replied. "You weren't too bad yourself."

Trent smirked, taking a sip of water. "You think they'll be talking about this in twenty years?"

Perry leaned back, his grin widening. "Oh, they'll be talking about this for a hell of a lot longer than that."

And as the tour rolled into its final stretch, the bond between the two bands deepened, a mutual respect forming between them. Perry and Trent, two icons from different corners of the same musical universe, found themselves drawn to each other's energy, their shared love of pushing boundaries creating a connection that felt both natural and inevitable.

On the last night of the tour, as the final notes of "Stop!" rang out and the crowd's cheers echoed through the venue, Perry stood at the edge of the stage, looking out over the sea of faces. For a moment, he allowed himself to feel the weight of it all, the history, the music, the people who had stuck with them through everything.

As he walked offstage, he turned to Dave, Stephen, and Chris, his voice steady but filled with emotion. "This is just the beginning, "he said. "We're not done yet."

They nodded, their expressions a mix of exhaustion and determination. The tour had been a triumph, but Perry knew there was more to come. The future was uncertain, as it always was, but for the first time in a long time, it felt like something worth chasing.

The tour rolled on like a freight train, unstoppable and relentless, leaving a trail of sold-out venues and blown-away audiences in its wake. Night after night, Perry would step onto the stage and feel the heat of the lights, the roar of the crowd washing over him like a tidal wave. It was intoxicating. For the first time in years, he felt fully alive, fully present, and fully himself.

Trent and Perry often found themselves talking late into the night, long after the venues had emptied and the adrenaline had started to fade. Backstage in some forgotten green room, they'd share stories, trade philosophies, and marvel at how their paths had converged.

"You know, "Perry mused one night, leaning back in a folding chair, his voice thoughtful, "we could've done this years ago. Jane's and NIN, side by side. Would've been fucking huge."

Trent, nursing a glass of whiskey, smirked. "Yeah, but back then, we'd probably have killed each other before the first gig. Or at least you and I would've ended up in some gutter, strung out, bitching about the other."

Perry laughed, the sound deep and genuine. "True enough, brother. Timing's a funny thing, huh?"

Trent nodded, his expression softening. "Yeah. But this? This feels right. Like all the shit we went through actually led somewhere. For once."

Perry raised his water bottle, a mock toast. "To survival, then. Against all fucking odds."

They clinked their drinks, the unspoken weight of everything they'd endured hanging in the air between them.

The camaraderie extended beyond the two front-men. Backstage, the bands mingled freely, their shared experiences bridging the gaps between them. Stephen and NIN drummer Josh Freeze often talked shop, geeking out over gear and technique. Chris and NIN bassist Jeordie White, formerly Twiggy Ramirez of Marilyn Manson, found a rhythm of their own, exchanging stories about life on the road and the unglamorous reality behind the scenes.

For Dave, though, the tour was both a redemption and a challenge. The clear-eyed discipline he'd worked so hard to maintain was put to the test every night, surrounded by the intoxicating energy of the road. Yet he stayed steady, his focus sharper than it had ever been. Onstage, he was a force of nature, his guitar work raw and visceral, the emotional core of every song. Offstage, he kept to himself more, often retreating to his hotel room to sketch or noodle on his guitar in private.

Perry noticed, pulling him aside one night after a particularly fiery set. "Hey, "he said, clapping a hand on Dave's shoulder. "You good? You've been killing it out there, but... I don't know. You seem quieter these days."

Dave looked at him for a long moment, then nodded. "I'm good, man. Just... keeping my head on straight, you know? The old me wouldn't have survived this. Hell, the old me would've fucked it all up by now."

Perry grinned, a flicker of pride in his eyes. "Well, for what it's worth, I'm glad you're here. Wouldn't be the same without you."

Dave's lips twitched into a small smile. "Thanks, Perry. Means a lot."

As the tour hit its final stretch, the shows only grew more intense. The crowds seemed larger, louder, as if they could sense the end was near and wanted to wring every last drop of energy from the performances.

The penultimate show in Los Angeles was particularly charged. Playing in their home city added a layer of emotion to the night, and both bands brought their absolute best. For the encore, Trent and Perry joined forces, performing a searing duet of NIN's "Hurt" that left the crowd in stunned silence, followed by a thunderous, defiant rendition of "Mountain Song" that shook the venue to its core.

Backstage afterward, the mood was jubilant but tinged with bitter-sweetness. "One more show, "Stephen said, slumping onto a couch, his drumsticks still clutched in his hand. "I can't believe it's almost over."

Perry, towel draped around his neck, nodded. "It flew by, huh? Feels like we just started."

Chris, sipping a Gatorade, smirked. "Guess time flies when you're blowing people's minds every night."

Trent appeared in the doorway, his expression unreadable as always, but there was a flicker of something softer in his eyes. "Hell of a show, guys, "he said simply. "Let's make the last one count."

The final night in Las Vegas felt surreal, like the culmination of something bigger than any of them could fully grasp. The stage was massive, the lights brighter, the energy crackling with an almost unbearable intensity. Perry could feel it in his bones, the weight of everything they'd built, everything they'd survived, and everything they were about to leave on that stage.

As the last notes of "Jane Says" faded into the desert night, the crowd erupted into a roar that seemed to stretch on forever. Perry stood at the edge of the stage, looking out at the sea of faces, his heart pounding with something he couldn't quite name. Gratitude, maybe. Or closure. Or just the simple, overwhelming joy of being alive, of still being able to do this after everything.

Backstage, as the cheers echoed faintly in the distance, Perry turned to Trent, who was sitting on a crate, wiping sweat from his face. "You think we did it?" Perry asked, his voice quiet.

Trent looked up, his gaze steady. "Did what?"

"Made something that'll last, "Perry said, gesturing vaguely toward the stage.

Trent's lips quirked into a small smile. "Oh, yeah. We did. And they'll be talking about it for a long fucking time."

Perry nodded, a sense of peace settling over him. "Not bad for a couple of old rockers, huh?"

Trent laughed, shaking his head. "Not bad at all."

As the band packed up and the crew began to dismantle the set, Perry lingered for a moment, looking out at the emptying venue. The tour was over, but the music, their music, felt eternal. And for now, that was enough.

A New Creative.

The recording studio in 2011 had an entirely different energy than the messy, dark, smoke-filled rooms of Jane's Addiction's early years. This was no longer the volatile environment of their youth. The atmosphere was focused and professional, with an undercurrent of calm determination that had been absent for decades. The walls of the studio were lined with sleek equipment, the faint hum of amplifiers filling the room as the band worked meticulously on what would become, *The Great Escape Artist*.

Dave leaned over his guitar, adjusting the knobs with practiced precision. His movements were deliberate, his focus sharp. This wasn't about proving anything to anyone, it was about making music that mattered, music that reflected who they had become. As he glanced toward a camera documenting the process, he paused, his expression thoughtful yet intense.

"We're not trying to be what we were, "he said, his voice steady but firm. "We're fucking finally becoming what we could be."

It wasn't just a statement; it was a declaration of intent, a line in the sand that marked the band's evolution.

Perry stood at the mic, his voice filling the room with a richness and clarity that spoke to years of growth, both personal and artistic. He no longer prowled the studio with the manic energy of his younger days. Instead, he commanded the space with a quiet confidence, his movements purposeful. Beside him, Stephen Perkins kept the rhythm tight, his drumming as precise as it was passionate, while Chris Chaney's bass lines wove through the music, grounding it with a sophistication that elevated their sound.

This was Jane's Addiction redefined, not a relic of the past but a band that had risen from the ashes, stronger and more grounded.

The release party for *The Great Escape Artist* was held in a sleek, intimate venue in downtown Los Angeles, its walls bathed in soft, golden light. The room buzzed with anticipation, a mix of die-hard fans, industry insiders, and old friends all gathered to celebrate Jane's Addiction's long-awaited return. Cameras flashed as the band entered, dressed to the nines but carrying themselves with the ease of men who'd survived the trenches and come out the other side.

Perry led the way, his sharp suit offset by his trademark swagger, the kind of confidence that seemed effortless but had been hard-earned over decades. Dave followed close behind, a quiet intensity in his eyes as he acknowledged the crowd with a brief wave, his black leather jacket catching the light. Stephen and Chris brought up the rear, their smiles wide and genuine, the kind of smiles that came from knowing they'd created something real, something worth celebrating.

As soon as they hit the floor, the room erupted in cheers. Fans held up their phones, snapping pictures and recording videos, their excitement palpable. Perry raised a glass in salute, his grin wide as he scanned the crowd.

"Alright, "he said, his voice cutting through the noise as he leaned into the mic set up for the occasion. "We've been through a lot of shit to get here, but this… this feels fucking good."

The crowd roared in response, the energy in the room rising like a wave. Perry chuckled, stepping back to let Dave take the mic.

"We couldn't have done this without you guys, "Dave said, his tone more subdued but no less sincere. "You've stuck with us through everything, and we don't take that for granted. So, thank you, for real."

The rest of the night was a blur of laughter, drinks, and stories, the kind of celebration that felt like a homecoming. Fans swarmed the band, asking for autographs and selfies, their excitement infectious. Perry moved through the crowd like a man at ease, shaking hands and hugging old friends, his charm as magnetic as ever.

At one point, a young woman approached him, clutching a vinyl copy of the new album. "This saved me, "she said, her voice trembling slightly. "I've been in such a dark place, and this… it gave me hope."

Perry's grin softened, his eyes kind as he signed the record. "That's the magic of music, isn't it?" he said, handing it back to her. "It saves us as much as it saves you."

The critical response to *The Great Escape* Artist was immediate and overwhelmingly positive. Headlines flooded music blogs, magazines, and newspapers, with critics marveling at the band's ability to evolve without losing their essence.

"Jane's Addiction proves they're more than just a relic of the '90s, "*Rolling Stone* declared in a glowing four-star review. "*The Great Escape Artist* is an audacious return, blending the band's signature rawness with a newfound sophistication that feels entirely their own."

Pitchfork, known for its often brutal reviews, praised the album's experimentation and depth. "It's rare for a band this far into their career to create something that feels both fresh and vital. Jane's Addiction has done just that."

Even *The New York Times* weighed in, calling the album "a masterclass in reinvention, a testament to the enduring power of artistry in an industry that often demands conformity."

The reviews weren't just kind; they were celebratory. Critics highlighted Perry's introspective lyrics, Dave's intricate guitar work, Stephen's relentless drumming, and Chris's seamless integration into the band. Each element felt deliberate, honed, as if the band had finally unlocked the potential they'd always hinted at but never fully realized.

The album's lead single, "Irresistible Force, "became a breakout hit, climbing the charts with a relentless momentum that surprised even the band. The accompanying music video, a swirling, surrealist visual feast, dominated MTV's remaining music programming and spread like wildfire online, introducing Jane's Addiction to a new generation of fans.

The phone buzzed on the glass coffee table in Perry's living room, the sound echoing faintly against the high ceilings. Perry, still in his yoga pants from his morning session, leaned forward and grabbed it. His eyes lit up as he read the text from his agent, Marc.

"Check Rolling Stone. You're trending."

Perry smirked, tossing the phone onto the couch before walking over to his laptop. As the screen lit up, his fingers moved deftly over the keyboard until the Rolling Stone homepage loaded. There it was, a bold headline plastered at the top:

"*The Great Escape Artist*: Jane's Addiction's Boldest Move Yet"

Perry leaned back in his chair, the words washing over him like a cool ocean breeze. He clicked on the article and began to read, his eyes scanning the glowing review.

"Jane's Addiction hasn't just returned; they've evolved. With 'The Great Escape Artist,' the band has abandoned the raw chaos of their early days for a sound that's refined but no less electric. Perry Farrell's introspective lyrics, Dave Navarro's intricate guitar work, Stephen Perkins' dynamic drumming, and Chris Chaney's polished bass lines come together to create something both modern and timeless."

"Modern and timeless, "Perry murmured to himself, his voice carrying a mix of pride and disbelief. He heard Etty's footsteps approaching from the kitchen, the soft padding of bare feet on the hardwood floor.

"What's got you smiling?" she asked, leaning over his shoulder to glance at the screen.

"Rolling Stone, "Perry replied, tilting the laptop toward her. "They love the album."

Etty scanned the review, her brow raising in surprise. "Wow, "she said, her tone teasing. "They almost sound like they're ready to kiss your ass."

Perry laughed, the sound full and genuine. "I don't mind a little ass-kissing every now and then, "he admitted.

Just then, Perry's phone buzzed again. This time, it was a call. He picked it up, glancing at the screen before answering. "Dave, "he said, his grin widening. "You see the reviews?"

On the other end, Dave's voice came through, calm but with a hint of satisfaction. "Yeah, man. Even Pitchfork gave us a good review. I didn't think they liked anything that wasn't recorded in a basement."

Perry chuckled. "I guess miracles do happen. Did you see what Rolling Stone called us? 'Modern and timeless.'"

"Not bad for a bunch of old guys, "Dave quipped.

"You mean seasoned, "Perry corrected, leaning back in his chair. "We've got layers now."

Dave snorted. "Yeah, layers of wear and tear."

Their laughter was interrupted by another call coming through on Perry's phone. He glanced at the screen again. "Hang on, it's Stephen. I'll merge him in."

Moments later, Stephen's cheerful voice joined the conversation. "You two reading the same shit I am? They're calling us the architects of alt-rock again. I mean, I'll take it, but I don't remember building anything."

Perry grinned. "You built it, all right. You and those drums, keeping us in line all these years."

Stephen laughed. "Well, somebody had to. But seriously, man, this feels good. Like, we're finally getting our due."

"Better late than never, "Dave said. "But don't let it go to your head, Perry. You're already insufferable enough."

"Please, "Perry shot back, his tone playful. "I've been insufferable since 1987. This changes nothing."

Chris's name popped up on Perry's screen next, and he added him to the call. "Chris, you're late to the party, man, "Perry greeted him. "We're basking in the glow of critical-fuckin' acclaim over here."

"Yeah, I saw, "Chris said, his voice carrying a note of modesty. "You know, I wasn't sure how people would react to the new sound, but… it feels good. Like we did something right."

"We did more than that, "Perry said, his tone turning serious for a moment. "We proved that we're not just a band from the past trying to relive our glory days. We're still creating, still pushing boundaries. That's not something every band can say."

"True, "Stephen agreed. "But I think what's really hitting me is how much fun this is again. Like, no drama, no bullshit. Just… the music."

Dave chuckled. "Yeah, give it another few months. We'll find something to fight about."

"Don't jinx it, "Chris warned.

The conversation shifted to their upcoming plans, a new tour to support the album, appearances on late-night shows, and maybe even a few festival slots. The energy was infectious, a mix of relief, pride, and renewed excitement.

Later that night, Perry sat on his balcony, a glass of wine in hand as he looked out at the ocean. The waves crashed softly against the shore, their rhythm steady and unchanging, a stark contrast to the whirlwind of his life.

Etty joined him, sitting beside him and resting her head on his shoulder. "You seem happy, "she said softly.

"I am, "Perry admitted, his voice thoughtful. "For the first time in a long time, I feel like we're exactly where we're supposed to be."

Etty smiled, her hand finding his. "Then let's stay here for a while."

And for the moment, Perry was content to do just that. But deep down, he knew the journey was far from over. There was always another idea, another challenge, another chapter waiting to be written. For now, though, he let himself savor the moment, the glow of the music, the praise, and the feeling that, against all odds, Jane's Addiction was truly back.

The Escape.

The lights dimmed, and the sold-out crowd at The Pageant in St. Louis erupted in a deafening roar. It was the kind of electric anticipation that only came when legends took the stage. Jane's Addiction was back, not just with a new album, but with something to prove.

Backstage, Perry Farrell paced, his energy already vibrating at performance-level. His voice coach had warned him earlier to save his breath, but Perry wasn't the type to sit still, especially not on opening night. His hands fluttered over a table of crystals and incense he'd laid out, the ritual now second nature. Beside him, Dave Navarro adjusted his leather jacket, casually leaning against an amp as if the screams of thousands were just background noise.

"Fuck, you'd think after all this time I wouldn't get nervous, "Perry muttered, shaking his hands out.

"You're not nervous, "Dave said, smirking as he tuned his guitar for the umpteenth time. "You're wound up. There's a difference."

Stephen was off to the side, quietly tapping out a complex rhythm on the edge of his drumsticks, his calm demeanor grounding the room. Chris Chaney, ever the professional, checked his bass, his fingers moving with the precision of a surgeon.

Perry turned to the others, his voice loud and clear. "Alright, boys. Let's show them we're still the best thing they've ever seen."

A stagehand gestured to the band, signaling it was time. Dave pulled his guitar strap over his shoulder, Stephen gave one last stick flourish, and Perry, ever the showman, strode forward, pulling on a sequined blazer as if he were donning armor.

The band hit the stage with a ferocity that blew the crowd back before the first verse of "Underground" was even finished. The opening track from *The Great Escape Artist* felt massive, the pulsing bass-line ricocheting through the venue as Perry's voice soared.

Perry prowled the stage like a lion surveying its domain, his every move choreographed chaos. He leaned into the audience, locking eyes with fans in the front row, his hands gesturing dramatically as if he were casting a spell over them. Dave stood a few steps back, his fingers dancing over the strings of his PRS guitar, creating a soundscape both ethereal and raw. His solos were sharp, deliberate, and uncompromising, a reminder that he wasn't just playing music, he was sculpting it.

The set-list was a masterful blend of old and new. They transitioned seamlessly from the dark, brooding "Twisted Tales" into the frenetic energy of "Ain't No Right, "the latter igniting the crowd in a way that only their classics could. Fans screamed the lyrics back at Perry, fists pumping in the air.

Stephen's drumming was thunderous, each beat a declaration of intent. During "Ted, Just Admit It…, "his intricate fills drove the band forward with precision and flair. Chris's bass-lines grounded the performance, his subtle flourishes adding depth to the newer material while doing justice to Eric Avery's iconic lines on the older tracks.

"St. Louis!" Perry shouted mid-set, his voice dripping with theatricality. "You're fucking beautiful tonight!" The crowd roared in response, the connection palpable. "This next one's for all you lost souls out there!" he added, launching into "Irresistible Force." The haunting melodies and lush production of the studio version translated beautifully live, the audience swaying as Perry's voice filled the venue.

Between songs, the band regrouped briefly backstage, dripping with sweat but grinning like maniacs.

"That was fucking tight, "Dave said, grabbing a towel and dabbing at his forehead. "Crowd's eating it up."

Perry, still buzzing, pointed at Chris. "Chaney! That bass-line on 'End to the Lies'? Fucking nasty, man. Keep it coming."

Chris grinned, adjusting his strap. "Hey, just trying to keep up with you lunatics."

Stephen laughed, twirling his sticks. "Alright, enough with the love fest. Let's finish this thing strong."

The second half of the set leaned heavily on their classic *Ritual de lo Habitual* material. "Three Days" stretched into a sprawling epic, with Dave unleashing one of the most transcendent solos of the night, his guitar crying out like a living thing. Perry stood at the center of it all, his arms raised, eyes closed, fully immersed in the music as the crowd swayed with him.

When they broke into "Been Caught Stealing, "the crowd erupted, the energy hitting its peak. Perry strutted across the stage, mimicking the exaggerated movements of a mischievous thief, drawing laughter and cheers from the audience. Dave's riff tore through the room, the infectious groove impossible to resist. Even Stephen couldn't help but flash a grin as the fans jumped and danced in unison.

As the night wound to a close, Perry grabbed the mic stand and addressed the audience, his voice hoarse but filled with emotion.

"Listen, "he said, pacing the stage. "This… this is why we're still here. Because of you. Because you believe in the music. You give us life, you crazy motherfuckers!" The crowd roared, and Perry's grin widened. "Now let's drill this place into the fucking ground."

The opening chords of "Stop!" sent the audience into a frenzy. The band gave it everything they had, the energy onstage matching the chaos in the pit below. Perry belted out the lyrics like a man possessed, while Dave's guitar screamed and wailed, a perfect embodiment of the raw power that had always defined Jane's Addiction.

When the final notes rang out, the band stood together at the edge of the stage, arms around each other as they took in the thunderous applause. Perry raised his mic stand in the air like a trophy, his face a mix of triumph and gratitude.

Back in the green room, the air was thick with exhaustion and satisfaction. Perry collapsed onto a couch, downing a bottle of water in one long gulp.

"That, "he said, panting, "was a goddamn good night."

Stephen raised his drumsticks in a mock toast. "Here's to us not fucking it up."

Dave chuckled, lighting a cigarette. "It's like riding a bike, man. A very loud, slightly dangerous bike."

Chris leaned against the wall, shaking his head with a grin. "You guys are insane. But I fucking love it."

Perry looked around the room, his band-mates laughing, the adrenaline still pumping through them. For the first time in years, it felt like they were exactly where they were meant to be. And as he sat there, soaking it all in, he couldn't help but think that this was only the beginning.

Reflection and "Ritual at 25"

Perry Farrell slouched on the couch in his living room, a half-finished glass of wine resting precariously on the armrest. The room was comfortably-eccentric, filled with mismatched furniture, stacks of vinyl records, and the faint hum of his latest experimental track playing softly in the background. He held the remote in his other hand, aimlessly flipping through channels, his expression a mix of boredom and restless energy.

From the kitchen, Etty appeared, carrying a bowl of popcorn. Barefoot and relaxed, she moved with the kind of calm that perfectly offset Perry's jittery unpredictability. She leaned against the doorway for a moment, watching him with an amused smile.

"You're gonna miss it if you keep flipping like that, "she said, her voice light but teasing.

"Relax, "Perry replied without looking up, his thumb still hammering the remote. "I'll find it."

Etty rolled her eyes and crossed the room, settling down beside him on the couch. Just as she did, the screen flashed to a press conference. Perry paused mid-flip, leaning forward slightly as the image of Ana Martinez, the Hollywood Walk of Fame producer, filled the screen. The chyron below her read: "Jane's Addiction Honored with Hollywood Walk of Fame Star."

"We are thrilled to honor Jane's Addiction, "Ana said, her polished voice filled with excitement. "One of the most influential rock bands of their time. Tomorrow, we'll unveil their star right here on Hollywood Boulevard, and we're expecting a massive turnout."

The broadcast cut to a montage of screaming fans already lined up outside the event location, clutching vinyl albums, T-shirts, and handmade signs. The sight of it all made Perry chuckle, shaking his head in disbelief.

Etty nudged him gently. "See? They still love you, my dumb rock star."

Perry smirked, leaning back into the cushions. "Yeah, well… it's about damn time."

The news cut to a commercial, but Perry didn't move. He stared at the now-muted screen, his expression softening as he took a slow sip of wine.

"A star on the fucking Walk of Fame, "he muttered, almost to himself. "Who would've thought? After everything…"

Etty set the popcorn bowl aside and rested a hand on his shoulder. "You earned this, Perry. You all did."

He turned to look at her, his eyes searching hers for a moment before he nodded. "Yeah, "he said quietly. "I guess we did."

Hollywood Boulevard was buzzing with life, the sidewalks packed shoulder-to-shoulder with fans, journalists, and curious onlookers. Cameras flashed incessantly as people jostled for position, their voices blending into an excited hum. A stage had been set up outside the Playmates of Hollywood store, adorned with banners bearing the Hollywood Walk of Fame logo.

At the center of it all stood Perry, Dave Navarro, Stephen Perkins, and Chris Chaney, each of them dressed sharply but still carrying their unmistakable rock star edge. They waved to the crowd, their smiles easy but tinged with disbelief at the sheer magnitude of the moment.

Ana Martinez stepped up to the podium, her own smile as bright as the California sun. She gestured to the crowd, her voice amplified by the speakers. "Ladies and gentlemen, welcome to this very special occasion! Today, we honor a band that reshaped rock music, inspired generations, and brought their unique artistry to the world stage. Please join me in celebrating Jane's Addiction!"

The crowd erupted into cheers, their voices rising in a deafening wave. Perry squinted into the sea of faces, catching glimpses of old fans holding up "Nothing's Shocking" vinyls and younger ones wearing shirts from the band's recent tours.

Ana continued, gesturing to the side of the stage. "We have a few special guests today who'd like to say a word about our honorees. First, please welcome a legend in his own right, John Densmore!"

The drummer for The Doors stepped up to the mic, his presence commanding yet approachable. His eyes twinkled as he looked out at the band.

"It's an honor to be here today, "Densmore began, his voice steady. "To celebrate a band that didn't just break the rules, they rewrote them. Perry, Dave, Stephen, Chris… you've given us music that's raw, real, and timeless. Los Angeles is proud of you. The world is proud of you."

The crowd roared their approval, and the band nodded their thanks, visibly moved.

Ana returned to the mic, her enthusiasm unflagging. "And now, please welcome another rock icon, Taylor Hawkins!"

Taylor bounded onto the stage, his energy infectious as he grabbed the mic. "Let's hear it for Jane's Addiction!" he shouted, grinning as the crowd cheered again.

"They're fucking legends, "he said, his voice loud and clear. "When I was a kid growing up in California, this band was everything. They weren't just a soundtrack, they were a lifeline. Perry, you crazy bastard, you made music feel like art and rebellion all wrapped up in one. Dave, your riffs are untouchable. Stephen, as a drummer, man, you're my hero. And Chris, you stepped in and kept the heartbeat alive when it mattered most. We owe you."

He turned to the band, his grin softening into something more genuine. "Thank you for giving us music that didn't just exist, it fucking mattered. This is your day. Enjoy it. You've earned it."

The crowd's applause swelled as Taylor stepped back, clapping along with them. Perry exchanged glances with Dave, Stephen, and Chris, each of them sharing a moment of unspoken pride.

Finally, Ana returned to the mic. "And now, the moment we've all been waiting for. Let's unveil the star!"

The band gathered around the covered star on the sidewalk, their hands gripping the cloth. Cameras clicked furiously as they pulled it back, revealing the brass and terrazzo emblem etched with "Jane's Addiction."

The crowd erupted into cheers, the sound echoing down Hollywood Boulevard. Perry stepped forward, his hand brushing over the star before he turned to the mic.

"I never thought we'd end up here, "he began, his voice steady but emotional. "Not in a million years. Not a bunch of stubborn, chaotic, misfit cats like us. But here we are."

He paused, scanning the crowd. "This star isn't just for us, it's for you. For every one of you who stuck with us through the highs, the lows, and everything in between. We're proof that no matter how fucked up life gets, you can still create something beautiful. Thank you for being part of this journey. We love you."

As the crowd roared their approval, the band posed for photos, their hands resting on the star. For a moment, time seemed to freeze, the weight of their journey culminating in this one surreal, unforgettable moment.

The late afternoon sun poured into Perry Farrell's home, spilling across the open floor plan where his two teenage sons, Izzadore and Hezron, were sprawled across the couch. The faint hum of music played in the background, something Hezron had queued up earlier that neither of them were paying attention to.

"I'm telling you, "Izzadore said, his voice climbing, "if you really think Radiohead's better than Zeppelin, you've got no taste. It's embarrassing, dude."

"Zeppelin's good, but they're old, man, "Hezron shot back. "Radiohead actually did something new."

Perry wandered into the room, mug of tea in one hand, looking amused. "What are we arguing about now? Lemme guess, neither of you thinks Jane's belongs in the conversation?"

Hezron grinned slyly, leaning back into the couch. "You're trying too hard, Dad. You know Ritual is a classic. But Radiohead's better."

Perry rolled his eyes. "You kids don't know shit. Let me tell you something, when 'Three Days' dropped live, people were having full-on out-of-body experiences. That's not just music; that's history."

Izzadore crossed his arms, a smirk tugging at his lips. "Pretty sure no one's tripping out when you're yelling about picking it up in the kitchen."

"Smart ass, "Perry muttered.

The house had been calm lately, unusually calm, and it made Perry restless. For decades, he'd thrived on the chaos of the road, the constant motion, the adrenaline of creating something bigger than himself. But here, surrounded by the quiet rhythm of family life, he found himself itching for the stage again.

He sat down in the chair nearest to the boys, staring off toward the window. "What would you say if I told you I'm thinking about playing Ritual live again?"

Hezron perked up. "The whole thing? Like, in order?"

"That's the idea, "Perry said, sipping his tea. "Front to back. Just like the record. Film it, make a night out of it."

"'Three Days' is, like, fifteen minutes long, Dad, "Izzadore pointed out. "You think people want to stand through that now?"

Perry smirked. "Kid, people pay to stand through that. It's the highlight of the album." He paused, tapping the mug against his knee as he let the idea roll around in his head. "I don't know. It's been a long time. Not sure if it'd still feel the same."

The boys exchanged a look but didn't say anything. They could tell their dad's wheels were already turning.

Later that evening, Perry sat in his home office, flipping through a stack of old notes and memorabilia from the 'Ritual era'. His phone buzzed on the desk, interrupting his thoughts.

"You're quiet, "Dave Navarro said when Perry picked up.

"Just thinking, "Perry replied.

Dave chuckled dryly. "Uh-hu, as usual. Whats on your mind Per?"

"I've got an idea. Yea I know, 'No way! Fucking Perry has an idea? Really?" Perry said sarcastically, leaning back in his chair. "The 25th anniversary of *Ritual de lo Habitual* is coming up. I'm thinking about a tour. Something different this time. Whole album, start to finish, possibly even in fuckin' order."

There was a long pause on the other end of the line. There's a sigh. "You serious?" Dave asked finally.

"Dead serious, "Perry said, his voice steady.

Dave let out a low whistle. "That's a tall order, man. I mean, fuck, can we even pull that off anymore?"

"I don't know, "Perry admitted. "But I think we've got to try. It feels… important, you know? Like something worth doing."

Dave was quiet for a moment before replying, "Alright. If you're in, I'm in. Let's see if we can still make some magic."

The rehearsal room was a mix of calm and anticipation, the kind of quiet that held the weight of everything they'd been through. Perry sat cross-legged on the carpeted floor, his hands resting loosely on his knees, eyes closed. The faint scent of incense lingered in the air, and the soft hum of a tuning guitar filled the background. He was meditating, his breathing steady, his mind trying to center itself amid the emotions swirling inside him.

Nearby, Dave stood by his rig, meticulously tuning his guitar. His fingers moved with practiced precision, the faint twang of each string cutting through the stillness of the room. His face was a mask of quiet focus, his usual smirk replaced by a look that bordered on solemnity. Behind him, the walls were lined with framed platinum records, each one a silent testament to the journey that had brought them here.

Stephen sat at his kit, twirling a drumstick between his fingers. He tapped out rhythms on the edge of a snare, his movements calm and collected, but his mind clearly working. The gentle, syncopated beat he played seemed to keep the room grounded, a steady pulse that tied everything together.

Perry opened his eyes, his gaze drifting around the room. For a moment, he simply observed, Dave's concentrated precision, Stephen's rhythmic calm. Nostalgia tugged at the corners of his thoughts, mingling with a deep sense of pride. Finally, he broke the silence.

"Remember the first time we played here?" Perry asked, his voice soft but laced with humor.

Dave chuckled, looking up from his guitar. "Ha. Christ. Barely. Feels like another lifetime, Brother."

Stephen laughed from behind his drum kit, shaking his head. "We were so fucked up."

Perry grinned, the memory of their younger, wilder selves bringing a flicker of mischief to his face. "Shit. No joke." He glanced between them, his voice taking on a note of wonder. "Look at us now."

Dave leaned against his amp, a small, reflective smile pulling at his lips. "Who the hell would've thought?" he said, almost to himself, before setting down his guitar and walking toward the hallway.

Perry watched him go, his expression softening into something deeper, something filled with gratitude. "I did, "he murmured, more to himself than anyone else. "Always did."

The faint, distant roar of the crowd began to filter into the room, growing louder with every passing second. Twenty thousand people, maybe more, waiting just outside the walls for them to take the stage. The energy was palpable now, the buzz of anticipation seeping into the air around them.

Stephen set his sticks down and stood, rolling his shoulders. He nodded toward the door. "They're ready."

Perry pushed himself to his feet, his movements fluid despite the years. He stood for a moment, looking at Stephen, then back at the empty space where Dave had been. Finally, he turned to face the room, as if addressing not just his band-mates, but the years of history that had brought them here.

"We all are, "Perry said, his voice low but steady.

The three of them moved toward the door, their steps deliberate, each one carrying the weight of everything they had endured, everything they had created. But just as Perry reached the threshold, he stopped, turning to glance back at the band members. His gaze seemed to break through the fourth wall, locking onto something unseen.

"People ask if I have regrets, guys" he said, almost conversationally, as if he were speaking directly to the audience of life that had followed their journey. "Sure. But fucking regret's just wisdom wearing mourning clothes. It's what you do with it that matters, right?"

He lingered for just a moment longer before turning back toward the hallway. The roar of the crowd was deafening now, a living, breathing force that seemed to vibrate through the walls.

The opening notes of "Stop!" began to echo faintly from the stage, and as they stepped into the spotlight, the crowd erupted into cheers so loud it felt like an earthquake.

The band tore through their set with a ferocity that made it clear they were more than just a group of rock stars, they were survivors, legends who had defied the odds and lived to tell the tale. Perry prowled the stage, his voice raw and electrifying, commanding the attention of every single person in the audience.

Dave's guitar screamed through the night, each riff sharp and deliberate, carrying the weight of decades of evolution. Stephen was locked in, his drumming precise but unrelenting, a force that seemed to push the entire performance forward. And Chris Chaney, ever the quiet anchor, held the rhythm steady with a subtle brilliance that reminded everyone why he was there.

The massive video screens captured every detail, the sweat dripping down Perry's face, the raw intensity in Dave's eyes, the way Stephen's hands blurred over the drums. The audience was mesmerized, their faces lit up with a mixture of awe and sheer joy. They weren't just watching a concert; they were witnessing something profound, a celebration of resilience and artistry.

As the final notes of "Classic Girl" faded into the night, the crowd's cheers reached a crescendo. Perry stood at the edge of the stage, looking out at the sea of faces, his chest rising and falling as he caught his breath.

For a moment, the world seemed to pause. And in that stillness, it was clear to everyone, on stage and off, that this wasn't just another show. This was a testament to the power of music, to the bonds they had forged, and to the simple, undeniable fact that Jane's Addiction still had the ability to captivate, inspire, and transcend.

Family and Heaven's Kind

The sun broke over the Pacific, painting the water in shimmering gold and orange. Perry Farrell stood on the shore, barefoot in the cool morning sand. The years had deepened the lines on his face, but his eyes carried the same vibrant spark, as though some part of him had never left the stage. He watched his 15-year-old son, Hezron, paddling out, scanning the horizon for the perfect wave. The boy moved with an ease that spoke to countless mornings like this, each one quietly stitching together the fabric of their bond.

A swell rose, and Hezron turned, paddling hard before catching the wave and riding it cleanly to shore. His posture was confident but not cocky, his balance smooth, a natural rhythm coursing through him. Perry grinned, clapping as Hezron stepped off the board and dragged it onto the sand.

"Did you see that, Dad?" Hezron called, breathless but beaming.

Perry nodded, his smile stretching wide. "Perfect form, kid. Better than mine already."

Hezron laughed, shaking his head. "Yeah, right. Mom showed me the old videos of you surfing in Hawaii. You looked like you were holding on for dear life."

"That's bullshit, "Perry replied, grinning. "Those waves were twice the size of this one. At least."

"They were smaller, and you know it, "Hezron shot back, grinning as he hauled his board onto the sand.

A few yards down the beach, 13-year-old Izzadore sat cross-legged, his focus entirely on the guitar in his lap. His fingers danced across the frets, experimenting with chords and melodies, his concentration so intense it almost felt contagious. Without looking up, he called out, "Everything was bigger in Dad's stories."

"Smart-ass, "Perry muttered, though his tone was warm. He turned to glance between his sons, the scene filling him with a peace he hadn't known in years. This, this was his life now. The waves, the music, the family. The chaos of the past seemed like a distant echo, muted by peace.

Perry found himself balancing two worlds: the demands of family life and the creative pull of the studio. On one side, he was a devoted father, spending afternoons on the California coast with his boys. On the other side, he was an artist deep in the process of recording *Kind Heaven*, his second solo album. It was a project that consumed him, a sprawling, genre-defying record that blended rock, electronica, orchestral arrangements, and storytelling in ways he hadn't explored before.

By day, Perry was present for his family, helping with school projects, catching waves, and laughing with Etty over dinner. But by night, he retreated to the studio, headphones on, surrounded by vintage gear, chasing the sounds in his head. The music on *Kind Heaven* felt different, more expansive, as if it belonged not just to him but to the dream he was building.

Etty would occasionally join him, sitting quietly on the studio couch, watching as Perry poured himself into the music. She would sometimes tease him about how "intense" he still was.

"You're not 25 anymore, you know, "she said one evening, watching him pace the room, tweaking lyrics.

Perry grinned, glancing at her. "And what exactly is your point?" Smiling, "Maybe not, but the fire's still fuckin' there, E. Just burns a little slower."

She laughed, shaking her head. "That's what I love about you, Perry. You'll never stop."

In the heart of Las Vegas, Perry pitched his vision to a room full of investors. He stood in front of a massive screen displaying 3D renderings of Kind Heaven, a sprawling, immersive entertainment venue that blended music, art, and technology into something entirely new.

He gestured animatedly as he spoke, his passion palpable. "This isn't just another club or theater, "he said, his voice commanding the room's attention. "This is a journey. A place where people can lose themselves in the beauty of sound and light. It's a celebration of the senses, a temple for modern creativity."

The investors exchanged glances, some intrigued, others skeptical. But Perry pressed on, his words weaving a narrative so compelling that even the most doubtful among them found themselves leaning forward in their seats.

By the end of the presentation, the room buzzed with excitement. One investor stood up, clapping slowly, a smile breaking across his face. "Alright, Farrell. You've got something here. Let's talk numbers."

Perry grinned, his confidence unshaken. He could feel it, the dream taking shape, step by step.

The album, *Kind Heaven* was released on June 7, 2019. The record was ambitious and bold, a reflection of Perry's fearless artistic spirit. Reviews were mixed, with some critics praising its boundary-pushing experimentation and others struggling to categorize its eclectic sound. But Perry wasn't chasing accolades, he was chasing creation.

The album's release party was a celebration of both past and future. Held in an intimate venue in Los Angeles, it was attended by old friends, collaborators, and young musicians who'd grown up idolizing Perry. He performed tracks from the album, his voice as commanding as ever. Watching him onstage, Etty couldn't help but feel a sense of pride, knowing how much of himself he'd poured into this record.

By early 2020, Perry was already looking ahead. He'd begun discussions about live performances tied to *Kind Heaven*, with his project, The Kind Heaven Orchestra as well as talks about reviving the larger-than-life, immersive entertainment project in Las Vegas. His days were packed with family, creative meetings, and studio time.

But in February, whispers of a strange new virus began dominating headlines. At first, it seemed distant, a problem far from California. But as March rolled around, those whispers became roars. COVID-19 hit the United States, and by April, the world as Perry knew it had come to a standstill.

The Farrell household, once a revolving door of creative collaborators and buzzing projects, became a bubble. Surf trips were replaced with backyard hangouts, and the home studio became the family's refuge. Hezron, now 15, and Izzadore, 13, spent hours jamming with Perry in the studio, experimenting with sounds, their laughter and clumsy riffs breaking through the heavy silence of quarantine life.

One afternoon, as Izzadore sat behind the drum kit and Hezron strummed Perry's old acoustic guitar, Perry leaned against the control board, watching them with a small smile.

"You know, "he said, arms crossed, "when I was your age, I didn't have all this. I had to scrape by with borrowed equipment and basements."

Hezron smirked, not looking up from his playing. "Yeah, but when you were my age, you were already famous."

Perry laughed, shaking his head. "Fair point, kid. Fair point."

Despite the forced stillness, Perry refused to stop creating. He spent long nights in the studio, crafting songs that captured the strange, surreal moment the world was living through. Some tracks were tender and hopeful; others were filled with the anger and frustration of being locked down.

He found solace in his family, even as the uncertainty of the world pressed in. Etty took on the role of teacher as the boys adjusted to online school, while Perry became the anchor that kept their creative spirits alive.

"What do you think it all means?" Etty asked one evening as they sat on the deck, watching the sunset.

Perry took a sip of wine, gazing at the horizon. "Maybe it's a reset, "he said softly. "A chance to rethink everything. What we value, what we create, how we connect. I don't know… but it feels like we're being forced to slow down for a reason."

Etty nodded, resting her head on his shoulder. "As long as we're together, we'll figure it out."

As the months dragged on, Perry found himself reflecting more and more on his journey, the chaos of Jane's Addiction, the triumphs of Lollapalooza, the dreams he'd chased and the ones that had slipped away. He shared these reflections with his sons, passing down lessons learned from decades of wild highs and crushing lows.

"Dad, "Izzadore asked one evening, pausing mid-drumbeat, "do you ever wish you'd done anything differently?"

Perry leaned back in his chair, considering the question. "Yeah, "he admitted, "but regrets aren't the point. It's what you do with them that matters."

Etty, overhearing, rolled her eyes as she walked into the studio with a tray of tea. "Here we go, "she teased, setting the tray down. "Wisdom from the rock god."

Perry grinned, reaching for a cup. "Hey, I earned it."

Perry leaned back in his chair, in the vast, open yet dimly-lit conference room of Artist Group International. The band had collectively decided to leave William Morris Endeavor. It was nothing against Marc or his team, but Perry needed new direction, as far as his solo career, and upon AGI's pitch to represent the band as a whole as well, they all agreed. AGI's vision and agreements, were what they all felt was best moving forward, both financially and creatively.

Perry sat, twirling the last sip of wine in his glass as he glanced over the paperwork spread across the table. Across from him, Dave was flipping through the contract, brow furrowed, while Stephen stretched out in his seat, arms crossed over his chest. Eric sat quietly, fingers tapping restlessly on the table.

Michael Arfin and Marsha Vlasic sat at the head of the table, their expressions patient but expectant.

"So, this is it?" Perry finally said, setting his glass down. "Artist Group International. You guys are gonna take care of us?"

Michael smiled. "We don't sign bands unless we believe in them. You still have unfinished business. We're here to help you take care of it."

Dave scoffed lightly, shaking his head. "Yea but Mike, we've all heard that one before....more times than I care to recall."

Marsha leaned forward. "Look, Gentlemen, nobody's trying to sell you a dream. We're offering structure, stability. Whatever the hell is next for Jane's Addiction, whatever you guys might cook-up, well...you need the right people behind you. And that's us. I assure you, that's us."

Eric let out a quiet laugh, finally speaking. "Structure, huh? Might be a little late for that."

Perry smirked, running a hand through his hair. "Yeah, well... better late than never."

Stephen nodded, exhaling slowly. "Alright then. Let's do this. I got to pick up my Niece at school."

Perry picked up a pen, twirling it between his fingers for a moment before pressing it to the page. As he signed his name, he glanced at Dave, Eric, and Stephen.

"This is for whatever the hell comes next, "he said.

By late 2021, as vaccines rolled out and the world began to reopen, Perry felt a spark reignite. He began discussing small, socially distanced shows and brainstorming ways to keep the spirit of *Kind Heaven* alive. Jane's Addiction started talks about reuniting for festival appearances, and Perry's heart soared at the thought of being back onstage.

At this time,

One evening, as the family sat around a fire pit on the beach, Hezron strummed the opening chords to "Jane Says." The familiar melody floated on the breeze, and Perry smiled, feeling a sense of peace he hadn't felt in months.

"You know, "he said, looking at his sons, "the world's been through hell, but music… music always finds a way."

Though Kind Heaven dominated much of his attention, Perry never let Jane's fall entirely by the wayside. The band played occasional shows, often in intimate venues where the energy crackled with the same raw intensity as their early days.

One night, in a small, packed club, Perry leaned into the mic, his voice cutting through the noise. "It's been a hell of a ride, "he said, his gaze sweeping over the crowd. "And we're not done yet."

The audience roared, their energy feeding into the band's performance. As the final notes rang out, Perry felt a surge of gratitude. Jane's wasn't just a band, it was a living, breathing piece of his soul.

At home, Izzadore practiced Perry's iconic stage moves in the studio, mimicking his father's swagger with surprising accuracy. Perry watched from the corner, laughing.

"Not bad, kid, "he said, clapping. "But you've got to mean it. The crowd can tell when you're faking it."

Izzadore nodded, adjusting his stance. "Like this?"

"Better, "Perry said, grinning. "You're getting there."

Hezron, meanwhile, had taken an interest in meditation, joining Perry on the beach for morning sessions. They sat cross-legged in the sand, the sound of the waves providing a natural rhythm.

"Still your mind, "Perry said softly, his eyes closed. "Let the world fall away."

Hezron peeked at his dad, a smirk tugging at the corner of his mouth. "Easier said than done."

Perry chuckled, shaking his head. "You'll get there. Just takes practice."

As 2022 approached and the "covid scare" was starting to be a thing of the past, the Farrell family found themselves in a place of balance. The insanity of Perry's early career had given way to something richer, a life where creativity and family coexisted, feeding off each other in a way that felt both natural and hard-earned.

A Pumpkin' s Spirit .

Perry sat in his home studio, surrounded by the warm glow of vintage instruments and the hum of creativity that seemed to live in the walls. He was tinkering with a synthesizer, headphones slung around his neck, completely absorbed in a new melody. The sun peeked through the blinds, casting a soft light over the room, but the tranquility was interrupted by the buzz of his phone on the desk. He glanced over, his curiosity piqued as the name Billy Corgan flashed on the screen.

He chuckled, pulling the headphones off and grabbing the phone. "Billy fuckin' Corgan! What's up, man?"

On the other end, Billy's voice came through, dry and unmistakable. "Perry. You busy saving the world, or can I pitch you something insane?"

Perry laughed, leaning back in his chair. "Always got time for insane. Hit me."

Billy's tone shifted slightly, tinged with excitement. "Alright. You, me. Pumpkins and Jane's Addiction. One tour. One stage. Let's make some noise, buddy."

Perry raised an eyebrow, intrigued. "You want Jane's to support your tour? Man, you don't think we'd ruin the whole idea before the second night?"

Billy let out a dry laugh. "That's the fun part, isn't it? But no, I wouldn't say, 'support us' but more like, well, 'join us.' And sure madness, but controlled madness, Sir. We call it the 'Spirits on Fire tour', cause let's be honest, neither of us has really mellowed out."

Perry leaned forward, his fingers tapping the desk as the name rolled around in his mind. "Spirits on Fire… I like it. North America?"

"Yep, "Billy confirmed. "October and November. Big venues. Big energy. Both bands at their best. We'll kill 'em."

Perry grinned, already envisioning the madness. "Shit, Billy. I don't know whether to hug you or be terrified. The thing is… 'the guys.' I gotta talk those cats into it, brother." He pauses, stands up, "And Michelle? Mike? What does AIG think? Have your folks talked to these cats?

Billy laughed again, this time more knowingly. "Look, Perry. I, uh… I already talked to Dave and Stephen. They're in. Eric? Not sure yet. Your management is in talks with mine, but I wanted to gauge your interest first, pal. And here's the thing, it'll be huge. More importantly and frankly, honestly, I'd be honored, buddy. You know how much Janes means to Pumpkins and well… I want you on this. Are you in?"

Perry let out a long sigh, rubbing his temple as he processed the offer. "Jesus, man, you've been fucking busy." He paused, the weight of the decision hanging in the air. "If I say yes, you better be ready to keep the fuck up. You know Jane's doesn't hold back."

Billy's voice turned serious, but there was a playful edge. "Perry, my man, I wouldn't have called you if I wasn't ready to go to war."

A smirk tugged at Perry's lips. "Alright then. Spirits on Fire. Let's set this thing ablaze."

They both laughed, the kind of laughter that came from two legends who knew exactly what kind of storm they were about to unleash. As the call ended, Perry leaned back in his chair, staring at the ceiling, a spark of excitement igniting within him.

"Guess I got a call to make, "he muttered to himself, sighing deeply. "Fuck… Eric."

Three weeks later, Perry found himself back on the airwaves, this time sitting in front of a mic in the Howard Stern studio. Howard, Billy and Perry all go way back and the energy in the room was fun and silly…as always.

Howard leaned in, his sharp eyes darting between Perry and Billy, who sat side by side, exuding a calm confidence that only came from decades in the spotlight.

Howard grinned. "We've got two absolute legends here today, Billy Corgan and Perry Farrell. And from what I hear, you've got something big to announce. Don't keep us waiting, what's the deal?"

Billy leaned into the mic, his tone steady but brimming with anticipation. "Alright, Howard, here it is. This fall, The Smashing Pumpkins and Jane's Addiction are teaming up for the Spirits on Fire tour."

Howard's eyebrows shot up in surprise. "No shit? Both of you? Together? That's fuckin' massive!"

Perry, his trademark smirk firmly in place, leaned closer to the mic. "It's been a long time coming, man. Two bands, one tour. It's gonna be raw, it's gonna be loud, and it's going to blow some fucking minds. And hopefully, you know, spread a little love around. Some happiness, God-willing.

Howard laughed, shaking his head. "So, who closes? You or Billy?"

Billy shrugged with a sly grin. "We might be switching it up, night to night. Haven't really gotten to that point, but no egos. Its just two bands doing they're thing together. Its Just music."

Howard rolled his eyes. "No egos? Yeah, right. You two fucking guys? C'mon."

Perry leaned in, his smirk turning into a full grin. "Hey Howard, this isn't a dick-measuring contest. We're here to put on a show people will never forget."

The interview went on for hours with Billy expressing the influence of Janes on the Pumpkins and himself, while Perry expressed his admiration for Billy's musical talent and how honored he was to be asked to join the Smashing Pumpkins on the tour.

Finally, as Howard's laughter filled the studio, "Alright, alright. Spirits on Fire. Big venues, two iconic bands. All four original members of Jane's Addiction back onstage for the first time in 13 years. Yes, that means Eric Avery as well. Tickets are gonna no doubt, sell like fuckin' crazy folks. Anything else you want to say before we wrap?"

Perry's tone turned serious as he addressed the mic. "Just this: If you've ever felt like rock's been missing something, especially lately, come out to the gig. We're bringing all the magic, the passion…you know? All that good stuff. We're fucking bringing it all back, Howard."

Billy nodded, his expression sincere. "Couldn't have said it better."

Howard leaned back in his chair, a grin plastered on his face. "Ladies and gentlemen, Billy Corgan and Perry Farrell. Spirits on Fire. Don't miss it."

As the segment ended, the energy in the room was electric. Perry and Billy exchanged a look, a silent understanding passing between them. They weren't just planning a tour, they were planning a fucking revival.

Dave sat hunched on the edge of his couch, the phone gripped tightly in his hand, his leg bouncing with nervous energy. The room was dim, the faint glow of a lamp catching the edge of his untouched guitar leaning against the wall. He'd been staring at the phone for ten minutes, rehearsing what to say, willing the right words to come. Finally, he took a deep breath and dialed.

After a few rings, Perry Farrell's voice answered, full of its usual buoyant energy.

"Davey! What's up, brother?" Perry's tone immediately lifted the room, but it only made Dave's stomach tighten.

"Hey, man, "Dave said quietly, his voice almost a whisper. "Got some shit - news."

Perry's mood shifted in an instant, the warmth in his voice replaced by concern. "What's going on?"

Dave exhaled heavily, running a hand through his hair. "Doctor says I've got… 'long-haul COVID.'" He forced the words out, his voice flat, like saying it would make it more real.

There was silence on the other end of the line. Perry didn't respond right away, and when he did, his voice was soft, deliberate.

"…Shit, Dave." He paused. "Nevermind the fucking tour, are you gonna be okay?"

Dave let out a bitter laugh, one that didn't reach his eyes. "Yeah… I mean, fuck, I don't know. But no tour for me. I can't do it, man. I'm fucking sorry, Per."

Perry sighed, the sound heavy with both disappointment and understanding. "Hey, man, get the hell outta here. It's alright. We'll figure something out." He paused, his tone softening. "You just focus on getting better, okay?"

"It's not just the tour, man, "Dave said, his voice cracking slightly. "It's… everything. This isn't just me being out for a couple of weeks. It's fucking scary, Perry."

"I know, man. I know." Perry's voice was quiet now, laced with worry.

The silence stretched between them, thick with the weight of the news. Neither of them spoke for a long moment, both processing what this meant, not just for the tour, but for Dave.

"But listen, "Perry finally said, breaking the silence. His voice was steady now, almost commanding. "You're still part of this. No matter what. You hear me, Dave? You're still part of this band. You always will be."

Dave choked out a weak laugh, his voice tinged with emotion. "Yeah, well, someone's gotta play the damn guitar."

Perry's tone shifted, snapping into action mode. "Don't you worry about that. I'll make a call."

"Who you thinking?" Dave asked, a mix of curiosity and resignation in his voice.

"Josh, "Perry said immediately. "Josh Klinghoffer."

"Josh? From Chili Peppers?"

"Yeah, man. That kid's a fucking machine. He's a true musician, Davey. And he's got heart. He'll hold it down while you get back on your feet."

Dave let out a deep breath, relief mingling with the ache of stepping aside. "Thanks, Perry."

"Don't thank me yet, "Perry said, a small grin creeping into his voice. "You just focus on kicking this thing's ass. And when you're ready… you come back swinging, alright?"

"Alright, "Dave murmured, his voice steadier now. "I'll hold you to that."

"Good, "Perry said firmly. "Now get some fucking rest, man. Call me if you need anything."

"Will do, "Dave replied, a faint smile tugging at his lips.

As the call ended, Dave sat back on the couch, staring at the guitar in the corner. For the first time in weeks, he felt a flicker of hope. Meanwhile, Perry leaned back in his chair, already scrolling through his contacts. He'd make this work, he always did. But his mind never left Dave, his brother, his band mate, and the battle he was about to fight.

An hour later, Perry was pacing the room, his phone clutched tightly to his ear. The desk was a complete mess of scattered papers, guitar picks, and scribbled notes, while a faint, unfinished track played softly in the background. He ran a hand through his hair as the line rang, his mind racing with a thousand thoughts.

Finally, Josh Klinghoffer's voice came through, casual and warm, carrying a calm that Perry envied in the moment.

"Perry! Been a while. What's up, man?"

Without preamble, Perry launched straight in. "Josh, I need a favor. A big one."

Josh laughed lightly, but there was a trace of curiosity in his tone. "Uh-oh. What kind of favor?"

Perry stopped pacing, gripping the phone a little tighter. "Dave's out. Long-haul COVID. He can't tour."

The line went quiet for a moment before Josh's voice returned, filled with concern. "Shit. How's he holding up?"

"Not great, "Perry admitted, his voice quieter now, the weight of it all pressing down on him. "But we've got a tour lined up. It's huge, Josh. And I need someone who can step in. Someone who can do Dave's parts justice."

Josh didn't respond immediately, and Perry could almost hear the gears turning in his head. "You're asking me to fill in for Navarro?" Josh finally said, his tone tinged with both surprise and hesitation.

"Yeah, "Perry said, exhaling slowly. "I know it's a lot. But you're one of the few people who can handle it. You've got the chops, the vibe… and you're already family."

Josh was quiet for a moment, the gravity of the ask washing over him. Finally, he sighed, his voice calm but resolute. "Alright, Perry. I'm in."

Perry let out a breath he hadn't realized he'd been holding, a wave of relief washing over him. "Fuckin' knew I could count on you, "he said, a grin spreading across his face for the first time that day.

Josh chuckled softly. "Shit, man, I owe you. Big time."

Perry laughed, the tension in his voice easing. "Nah, *I* owe you. Thanks, Josh. Really."

As Perry ended the call, he leaned back in his chair, exhaling deeply. His eyes drifted to a framed photo on the wall of Jane's Addiction in their prime, the four of them standing together, a reminder of the legacy they'd built.

The studio was alive with kinetic energy, the faint hum of amps warming up mingling with the sound of instruments being tuned. Josh stood in the center of the room, guitar in hand, his posture relaxed but focused. Stephen sat behind the drum kit, tapping lightly on a tom as he adjusted his stool. Eric was fiddling with his bass, tightening a string with practiced precision. Perry leaned against the wall, arms crossed, his eyes fixed on Josh with a mixture of nervous energy and hope.

Josh glanced at Stephen, a small smile tugging at the corner of his mouth. "Alright, let's start with 'Mountain Song, '" he said, his voice calm but firm.

Stephen grinned, twirling a drumstick in his fingers. "Let's see what you've got, man."

Josh nodded, adjusting the strap on his guitar. Then, without hesitation, he launched into the opening riff. The sound was crisp, powerful, and unmistakably Jane's Addiction. Perry's face lit up immediately, a grin spreading as the room seemed to come alive.

As Stephen and Eric joined in, the music swelled, filling the space with a raw energy that felt almost electric. Josh's playing was confident and fluid, his fingers moving across the fret board with ease. Perry couldn't help but half-shout over the music, his voice filled with a mixture of pride and excitement. "Knew you were the guy for the job!"

The song built, the band locking into a groove that felt natural, almost effortless. For the first time in weeks, the weight that had been pressing on Perry's shoulders seemed to lift, replaced by a renewed sense of purpose.

As the final notes rang out, the room fell silent for a brief moment, the air heavy with the kind of magic that only came from truly great music.

Stephen leaned back on his stool, grinning. "Well, shit. I think we're gonna be just fine."

Josh smirked, his eyes glancing at Perry. "Think Navarro'll be pissed I'm stealing his thunder?"

Perry laughed, shaking his head. "Nah. He'll be proud as hell when he sees this."

The tension that had lingered since Dave's news melted away, replaced by something stronger, determination. Perry knew they still had mountains to climb, but for the first time in a while, it felt like they had the tools to make it to the top.

The consistent sound of tires on the road was a steady rhythm beneath the conversation inside the bus. Perry sat at the small kitchenette, flipping through a notebook filled with scribbled set-lists and ideas. Across from him, Josh tinkered with his guitar, playing a quiet riff under his breath.

Stephen leaned against the counter, a cup of coffee in hand. "You know, I wasn't sure how this was gonna work, "he admitted, his voice thoughtful. "But... damn, Josh. You're killing it."

Josh looked up, smiling faintly. "Thanks, man. Means a lot coming from you guys."

Perry closed his notebook, looking around at his band-mates. "We're gonna fucking own this tour, "he said, his voice carrying a quiet confidence.

Stephen raised his cup in a mock toast. "Damn right we are."

As the bus rolled on into the night, the band sat together, their bond stronger than ever. The road ahead wasn't easy, but for the first time in a long time, it felt like they were ready for whatever came their way.

The podcast studio was a small, intimate space, lined with vinyl records and posters of legendary bands. Perry Farrell sat across from the host, his energy electric, a pair of headphones perched over his wild, untamed hair. The host leaned forward, clutching a coffee mug, his eyes wide with admiration as he soaked in the presence of the rock legend sitting across from him.

"So, Perry, "the host began, his voice laced with excitement, "let's talk about the tour. How's it been working with Josh Klinghoffer?"

Perry grinned, leaning back in his chair, his posture relaxed but his words charged with sincerity. "Oh man, where do I start?" He shook his head, smiling as if replaying the entire experience in his mind. "Josh has been... I mean, he's a goddamn inspiration. He's not just a musician, he's a true musician. You throw him into any situation, any genre, and the guy just fucking gets it."

The host raised an eyebrow, impressed. "That's high praise, especially coming from you."

"It's the truth, "Perry said, his grin widening. "Look, when Dave had to sit this one out, we were in a tough spot. And I mean tough. But Josh stepped in like he'd been playing these songs his whole life. And it's not just about him replicating Dave's parts, he's making them his own while still respecting the band's legacy."

The host nodded, clearly intrigued. "That's gotta be a tough act to follow, though. I mean, Navarro is iconic."

"Absolutely, "Perry replied, tilting his head thoughtfully. His voice softened, tinged with emotion. "But Josh has this… grace, you know? He's been a godsend, especially with everything going on. He's kept the flame alive while Dave's been working his ass off to get back."

The host leaned in, his curiosity growing. "How's Dave doing? I know this has been tough for him."

Perry exhaled deeply, his expression a mix of pride and concern. "Man, Dave is fighting. Every time I talk to him, he's got his guitar in hand, relearning all the old parts, pushing himself harder than I've ever seen. It's fucking inspiring, you know? He's not the kind of guy who gives up."

Dave Navarro sat in his home studio, the dim glow of a desk lamp illuminating the cluttered space. Amps and pedals were scattered across the floor, a well-worn guitar perched on his lap. His brow glistened with sweat as his fingers moved over the fret board, struggling through the riff of "Three Days."

The familiar notes faltered, a sour chord ringing out, and Dave cursed under his breath, slamming his hand against the strings in frustration.

"Come on… come the fuck on, "he muttered, his voice low and filled with determination.

He took a deep breath, shaking out his hands, and started again. This time, the notes came out smoother, but his expression remained tense. A stack of handwritten notes lay beside him, scribbled reminders like "Slow it down" and "Focus on transitions" staring back at him like a to-do list from hell.

Pausing, Dave reached for his phone and opened a video of Jane's Addiction performing live. The camera lingered on his younger self, commanding the stage, his playing effortless and raw. He stared at the screen, his jaw tightening, a mixture of longing and frustration etched across his face.

"I'm getting back, "he whispered to himself, his voice barely audible but laced with conviction. "I'm fucking getting back."

Setting the phone down, he picked up the guitar again, his hands steadier this time. The notes came together, piece by piece, the melody rebuilding itself like a muscle slowly regaining strength.

In the sleek, modern recording studio, the atmosphere buzzed with energy. Perry stood in the vocal booth, headphones on, his body swaying slightly as he adjusted the mic. In the control room, Stephen and Eric tuned their instruments while Josh leaned back, casually strumming his guitar.

The door creaked open, and Dave walked in, guitar case slung over his shoulder. He looked stronger than he had in months, his presence instantly shifting the room's energy.

Perry glanced up from the booth, a grin spreading across his face. "Well, look who decided to join us!"

Dave smirked, setting his case down. "Miss me already, huh?"

Stephen grinned from behind the kit. "Hell yeah, man. About time."

Dave plugged in his guitar, adjusting the strap across his shoulder. Josh leaned over, a mischievous glint in his eye. "No pressure, "he said, smirking, "but I already nailed all your parts."

The room erupted in laughter, the tension breaking as Dave flipped him off with a grin. "Yeah, yeah, "Dave shot back. "Let's see if you can handle this."

He launched into the opening riff of "True Love, "the band's new song. The notes rang out, raw and emotional, filling the studio with a sound that was unmistakably Jane's Addiction. The rest of the band joined in, the music building into something powerful and undeniable.

In the vocal booth, Perry closed his eyes, his voice cutting through the track with raw intensity.

"True love… it's a fire that never dies…"

The song reached its crescendo, the chemistry between the band crackling like electricity. As the final note faded, the room fell silent for a moment, everyone catching their breath.

"Holy shit, "Stephen muttered, his voice low but filled with awe. "That's it."

Eric grinned, leaning back in his chair. "That's the one, guys."

Perry stepped out of the booth, wiping sweat from his forehead. He looked at the band, his gaze steady. "Alright, "he said, his voice firm. "Spirits on Fire is almost wrapped. After that… 2024. All four of us. Reunion tour."

The suggestion hung, the idea of it sinking in. Dave looked up from his guitar, his eyes locking with Perry's.

"You serious?" he asked, his tone cautious but hopeful.

"Dead fucking serious, "Perry replied without hesitation.

Josh leaned back, a smile tugging at his lips. "Well, "he said, smirking, "I guess I'll be in the crowd for that one."

"Hell no, "Perry shot back, grinning. "You're family now. You're coming with us on this road trip. I mean, if you want. We'd love to have you Josh. You've been a fucking life-saver. Come on."

The band laughed, the tension breaking as the room filled with excitement. For the first time in years, the future felt bright, the promise of what was to come lighting a fire none of them could ignore.

The arena pulsed with life, a sold-out crowd of thousands roaring as Jane's Addiction took the stage for the final night of the Spirits on Fire tour. Perry Farrell stood front and center, commanding the crowd like a shaman, his voice rising over the deafening cheers. Eric Avery's bass rumbled through the venue, locking into a tight groove with Stephen Perkins' thunderous drumming. The rhythm was hypnotic, primal, the foundation of the band's unmistakable sound. Josh Klinghoffer, filling in for Dave Navarro, tore into the opening riff of "True Love, "playing with precision and heart, adding his own flare while respecting the song's spirit.

Perry leaned into the mic, sweat glistening on his face as he belted out the lyrics. His energy was contagious, electrifying the already ecstatic crowd. The fans screamed along, arms raised, their voices merging into one as the band delivered a performance that felt raw, triumphant, and cathartic.

Backstage, Dave Navarro stood in the shadows, watching from the wings. His hair was pulled back, and though he looked stronger than he had in months, his hands rested on the cane he occasionally used to steady himself. He nodded along to the music, a small smile tugging at the corners of his mouth. Despite not being onstage, he was proud. Proud of the band, proud of Perry for holding it all together, and proud of Josh for stepping into an impossible role and making it his own.

The crowd erupted as the song ended, their cheers shaking the rafters. Perry turned to face his band-mates, giving them a nod of approval before stepping back to address the audience.

"How we doing tonight, Los Angeles?" he shouted, his voice echoing through the venue. The response was deafening. "I gotta say… This tour, this moment, it's been fucking unreal. And we couldn't have done it without you crazy bastards."

The crowd roared again, their love for the band palpable. Perry looked over at Eric, who gave him a small, knowing grin. It had been a long journey to get the original members of Jane's Addiction back together, and tonight, it all felt worth it.

The celebration after the show was as electric as the performance itself. Backstage, the band gathered in a private room with their families, close friends, and Billy Corgan, who had joined them for the tour. Champagne flowed freely, and the air buzzed with the kind of energy that only comes from the culmination of something extraordinary.

Perry leaned against a table, holding a glass of champagne, his arm slung casually around Etty. Across the room, Stephen and Eric stood together, laughing as they recounted tour mishaps. Josh was off to the side, quietly strumming an acoustic guitar, while Dave sat on a couch, his fiancée beside him, a relaxed smile on his face.

Billy approached Perry, holding a whiskey glass. "Hell of a way to close it out, "he said, clinking his glass against Perry's.

Perry grinned. "Yeah, it felt right. Thanks for dreaming this up, Billy. You really kicked us in the ass."

Billy smirked, taking a sip. "Hey, I just lit the fire. You guys are the ones who burned the fucking playground down."

Eric wandered over, overhearing the comment. "It was chaos, "he said with a wry smile. "But the good kind."

Billy nodded. "Controlled chaos. That's what makes it great."

Etty joined in, freshly-showered, smiling warmly. "It's been a trip watching you guys out there. You still have that magic, you know."

Perry kissed her cheek. "We've still got a few tricks left."

As the group continued to laugh and reminisce, Dave tapped his cane lightly against the floor to get everyone's attention. "Alright, alright, "he said, standing with a little effort but a lot of determination. "I just want to say something."

The room quieted, all eyes on him.

"You know, sitting this one out fucking sucked, "Dave began, his voice steady but emotional. "But watching you guys… Watching Josh… It reminded me why we do this. Why we've kept coming back to it, despite all the bullshit. It's because what we've built is bigger than any of us. And I can't wait to be back up there with you."

The room broke into applause, cheers of support echoing through the space. Perry raised his glass. "To Dave, "he said. "And to our future."

Everyone raised their glasses, the toast carrying a sense of hope and camaraderie.

Perry sat in his home office; the room quiet except for the faint hum of the city outside. A glass of wine sat on the desk beside him as he scrolled through mock-up ads for the band's 2024 reunion tour. The names stared back at him: Perry Farrell. Dave Navarro. Eric Avery. Stephen Perkins. For the first time in thirteen years, the original lineup would take the stage together.

Etty walked in, leaning against the door-frame. "Big plans?" she asked, her tone soft but teasing.

Perry looked up, a grin breaking across his face. "The biggest."

"You ready for this?" she asked, stepping closer.

Perry leaned back in his chair, exhaling deeply. "I've been ready for thirteen fucking years."

Etty smiled, placing a hand on his shoulder. "Then let's make it count."

Perry nodded, the weight of the past replaced by a renewed sense of purpose. The future stretched out before him, and for the first time in a long time, it felt limitless.

Imminent Redemption.

The small stage outside the venue was flanked by reporters, cameras flashing incessantly as the crowd of fans nearby cheered and clapped. Perry Farrell stepped up to the mic, dressed sharply but still carrying his signature edge. The rest of the band stood behind him, Dave Navarro, Eric Avery, and Stephen Perkins, all looking poised but relaxed, their camaraderie palpable.

Perry leaned into the microphone, his voice steady but charged with emotion. "It's been over a decade since the four of us made something new together. But here we are. A new album, a new tour, and the same spirit that's carried us through every fucking up and down."

The gathered press applauded loudly, flashes illuminating the band's faces as Perry stepped back slightly, giving Dave the floor. Dave moved forward, his expression calm but his voice carrying a quiet confidence.

"We're not just back, "Dave said, his words deliberate. "I think, I believe, we're better."

Eric crossed his arms, smirking slightly as he muttered just loud enough for the mic to catch, "Don't get cocky."

The crowd laughed, and even Dave cracked a smile, shaking his head.

Perry glanced back at his band-mates, his grin widening. "You hear that, folks? This is why it's taken us thirteen years."

The laughter rippled through the audience as the band exchanged glances, their bond evident in the shared humor.

A journalist raised their voice from the crowd. "Can fans expect a new album?"

Perry leaned back into the mic, his eyes gleaming. "Expect the unexpected. It's Jane's Addiction, after all. We're bringing everything we've got, our sound, our souls, and we're putting it all on the line. It's going to be raw. It's going to be real. And it's going to fucking rock."

The crowd burst into applause again, a mix of excitement and admiration filling the space as photographers leaned in to capture the band's energy.

The press event wrapped, the band retreating backstage to a quieter room. The energy of the announcement still lingered, but the atmosphere had shifted, less public, more personal. Perry paced slightly, a bottle of water in hand, while Eric leaned against a table, arms crossed.

"That went well, "Stephen said, plopping onto a couch and stretching his legs. "No one asked any stupid shit."

"Yeah, "Eric added dryly, "which is a miracle considering it's us."

Perry chuckled, turning to face them. "You know why? Because we've still got it. People fucking love us."

Dave, who had been quiet, sat down next to Stephen, resting his elbows on his knees. "They do. But that doesn't mean this is going to be easy. The fans have expectations. Big ones."

Perry shrugged, his grin unshaken. "Good. Let's give 'em a reason to keep those expectations high."

Eric tilted his head, his voice steady but thoughtful. "Just as long as we don't burn ourselves out trying to prove something."

His comment was a subtle reminder of the band's history, the highs, the crashes, and the resilience it took to get to this point.

Perry raised his bottle, breaking the tension with a smile. "To us. To the album. And to the most kick-ass tour this band's ever fucking done."

The others lifted whatever was in their hands, water bottles, coffee cups, even a pack of drumsticks, and tapped them together.

"To us, "Dave echoed, a rare softness in his voice.

"To us, "Eric and Stephen repeated, their voices overlapping.

The moment was brief but grounding, a quiet acknowledgment of everything they'd survived, and everything they still had left to do.

The noise of the crowd at Atlantic Union Bank Pavilion had barely subsided as the band stumbled offstage, sweat-drenched and riding the adrenaline high of their first show on the 2024 reunion tour. In the corner of the green room, Perry Farrell grabbed a bottle of wine, twisting the cap off with practiced ease. He drank deeply, his face flushed, eyes glittering with a mix of exhaustion and exhilaration.

Dave Navarro watched from across the room, his jaw tightening as Perry took another swig. He walked over, his frustration barely contained.

"Maybe slow down, man, "Dave said, his tone sharp but not unkind. "You're gonna burn out before we're halfway through this."

Perry turned, his sneer immediate and defensive. "Don't start with that shit, Dave. I'm giving people a show. I'm doing my fucking part."

"There's a difference between living and… whatever the hell this is, "Dave shot back, his voice tight.

Perry laughed bitterly, stepping closer. "Is that what Vanessa's been telling you? Look, brother, it's me. You know I love you. We're brothers, David. We always have been. Just… just get through this with me, okay? Like the ol' days?"

Dave's face hardened, his voice dropping. "I'll get through it, Perry, because it's my JOB. It's called balance, 'Brother.' Not that you'd know much about it."

Perry chuckled darkly, brushing past him, but the tension in the room lingered, thick and heavy.

Dave sat on the edge of his hotel bed, the room dimly lit except for the glow of his phone screen. Vanessa Dubasso's face filled the display, her expression a mix of concern and warmth as they Face-timed.

"You look tired, honey, "Vanessa said softly. "Everything okay?"

Dave forced a smile, but the fatigue in his eyes betrayed him. "Yeah… it's good. The shows are great. Just… Perry's been pushing it. I don't know if he'll hold up."

Vanessa sighed, shaking her head. "Dave, sweetie, I know you love him. I do too. And I get it, Perry is fucking awesome. Remember, I was a fan before I met you." She laughed lightly, but her tone quickly grew serious. "I just want you to come back in one piece. That's all. I need you here, too."

Dave's gaze softened, a mix of guilt and longing in his expression. "Look, physically I'm feeling great, and I miss you every day. This will be over before you know it."

As the call ended, Dave sat in silence, the weight of his words, and the tour, pressing down on him.

Another night, another show, another stumble backstage for Perry. His steps were uneven, his face drawn, hands shaking slightly as he reached for another drink. Eric Avery intercepted him, his expression tight with concern.

"Perry, this has to stop, "Eric said firmly, his voice low but carrying authority. "You're barely holding it together out there."

Perry rolled his eyes, brushing him off. "What are you, my babysitter now?"

Eric's jaw clenched, his frustration bubbling over. "Just trying to keep this from fucking blowing up in our faces, man."

Perry turned, his glare sharp and defensive. "I don't need a damn lecture. Just let me do my thing."

Eric stepped back, exhaling sharply, his voice tinged with exasperation. "Your 'thing' is screwing us all, Perry."

He walked away, leaving Perry swaying alone, the weight of his choices settling over him for a fleeting moment before he took another drink.

The polished morning show set gleamed under bright studio lights, the air buzzing with energy. Producers darted around the room, giving last-minute instructions to the camera crew, while Perry Farrell sat across from the host, leaning comfortably in his chair. His signature charm radiated through his weary frame, and despite the toll of the tour, his energy remained magnetic.

The host, a polished man in his forties with a sharp suit and a warm smile, adjusted his earpiece and leaned forward. "Perry, your latest single, 'Imminent Redemption, ' has been making waves. Critics are calling it raw, intense, and some of your best work in years. What can you tell us about it?"

Perry tilted his head, letting the question linger as he considered his answer. His fingers tapped lightly on the arm of the chair, keeping rhythm with a beat only he could hear. "It's about rebirth, "he said finally, his voice calm but charged with meaning. "About finding clarity in chaos. We've all been through some shit these past few years, pandemics, distance, loss. 'Imminent Redemption' is about walking through that fire and coming out the other side, scarred but alive."

The host nodded, visibly impressed. "And musically, it feels like classic Jane's but also… different. There's a new edge to it, a weight that feels deeply personal."

Perry smiled, leaning forward now, his voice more animated. "That's because it is personal. When we started writing this track, we weren't just jamming for the sake of it. Every note, every lyric came from someplace real. Eric laid down this bass-line that hit like a punch to the gut, and Stephen, "Perry paused, shaking his head in admiration, ", Stephen brought this primal, almost tribal rhythm. And then Dave, man… Dave came in like he had something to prove. You can feel the fight in every riff he plays on this one."

The host raised a curious eyebrow. "And where were you in all this?"

Perry grinned. "Me? I was trying to keep up with these ultra-talented cats, man, "he said with a laugh. "But seriously, I wanted the lyrics to cut deep, to be honest about the struggle and the hope. 'Imminent Redemption' isn't just a song; it's a statement. It's saying, 'Yeah, we've been knocked down, but we're still here.'"

The band's tour bus was quiet, the kind of silence that wasn't peaceful but heavy, like the air before a storm. They were parked in a lot near Pier 17 in New York City, the skyline sprawling out in the distance. Inside, Stephen Perkins sat at the small kitchenette table, absentmindedly tapping a drumstick against his thigh. Across from him, Eric Avery was scrolling through his phone, his face set in a grim expression.

"Jesus Christ, "Eric muttered, breaking the silence.

Stephen looked up, eyebrows raised. "What now?"

Eric turned his phone toward Stephen, showing him the screen. It was a thread on Reddit, filled with comments dissecting the previous night's performance. "What happened to Perry?" one post read. Another: "Jane's Addiction isn't Jane's anymore. This is just sad."

Stephen sighed, rubbing his temples. "Fuck me."

The door at the back of the bus opened, and Dave Navarro stepped in, his guitar slung over his shoulder. He looked at the two of them, then at the phone in Eric's hand. "I don't even need to ask, do I?"

Stephen shook his head. "It's bad, man. Last night was a train-wreck. Fans are losing their shit online."

Dave threw his guitar onto the couch and flopped down next to it, running a hand through his hair. "They're not wrong. Perry was... I don't even know what the fuck he was doing. Singing choruses during verses, missing cues, stumbling all over the place."

Eric leaned back in his chair, his expression dark. "This isn't just 'Perry being Perry.' Something's wrong."

Perry sat alone in the dressing room, staring at his reflection in the mirror. His face was pale, his eyes bloodshot. A bottle of water sat untouched on the table in front of him, next to a crumpled set-list from the night before. He could hear muffled voices outside the door, his band-mates, no doubt talking about him. He knew he'd fucked up. He could feel it in every fiber of his being. But instead of facing it, he leaned back in his chair, closing his eyes, trying to shut it all out.

The door creaked open, and Stephen stepped in, his expression a mix of concern and frustration. "Hey, man. You got a minute?"

Perry opened one eye, his voice flat. "If this is about last night, save it."

Stephen didn't move, crossing his arms. "It's not just about last night, Perry. It's about this whole fucking tour."

Perry sat up, glaring at him. "What the hell is that supposed to mean?"

Stephen took a deep breath, trying to keep his cool. "It means you're off, Per. And I don't mean a little off, I mean really fucking off. The fans see it. We see it. And we're worried."

Perry snorted, shaking his head. "Oh, you're worried? That's rich."

Stephen's patience snapped. "Yeah, we're worried, Perry! Because this band isn't just about you. We're out there every night, busting our asses, and you're… I don't even know what the fuck you're doing anymore."

Perry stood up, his chair scraping loudly against the floor. "I'm doing my job, Stephen. I'm giving people a goddamn show." He pauses, looks at everyone, the mumbles, "doesn't fucking help that the sound monitors are off! Constantly!"

Stephen stepped closer, his voice dropping. "Don't give us that bullshit! No, what you're giving is a disaster. And if you keep this up, there won't be a show left to give."

Later that night, the entire band sat together in the lounge area of the bus. The air was thick with tension. Eric was on one end of the couch, arms crossed, while Dave sat on the other, staring at Perry, who was slouched in the middle seat. Stephen leaned against the kitchenette counter, his arms folded.

Dave broke the silence first, his voice low but firm. "Alright, Perry. We need to talk."

Perry rolled his eyes. "Oh, great. An intervention. Just what I fucking needed."

Dave leaned forward, his elbows on his knees. "This isn't a joke, man. Last night… the fans noticed. They're talking about it. And not in a good way."

Perry waved a dismissive hand. "Fans are always talking shit. That's nothing new."

Eric, who had been quiet until now, finally spoke up, his tone sharp. "They're not just talking shit, Perry. They're saying they don't even recognize the band anymore, man. We've always been about the kids…the fans. I just, I can't let them down again. Ok?!"

Perry flinched at that, but his expression hardened. "I'm doing the best I fucking can, alright? You think this shit is easy?"

Stephen pushed off the counter, stepping closer. "No one said it's easy, but we're all out there giving 110%. We need you to meet us halfway, man."

Perry's voice rose, defensive. "I'm carrying this fucking band! I'm the one they come to see. Not you, not Eric, not Dave, me."

Dave's eyes narrowed, his voice cold. "That's bullshit, and you know it. This band is all of us. Always has been. And if you keep going like this, you're gonna destroy everything we've built."

The room went silent, the weight of the conflict was uncomfortable and tense. Perry looked around at his band-mates, his defiance wavering for just a moment. But instead of responding, he stood up abruptly and left the room, slamming the door behind him.

Perry sat on the edge of his bed, staring at his phone. He opened Instagram and scrolled through comments under a video clip from the previous night's show. "What the hell happened to Perry?" one comment read. "This isn't Jane's Addiction. This is a mess." Another: "I paid $200 for this? Never again."

He threw the phone onto the bed, burying his face in his hands. For the first time in a long time, the weight of his actions hit him. He wasn't just letting himself down, he was letting the band down, the fans down, everyone who had believed in him.

The band gathered in a small rehearsal space, the atmosphere tense but determined. Perry walked in last, his face pale but resolute.

"Alright, "he said, his voice quieter than usual. "Let's figure this shit out."

Eric exchanged a glance with Dave, who gave a small nod. It wasn't much, but it was a start. They picked up their instruments, the first notes of "Three Days" filling the room. The music was raw, imperfect and not "Jane's." Not by any means.

The curtains in the hotel suite were half-drawn, letting in just enough sunlight to bathe the room in a soft glow. The space was cluttered with the remnants of late-night brainstorming, scattered notebooks, an open laptop, and a nearly empty bottle of wine on the coffee table. Etty stood at the kitchenette counter, focused on frothing almond milk for her morning coffee. She moved with precision, her robe loosely tied around her waist, her hair pulled into a messy bun.

Perry sat at the small dining table nearby, staring into his half-full glass of wine. His hands drummed idly on the table, a nervous energy radiating from him. He looked up at Etty, his voice cutting through the quiet.

"I'm worried, babe." He swirled the wine in his glass before taking a sip, the words hanging in the air. "The sound, the production, the band, it's all off. Like… everything's unraveling."

Etty glanced over her shoulder, her brow furrowing as she studied him. "What do you mean? What's unraveling?"

Perry sighed, running a hand through his already-messy hair. "I mean us. The shows. Me." He gestured toward his glass with a self-deprecating chuckle. "This. I've been… self-medicating again. I think. Fuck, I know."

Etty set the milk brother down and turned to face him, arms crossed over her chest. "You're drinking wine at eleven in the morning, Perry. That's not thinking, that's knowing."

He winced but didn't argue. Instead, he took another swig, his expression distant. "I'm serious, Ett. Something's not right. I'm losing my grip on this whole thing."

Before Etty could respond, their oldest son, Hezron, padded into the room, still rubbing the sleep from his eyes. His hair stuck up in wild directions, and he wore an oversized T-shirt and sweats. He glanced between his parents, instantly picking up on the tension.

"Morning, "Hezron mumbled, heading straight for the fridge. He pulled out a bottle of orange juice and poured himself a glass before joining them at the table. "What's going on?"

Etty shot Perry a pointed look, one that clearly said, Your turn. Perry exhaled sharply, leaning back in his chair.

"Just… band stuff, "Perry said vaguely, avoiding his son's gaze.

Hezron raised an eyebrow, unimpressed. "You mean the band or you?"

Perry's eyes flicked to Etty, who gave him a small nod of encouragement. He turned back to his son, swallowing hard. "Me. Mostly me."

Hezron leaned back in his chair, sipping his juice. "Yeah, no offense, Dad, but… you look like shit lately."

Etty stifled a laugh, covering her mouth, while Perry groaned, running a hand down his face. "Thanks for the brutal honesty, kid."

"I'm just saying, "Hezron continued, shrugging. "You've been acting…well, 'strange.'. Everyone can see it. Even Uncle Dave said that…"

Perry looked at him sharply and cut him off. "Uncle Dave said something? (sarcastically) You think? Trust me, son, he's….they all have made me aware. Hence my concern. "

Hezron nodded. "Not to me. I mean, I overheard him talking to Mom on the phone the other day. He's worried about you."

"Thanks, son!" Etty says, holding up her hands defensively. "Don't look at me like that. He called because he cares. He's not trying to throw you under the bus."

Perry leaned forward, elbows on the table, burying his face in his hands. "Great. So now the whole fucking band thinks I'm a liability."

"Not a liability, "Etty corrected, her tone firm but gentle. She walked over and placed a hand on his shoulder. "But they're worried. And so am I."

Hezron set his glass down, leaning in. "You've gotta get it together, Dad. You're, like, the glue for this whole thing, right? The band, the shows… they don't work without you."

Perry looked up at his son, surprised by the blunt wisdom in his words. "That's a lot of pressure to put on one guy, don't you think?"

Hezron smirked. "You're Perry Farrell. You can handle it." He heads back to the bedroom while saying, "…But not if you're drinking wine for breakfast, Dude."

Perry let out a dry laugh, shaking his head. "Damn. My teenager's giving me life advice. What's next, therapy sessions?"

Etty squeezed his shoulder. "Maybe that's not the worst idea."

Perry looked between them, his family, his grounding force. He nodded slowly, his voice quieter now. "Alright. Maybe it's time to face some shit."

Etty leaned down, kissing the top of his head. "That's all we want, honey. Just face it. Come on? You We've got your back." She turns and walks toward the fridge then, "now get it together!"

Hezron raised his glass of orange juice in a mock toast. "To Dad getting his shit together."

Perry rolled his eyes but clinked his wine glass against his son's. "To me getting my shit together."

As the tension eased, Etty returned to her coffee, and Hezron grabbed a piece of toast from the counter. Perry sat back in his chair, the weight on his shoulders feeling just a little lighter.

Boston

Perry stumbled down the backstage corridor, a glass of wine in one hand, the other clenching and unclenching at his side. The muted buzz of the crowd seeped through the walls, a reminder that in mere moments he'd be expected to command an entire room. His walk was slightly unsteady, but he pushed through it, jaw tight, shoulders squared. He hadn't always needed the wine to take the edge off, but these days it felt like the only thing that could quiet the storm in his head.

A tech approached him cautiously, clipboard in hand, trying not to provoke whatever mood Perry had walked in with.

"Everything's ready to go, "the tech said, keeping his voice calm. "Sound check came through fine, feed's perfect."

Perry shot him a sharp look, his brow furrowing. "Perfect? Really? Then why the fuck does it sound like I'm singing in a tin can out there half the time?"

The tech hesitated, glancing nervously at the clipboard. "We've triple-checked it, Perry. It's all calibrated. Whatever issues there were last night, "

"Last night was a fucking disaster, "Perry interrupted, his voice rising. He took a step closer, the wine sloshing slightly in his glass. "And don't stand there and act like you didn't hear the same shit I did. It's the fucking monitors. They're all over the place."

Etty appeared from around the corner, her expression a mix of concern and composure. She carried herself carefully, like someone trying to walk a tightrope. "Perry, "she said softly, placing a hand on his arm. "The sound team is doing their best. Let's just… stay focused on the show, okay?"

He shook her hand off, not unkindly, but with the irritation of someone who didn't want to be handled. "You heard it too, Etty. Don't tell me you didn't. It's like they're sabotaging us out there."

Etty glanced at the tech, offering a small, apologetic smile, before turning back to Perry. "The crowd didn't notice, "she said firmly. "They were with you the whole time. You've got this."

Perry let out a bitter laugh, shaking his head. "That's the problem, isn't it? They don't notice. They don't hear what I hear. But I'm the one standing out there, looking like an idiot when shit's off."

The tech took a step back, clearly deciding now wasn't the time to argue. "I'll double-check everything again, "he said quickly, before retreating down the hallway.

Etty stepped closer, lowering her voice. "Babe, you're putting so much pressure on yourself. The monitors were fine last night. You're fine. Just… trust me, okay? It's all in your head."

He shot her a sharp look, his jaw tightening. "Don't fucking tell me it's in my head, Etty. I know what I hear."

There was a moment of silence between them, the tension palpable. She exhaled slowly, keeping her voice calm. "I'm not your enemy, Perry. I'm here for you. Always. But maybe…" She hesitated, choosing her words carefully. "Maybe take it easy on the wine tonight?"

He stared at her for a long moment, then downed the rest of the glass in a single gulp. "It's not the wine, "he muttered, handing her the empty glass as he brushed past her.

Etty stood there, holding the glass, watching him disappear down the corridor toward the stage. For a moment, she looked like she wanted to say something else, but she stopped herself, sighing instead. Turning, she set the glass on a nearby table and followed after him, her steps quiet but determined.

Back at the soundboard, the engineers huddled together, speaking in hushed tones as Perry approached. "Let's go over it again, "he barked, cutting through their conversation. "Start from the top. If I hear one goddamn hiccup out there tonight, someone's getting fired."

The head engineer nodded, trying to remain calm under Perry's scrutiny. "You've got it. We're running everything through a final check now."

"You'd better, "Perry snapped, turning back toward the stage entrance. He paused at the bottom of the stairs, running a hand through his hair and exhaling sharply. The faint hum of the crowd grew louder, a dull roar building as anticipation filled the venue.

Etty appeared behind him, placing a hand gently on his back. He didn't shrug her off this time, but he didn't turn to look at her either. "Okay, babe, they're out there waiting for you, "she said quietly. "Show them why they came. That's what you're best at. You ready? Me and the 'gals' are…" As she heads for the stage, "let's go 'skin n' bones!'" She stopped, suddenly, turned back, and looked her husband in the eye, "baby? I'll see you out there, okay?"

Perry nodded once, almost imperceptibly, before stepping onto the stairs. As the stage lights began to glow, he squared his shoulders.

The show opened with an intensity that promised something unforgettable. The band launched into "Kettle Whistle, "and the crowd erupted, their energy electric as they sang along to every word. Next came "Whores, "the gritty rhythm driving the audience into a frenzy. But as the first chords of "Ocean Size" rang out, the cracks that had been quietly forming began to widen.

Perry stumbled slightly as he approached the mic, his face flushed and his movements erratic. His voice, normally commanding, wavered as he sang the wrong verse, then jumped to the chorus too soon. The band tried to keep up, but the cohesion that had defined their earlier performances began to slip away.

Eric glanced toward Stephen, his expression tight with worry, while Dave focused intently on his guitar, his jaw clenched as he fought to keep the song together. Perry, however, was spiraling. His frustration bubbled over as he grabbed at his in-ear monitor and ripped it out, glaring toward the sound crew.

"Fuck you all!" Perry's voice boomed through the mic, his words dripping with venom. He gestured wildly toward the band. "And fuck all these guys!"

The crowd gasped, their cheers faltering into uneasy murmurs. Perry staggered across the stage, his eyes blazing as he made a beeline for Dave.

"You're fucking rushing it, Dave!" Perry snarled, his words slurred but sharp.

Dave didn't look up, his fingers steady on the fret board. "Stay in your goddamn lane." he muttered coldly, his voice barely audible over the hum of the amplifiers.

Perry's face twisted in rage, his breath coming in heavy bursts. "My lane? MY FUCKING LANE?!"

Without warning, Perry swung at Dave, his fist connecting hard with Dave's shoulder. The impact sent Dave stumbling backward, his guitar letting out a shrill burst of feedback as it clanged against the amp.

The entire venue seemed to hold its breath for a moment before the chaos erupted. Stephen threw his drumsticks to the ground, the sharp clatter echoing through the stunned silence. "What the fuck, Perry?!" he yelled, his voice trembling with a mix of anger and disbelief.

Eric, already yanking off his bass, stormed toward Perry. "That's it!" he shouted, shoving Perry hard in the chest. "What the fuck is wrong with you?!"

Perry staggered, clutching at his mic stand for balance. "The sound's fucked!" he shouted, his voice cracking. "I can't hear shit!"

Eric's voice cut through like a blade. "The sound isn't the problem, Perry. You are!"

Before Perry could respond, security and stage crew rushed in, separating him from the rest of the band. "Kill the lights!" someone from the crew barked, and the stage was plunged into darkness.

The crowd erupted into confusion, murmurs and scattered boos filling the air. A single spotlight remained on Perry, who stood at center stage, restrained by three crew members. The fury on his face began to fade as he looked out at the sea of faces, their excitement replaced by shock and disappointment. The realization of what he'd done dawned on him, his expression crumbling into something hollow and defeated. The spotlight cut out, leaving the venue in darkness.

The band stumbled offstage into the chaotic backstage area, the air thick with tension. Dave, still gripping his guitar, wiped sweat from his brow, his jaw tight, blood smeared at the corner of his mouth where his lip had split during the last set. He didn't look at Perry, but his whole posture radiated fury.

"What the hell was that, Perry?!" Dave's voice was low and sharp, cutting through the commotion of crew members trying to stay out of the blast radius.

Perry stood near the wall, his shoulders slouched, his face pale beneath the stage lights that still filtered backstage. He didn't answer, didn't even lift his eyes. His breathing was uneven, his hands twitching as though fighting an internal war. Eric stood nearby, watching the interaction unfold, his fists clenched at his sides.

Then, without warning, Perry broke free from the crew who had been hovering near him and lunged forward. His fist connected with Dave's face in a brutal swing. The sound of the impact, a dull, sickening thud, made everyone freeze. Dave staggered back, dropping his guitar. Blood smeared down his chin as he raised a hand to his face, his eyes wide with shock.

"Perry, what the fuck?!" Eric shouted, rushing forward to pull Perry away. Stephen followed, his face twisted with disbelief, as two crew members grabbed Perry by the arms and wrestled him back.

Dave stood frozen for a moment, wiping at his bloody lip. He didn't say anything at first, but his eyes glistened, not with rage, but with something far more painful, betrayal. Slowly, he gathered himself, his breath uneven, his shoulders trembling. Finally, his voice cracked as he whispered, "Goodbye, Per."

Perry's struggles ceased as he stared at Dave. "Davey! Dave, I'm fucking sorry!" His voice was raw and desperate, breaking under the weight of his emotions. "Don't leave! Don't fucking leave, man! It… it just happened!"

But Dave didn't look back. He walked away, his steps slow, his face crumpling as he disappeared down the hall, leaving his guitar behind.

Perry slumped onto the nearest sofa, his head in his hands, his body shaking with uneven breaths. He whispered again, almost inaudibly, "It just happened…"

Stephen, standing nearby, let out a sound of disbelief. He threw his drumsticks onto the floor, the clatter echoing through the space. "That's your excuse?" he demanded, his voice rising. "That's all you've got? 'It just happened'? You fuckin' prick! You couldn't keep your shit together for one night, Perry. ONE NIGHT!" His voice cracked, his hands trembling.

Perry lifted his head, his eyes rimmed with tears. "I didn't mean to…" he began, his voice faint.

Eric stepped forward, his expression a mix of frustration and exhaustion. "It's never about what you mean to do, Perry. It's about what you fucking do." He exhaled sharply, trying to contain his anger. "We've put up with a lot over the years. But this?" He gestured toward the space where Dave had stood moments ago. "This is too far. We're not doing this anymore. We can't."

Perry looked at Eric, his voice a hoarse whisper. "So what happens now? We just… we just leave it like this?"

Eric's voice dropped, firm and resolute. "What the hell did you expect? That we'd keep putting this band back together, keep cleaning up after your shit every time you screw it up? You think this is some goddamn movie where it always works out? It's not. This is real, Perry, and you just burned it all to the ground."

Stephen stood silent, his arms crossed tightly over his chest. Perry looked between them, his eyes searching for some semblance of forgiveness, but there was nothing left. Eric's next words cut through any last hope.

"It's over, Perry. We're done. We're all fucking done."

Perry flinched like he'd been struck again, his whole body sagging into the sofa. He opened his mouth to say something, anything, but no words came. The room was quiet except for the muffled sounds of the fans outside, still waiting, still hoping, still unaware that everything had just fallen apart.

Finally, Stephen turned and walked out, shaking his head. Eric followed, muttering to the crew to clear the space. Perry stayed seated, his face buried in his hands, drowning in the silence they left behind.

The Final Curtain?

The hotel lobby was cavernous and eerily silent, a stark contrast to the chaos and noise that had filled the venue just hours earlier. Perry wandered in, his steps slow and dragging, as though the weight of the night clung to him like a lead blanket. His shoulders were hunched, his face pale, the lines around his eyes deeper than ever.

The bartender, a young man in his mid-twenties with an air of practiced neutrality, watched him approach the bar. Perry collapsed onto a stool, running a hand through his damp hair. The bartender hesitated, his eyes flickering to the faint smear of blood still visible on Perry's knuckles.

"Drink?" the bartender asked, his tone cautious but professional.

Perry's gaze drifted to the row of bottles behind the bar, their colors glinting under the soft overhead light. His hand twitched involuntarily, and for a moment, he seemed ready to give in. His jaw tightened, his teeth grinding audibly. But then he exhaled deeply, closing his eyes and shaking his head.

"No... no, "Perry said, his voice hoarse and strained. "Just... just water."

The bartender nodded silently, grabbing a clean glass and filling it with water from the tap. Perry took the glass with a shaky hand, the condensation already chilling his fingers. He sipped slowly, the cool liquid offering little comfort. He stared into the glass as if it held some answer, his distorted reflection staring back at him.

He looked like a ghost, a man hollowed out by years of highs and lows, by triumphs and failures, by the relentless grind of a life lived on the edge.

Perry's hotel room was dark, save for the faint glow of the city lights outside. He sat on the edge of the bed, elbows on his knees, his head hung low. His phone rested on the nightstand, the screen lighting up every few minutes with notifications he refused to check.

Finally, unable to resist, he picked up the phone and began scrolling. Missed calls, text messages, and a flood of headlines assaulted his tired eyes:

"Jane's Addiction Implodes On Stage."

"Rock's Last Rebels Self-Destruct Again."

"Perry Farrell's Onstage Meltdown Ends Jane's Reunion."

The words blurred together, each headline cutting deeper than the last. His hand trembled as he set the phone down, letting it slip from his grasp and land with a soft thud on the carpet.

He buried his face in his hands, his breathing shallow and uneven. Regret clawed at his chest, suffocating and unrelenting. For the first time, Perry felt not just the consequences of his actions, but the sheer weight of his own self-destruction.

By morning, the room was bathed in harsh sunlight streaming through the half-open blinds. Perry hadn't moved from his spot on the bed. His eyes were bloodshot, his face pale and sunken. He stared at the ceiling, the events of the previous night looping endlessly in his mind like a broken record.

A knock at the door broke the suffocating silence. At first, he didn't respond, his body too heavy to move. But the knocking persisted, louder and more insistent. With a groan, he pushed himself to his feet and shuffled to the door.

When he opened it, he found Eric standing on the other side, his face unreadable.

Perry's lips parted, but the words came out barely above a whisper. "Eric… I'm so, "

"Save it, "Eric cut him off, his tone sharp but not cruel. "I'm not here for fuckin' apologies."

Perry flinched, his shoulders slumping further. He looked at Eric, searching his face for something, anything, that could offer a shred of reassurance. But Eric's gaze remained steady, unyielding.

"You've got to figure this out, Perry, "Eric continued, his voice firm but quieter now. "You can't keep burning everything down just because you're afraid of what's on the other side."

The words hit Perry like a blow. He nodded slowly, swallowing hard, but no response came.

Eric sighed, and for the briefest moment, his expression softened. "It might finally be too late for Jane's to exist, "he said, the weight of the admission hanging between them. "But it's not too late for you to do something right. For once."

Perry blinked, his throat tightening as Eric's words sank in.

"You don't have to be an asshole for the rest of what life you have left, "Eric added, his tone blunt but not unkind.

And with that, Eric turned and walked away, leaving Perry standing in the doorway. He watched as Eric disappeared down the hall, the echo of his footsteps fading into silence

For a long time, Perry didn't move. He stood there, staring down the empty corridor, Eric's words echoing in his mind. When he finally stepped back inside, the weight in his chest felt heavier than ever.

In the days following the Boston disaster, the media buzzed with headlines dissecting every detail of the meltdown. Fans speculated, critics opined, and social media exploded with theories and accusations. The band's silence was deafening, but soon enough, statements began to emerge, attempting to make sense of what had happened.

It started with an official statement from the band's PR team, concise and clinical:

"Due to unforeseen circumstances, Jane's Addiction regrets to announce the cancellation of the remaining dates of the reunion tour. We deeply apologize to our fans for this disappointment and thank you for your continued support. Refunds will be available at the point of purchase."

The press release offered no details, leaving fans to fill in the blanks.

On Instagram, Etty shared a photo of Perry from an earlier tour date, his arms outstretched on stage, bathed in light. Her caption was heartfelt yet carefully worded:

"To our incredible fans: We are heartbroken to have to cancel the rest of the tour. Perry has been under an immense amount of stress these past few months, and it all came to a head in Boston. The sound issues we've been dealing with night after night, combined with the pressure of performing, took their toll in ways we couldn't have anticipated.

I want to apologize to Dave, Stephen, and Eric for what happened onstage. Perry and I love you guys and always will. To the fans, I am so sorry we let you down. Please know Perry is taking this seriously and will be stepping back to focus on his mental health. Thank you for your understanding, love, and support. It means the world to us.

"The post was flooded with mixed responses, messages of support, anger, confusion, but Etty, as always, stood firm in her loyalty to Perry.

Perry's apology came the next morning on "X" raw and unfiltered. It read:

"To my band-mates, especially Dave, I owe you all the deepest apology. What I did in Boston was inexcusable. I let my emotions take over, and I crossed a line that should never have been crossed.

To the fans, I'm sorry I let you down. I know you've been with us through the highs and lows, and this is not how I ever wanted things to go. Canceling this tour is devastating, but I know it's the right thing to do. I need to step back and deal with my demons, demons that I've ignored for far too long.

I don't know what the future holds for Jane's Addiction. Right now, my focus is on getting mentally and emotionally right. Thank you for your patience, your love, and for believing in us when we didn't always deserve it. I'm deeply sorry. -Perry"

The fallout was immediate. Fans debated whether Perry's apology was enough, whether the band could survive yet another implosion. Articles dissected his words, speculating on the fate of Jane's Addiction.

Meanwhile, the band's members maintained their silence. Dave, visibly absent from social media, declined to comment. Eric re-posted the band's official statement but offered no additional thoughts. Stephen shared a cryptic image of his drum kit packed up, captioned, "Done for now."

Unbeknownst to the public, Etty reached out to Dave directly, her message full of emotion:

"Dave, I don't know if you'll read this, but I needed to say it. I'm so sorry for what happened in Boston. I know Perry hurt you, and it kills me to see the band like this. Please know that he loves you, even if he's too broken right now to show it. We both love you. I hope someday we can all find a way to heal from this. You mean the world to us."

Dave never responded, but Etty felt it was important to say her piece, even if the wounds were too fresh for reconciliation.

The band was quiet. The stages were dark. For the first time in decades, Perry Farrell was not preparing for the next tour, the next album, or the next chaotic chapter of Jane's Addiction. He was preparing for something different.

A Healing.

The small storage closet in the corner of Perry's sprawling Los Angeles home had been a chaotic mess for years, boxes haphazardly stacked, old gear shoved into the back, forgotten memories buried beneath layers of dust. Perry knelt on the floor, a faded bandanna tied around his head to keep his hair out of his face, methodically pulling items from the shelves.

It was a quiet morning, the kind he'd come to appreciate more these days. No rushing to sound checks, no frantic calls from managers, no looming deadlines. Just the soft rustle of cardboard, the faint hum of birds outside, and the occasional clang of metal as he moved something too quickly.

His hand landed on a weathered, leather-bound photo album tucked between a stack of vinyl records and an old tour poster. The spine cracked slightly as he opened it, the pages heavy with age. Inside were black-and-white snapshots from the early days of Jane's Addiction, grainy photos of their first gigs at dingy LA clubs, Perry with his wild curls and painted face, Dave with a cigarette dangling from his lips, Eric scowling at the camera, and Stephen mid-drum solo, a blur of movement.

Perry smiled, but it was a bittersweet kind of smile, one that spoke of both pride and loss. He lingered on a shot of the four of them crammed together on a ratty couch, beers in hand, laughing like they had the whole world ahead of them. And they had. But now? The weight of everything that had happened, every fight, every triumph, every mistake, settled heavily in his chest.

"Perry!" Etty's voice floated from the kitchen, pulling him out of his reverie. "Breakfast is ready!"

He closed the album carefully, placing it on top of a growing pile of things he wasn't quite ready to part with. "Coming!" he called back, brushing the dust from his hands as he stood.

The scent of fresh fruit and toasted nuts filled the air as he walked into the kitchen. Etty was by the counter, pouring pecan milk from her beloved homemade machine into a tall glass. She glanced over her shoulder at him, smiling.

"You've been at that stupid closet for hours. How's it going?" she asked, placing the glass on the table next to a bowl of freshly cut fruit.

Perry sat down, the corners of his mouth twitching into a faint grin. "It's…a trip. Found some old photos. You should see how ridiculous we looked back then."

Etty chuckled as she joined him at the table, her chair scraping softly against the floor. "I've seen the photos, remember? I married that ridiculous guy." She leaned forward, resting her chin on her hand. "Bittersweet?"

Perry nodded, taking a sip of the pecan milk. It was rich and slightly sweet, the way he liked it. "Yeah. Bittersweet's a good word for it." He paused, running a hand through his hair. "There's just… so much in those pictures. So much I didn't realize I'd forgotten."

Etty reached out, placing her hand over his. "That's the thing about memories. She pauses, "Babe, they wait for you to be ready for them." She leans back and takes a bite of an orange then continues, "It's like the fucking know when you need them."

He looked at her, his eyes softening. "You always know what to say, you beautiful goofball."

"I try, "she said, squeezing his hand before sitting back. "So, what's next? More organizing?"

Perry chuckled, the sound warm and genuine. "Maybe. Or maybe I'll just sit with it for a while. Let it all sink in." An alert goes off on his phone. "Speaking of."

Etty stands up, takes his and her plates, and heads to the sink. "What now?"

"Oh, just another therapy appointment, E, "he says as he rises from the kitchen table.

She nodded, understanding. "Cool. Take your time with it, Babe….and be honest."

Perry smiles, walks over, and kisses her on the forehead, then turns to walk out the door. "See ya later, love you."

Etty watches the love of her life. Her hero walked out the door to make an honest effort to change for the better. To improve. She smiles, then yells up the stairs, "Boys! Get your asses down here if you want to eat today."

Later that afternoon, Perry found himself sitting in his study, the photo album open on the desk in front of him. He thumbed through the pages slowly, each image pulling him deeper into the past. There was the band's first photo shoot, all leather and lace, trying so hard to look cool. A candid shot of Perry and Eric arguing backstage, their faces inches apart, passion and frustration written all over them. A grainy Polaroid of the entire band at Lollapalooza, arms around each other, sweaty and triumphant.

He ran his fingers over the edges of the photos, the memories sharp and vivid now. They weren't just a band. They were a family. A dysfunctional, chaotic, beautiful family. And despite everything, despite the fights, the breakdowns, the implosions, they had made something incredible together. Something that would outlive all of them.

The thought gave him a strange sense of peace.

He reached for his phone, scrolling through his contacts until he found Eric's name. His thumb hovered over the call button for a moment before he set the phone down. Not yet. But soon.

That evening, as the sun dipped below the horizon, painting the sky in shades of orange and pink, Perry stood on the balcony with a glass of water in hand. The waves crashed against the shore in the distance, steady and unrelenting.

Etty joined him, slipping her arm around his waist. "Feeling, okay?"

He nodded; his gaze fixed on the horizon. "Yeah. I think I am."

They stood in comfortable silence for a while, the weight of the day slowly lifting.

"What are you thinking about?" Etty asked softly.

Perry smiled, a real smile this time. "The future. And maybe, just maybe, making peace with the past."

Etty rested her head against his shoulder, her voice barely above a whisper. "Sounds like a good plan."

And for the first time in a long time, Perry believed it might just be.

A week later Perry, once again lay back on the plush chaise, the air around him heavy with a stillness he hadn't known in years. The faint hum of the ocean could be heard through the open window, mingling with the soft ticking of the therapist's clock. He stared at the ceiling, his arms crossed tightly over his chest, his face drawn with exhaustion.

The therapist, a calm presence seated across from him, waited with a patience that made Perry feel both exposed and oddly safe.

"Tell me about that moment on stage, "she finally said, her voice gentle but steady.

Perry's jaw clenched, and his eyes flicked briefly toward her before returning to the ceiling. "What's there to say?" he muttered. "I screwed up. Again. It's what I do best, right?"

The therapist didn't respond immediately; her silence was deliberate. It wasn't the kind of silence that judged or demanded, but the kind that made space for truth.

"And how does that make you feel?" she asked softly.

Perry let out a bitter laugh, the sound dry and sharp. "Relieved, "he said, surprising even himself.

The therapist leaned forward slightly, her brow furrowing. "Relieved?" she repeated, her tone curious.

He sat up, running a hand through his disheveled hair. His voice was quieter now, almost fragile. "Yeah. Relieved. I've been living on this tightrope my whole damn life. Terrified of falling. Terrified of screwing it all up. But when it finally happened…" He paused, his throat tightening as the words took shape. "It was almost peaceful. Like… maybe I don't have to keep fighting so hard to stay on that tightrope anymore. Maybe it's okay to fall."

The therapist studied him, her expression softening. "That's a powerful realization, Perry. So, what's next? What do you do with that?"

Perry stood, his movements deliberate, as if each step toward the window carried some invisible weight. He stopped in front of the glass, his hands resting lightly on the frame. Outside, the beach stretched endlessly, the waves crashing in a rhythm that felt ancient and reassuring.

"What's next?" he echoed, his reflection catching his eye. He stared at it for a long moment, taking in the lined face, the weary eyes, the man he had become. Then he smiled, a faint, almost imperceptible curve of his lips, but a smile nonetheless.

"I don't know, "he said finally, his voice steady. "But it's gonna be fucking brilliantly exciting. It has to be."

The therapist smiled at his back, sensing something shift in him, something raw but alive.

Perry turned from the window, a glimmer of determination lighting up the exhaustion in his eyes. For the first time in years, the tightrope didn't feel like a prison. It felt like a choice.

And for Perry Farrell, choices were where all the best stories began.

The End.

REFERENCES

Special thanks to the following authors, journalists, interviewers, writers, and webmasters, for their publications, articles, and content, which helped to make this book a reality:

Ahearn, Charlie. "Perry Farrell and Lollapolooza" Spin 10, no. 5 (January 1994): 56-62. Accessed September 12, 2024.

AllMusic. "Jane's Addiction: Songs, Albums & Bio" Accessed October 5, 2024. https://www.allmusic.com/album/janes-addiction-mw0000201212

AllMusic. "Jane's Addiction." Accessed October 5, 2024.

https://www.allmusic.com/artist/janes-addiction-mn0000806829

Avery, Eric and Thompson, Matt. "Eric Says." Spin. (November 12, 2024) Accessed November 8, 2024.https://www.spin.com/2024/11/eric-avery-on-janes-addiction/

Azerrad, Michael. Our Band Could Be Your Life: Scenes from the American Indie Underground, 1981-1991. Little, Brown, and Company, 2001.

Azerrad, Michael. "Jane's Addiction: The Lost Boys." Rolling Stone 615 (April 19, 1990): 54-58. Accessed September 21, 2024. https://janesaddiction.org/random/articles/

Bloom, Nate. "Jane's Addiction: Music, Madness, and the Myth of L.A." Mojo 197 (October 2011): 84-90.

Dome, Malcom. "The chaotic story of Jane's Addiction's Ritual de lo Habitual, the debauched masterpiece that changed music." Louder. (November 16, 2024.) Accessed December 17, 2024. https://tinyurl.com/4fkpx5m6

Kot, Greg. "Jane's Addiction: The Return of the Prodigal Sons." Chicago Tribune, (September 16, 2011.) Accessed November 8, 2024. https://www.chicagotribune.com/2022/06/26/chicago-history-timeline-revisiting-175-years-of-breaking-news-from-the-pages-of-the-chicago-tribune/

Kappes, John. "Something's Shocking." Alternative Press. (November 21, 1997) Accessed October 19, 2024. https://tinyurl.com/4tac9bf4

Kupiers, Dean, "Jane's Addiction." Spin 91 no. 6 (June 1991) Accessed September 8, 2024. https://www.spin.com/featured/janes-addiction-cover-story-1991/

Navarro, Dave. Don't Try This at Home: A Year in the Life of Dave Navarro. 1st ed. Harper Collins, Oct 9, 2012

Perry, Stephen. "Interview with Perry Farrell." Guitar World 12, no. 11 (November 1992): 48-54.

Spitz, Marc. "Interview with Dave Navarro." Spin 12, no. 1 (January 1996): 58-62.

Strong, Martin C., The Great Rock Discography. 7th ed. Canongate Books, 2004.

Weisbard, Eric. "Jane's Addiction: The Sound of the Apocalypse." Spin 11, no. 11 (November 1995): 76-82.

Green, Andy "Dave Says." Rolling Stone. (August 9, 2024.) Accessed October 19, 2024.

https://www.rollingstone.com/music/music-features/dave-navarro-janes-addiction-reunion-1235075416/

Thompson, D.(2011). Perry Farrell: The Saga of a Hipster. (April 1, 2011) St. Martin's Griffin

About the Author

Micah R. Guidry is a freelance blogger, journalist, screenwriter, and author. He wrote the San Antonio Independent Film Festival, award-winning screenplay for the "cult-classic" film, *Claustrophobia* (2008), wrote and directed two chapters of the short film, *Secrecy and a Sweet Hereafter*, and the New Orleans Film Festival, award-winning script, *Return to Everlong*. He is the author of the novels *5-Minutes, Wrights' Flight Four,* and his autobiography, *The Book of Micah: The Insane Memoirs of an American Good Guy,* is set for release in January 2026. He has recently adapted his Literary Nonfiction Book, *Jane's Addiction: SHOCKINGLY HABITUAL*, into a screenplay and is currently writing the script, *James*, a remake of the film *12 Monkeys*.

Micah is a father, Grandfather, Son, and friend to many, currently residing in South Texas.

www.ingramcontent.com/pod-product-compliance
Lightning Source LLC
Chambersburg PA
CBHW062008090426
42811CB00005B/791